SCIENCE VISUAL RESOURCES

PHYSICS

An Illustrated Guide to Science

The Diagram Group

CHELSEA HOUSE
PUBLISHERS
An imprint of Infobase Publishing

Physics: An Illustrated Guide to Science

Copyright © 2006 The Diagram Group

Author:	Derek McMonagle BSc PhD CSci CChem FRSC
Editors:	Catherine Gaunt, Jamie Stokes
Design:	Anthony Atherton, Richard Hummerstone, Lee Lawrence, Tim Noel-Johnson, Phil Richardson
Illustration:	Peter Wilkinson
Picture research:	Neil McKenna
Indexer:	Martin Hargreaves

Chelsea House
An imprint of Infobase Publishing
132 West 31st Street
New York NY 10001

For Library of Congress Cataloging-in-Publication Data,
please contact the Publisher

ISBN 0-8160-6167-X

Chelsea House books are available at special discounts when purchased in bulk quantities for businesses, associations, institutions, or sales promotions. Please call our Special Sales Department in New York at 212/967-8800 or 800/322-8755.

You can find Chelsea House on the World Wide Web at
http://www.chelseahouse.com

Printed in China

CP Diagram 10 9 8 7 6 5 4 3 2 1

This book is printed on acid-free paper.

Introduction

Physics is one of eight volumes in the **Science Visual Resources** set. It contains five sections, a comprehensive glossary, a Web site guide, and an index.

Physics is a learning tool for students and teachers. Full-color diagrams, graphs, charts, and maps on every page illustrate the essential elements of the subject, while parallel text provides key definitions and step-by-step explanations.

Forces and energy provides an overview of the fundamental forces and the basic forms of energy. This section discusses Newton's laws of motion, gravity, simple machines, and the relationship between energy and forces. Conduction, convection, and radiation are also explained as well as energy changes.

Waves, sound, and light explores the transfer of energy through waves. Superposition, interference, diffraction, reflection, and refraction are described in this section. The behavior of sound, light, and other electromagnetic waves is examined in detail. Other subjects covered in this section include seismic waves, noise and decibel ratings, the velocity of light, and the principles of lenses and other optical instruments.

Electricity is concerned with the phenomena associated with electrons and protons that are stationary or moving. The theories of electrostatics, electric current, and electromagnetism are the principal themes of this section. Practical applications such as the generation of electricity, AC and DC electric motors, and radio and television are also considered.

Electronics focuses on systems that function by directing or controlling the flow of electricity. The principles of electronic circuitry are the main theme of this section. There are expositions of Boolean algebra, combinational logic, and sequential logic, as well as detailed descriptions of electronic elements such as transistors, diodes, counting circuits, operational amplifiers, and rectifier circuits.

Units and measurements is a short section that gives details of the international system of units and measurements (commonly known as SI units) used by physicists and other scientists.

Contents

1 FORCES AND ENERGY

2 WAVES, SOUND, AND LIGHT

3 ELECTRICITY

4 ELECTRONICS

5 UNITS AND MEASUREMENTS

APPENDIXES

Key words

force
friction
gravity
inertia
mass

Newton's first law

- Newton's first law of motion states that an object will remain at rest or, if it is moving it will continue to move at a constant speed in the same direction, unless it is acted on by an external *force*. This might be a single force or the resultant of two or more unbalanced forces.

1 Effect of friction

- When the engine of a car is switched off, the car will eventually come to rest because *friction* and air resistance act on the car to slow it down. If these forces were absent the car would continue with a constant speed in a straight line.

2 Absence of friction

- In space there is no air. Once a rocket has escaped the *gravitational* pull of Earth it will continue to move with a constant speed in a straight line forever without needing any additional thrust from its engines.

3 Inertia

- All matter has an inbuilt opposition to being moved or, if it is moving, to having its motion changed. This property is called *inertia*.
- When the piece of card is flicked sharply it moves in the opposite direction to the flick but the coin remains where it is.
- The greater the *mass* of an object the greater its inertia. The greater its inertia, the more difficult it is to move when it is at rest and the more difficult it is to stop when it is in moving.
- Inertia provides a definition of mass. The mass of a body is a measure of its inertia.

Newton's first law of motion

1 Effect of friction

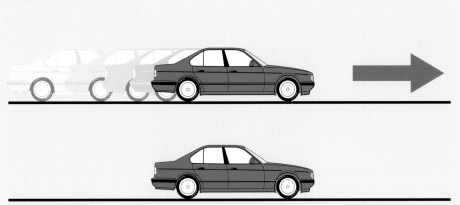

2 Absence of friction

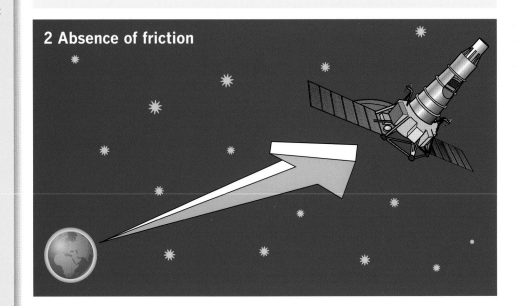

3 Inertia

coin   card

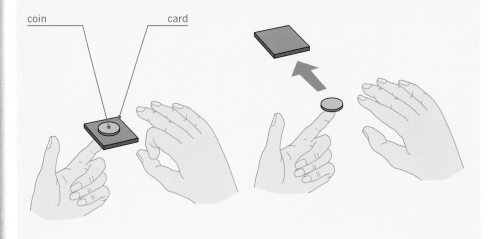

Newton's second law of motion

Key words

acceleration
momentum
velocity

1 Equipment and method

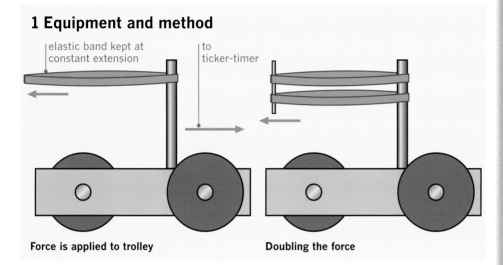

elastic band kept at constant extension

to ticker-timer

Force is applied to trolley

Doubling the force

2 Typical result

ticker-tape

Distance (in cm)

number of ticks

Time (in equal units of time)

3 Velocity/time graph

Velocity (in cm per tick)

Time (in equal units of time)

Newton's second law

- Newton's second law of motion states that an external resultant force changes the motion of an object in such a way that the rate of change of the object's *momentum* is proportional to the force, and in the same direction.
- This law may be expressed mathematically in two ways:
  force = mass x acceleration (F = ma)
  impulse = change of momentum

1 Equipment and method

- The paper strip attached to the trolley passes through a ticker-timer which places a dot on the paper at regular time intervals.
- Exert a steady force on the elastic band in the direction shown.

2 Typical result

- As the trolley accelerates, the distance between adjacent dots on the tape increases. The distance traveled by the trolley can be plotted on a graph.

3 Velocity/time graph

- The trolley's *velocity* (v) equals the distance traveled (d) divided by the time (t). v=d/t
- As the ticker-timer places dots on the paper at regular time intervals, the trolley's velocity at any point equals the distance traveled per dot.
- The *acceleration* (a) of the trolley equals its velocity divided by time. a=v/t
- The velocity time graph is a straight line indicating that acceleration is uniform. The trolley's acceleration is given by the gradient of the graph.
- Study the effect of increased force by increasing the number of elastic bands used in the experiment. With increased force, the gradient of the graph increases, showing that the force is proportional to the acceleration.

© Diagram Visual Information Ltd.

Key words

force
momentum

Newton's third law

- Newton's third law of motion states that when two objects, **A** and **B**, interact, the *force* exerted by **A** on **B** is equal in magnitude to the force exerted by **B** on **A**, but the forces act in opposite directions.

1 Example 1

- When a person steps forward from rest their foot pushes backwards on Earth and Earth exerts an equal and opposite force forward on the person. Two bodies and two forces are involved.
- The small force that a person exerts on Earth gives no noticeable acceleration to Earth because of its large mass. The equal force exerted on the person, who has a much smaller mass, causes them to accelerate.

2 Example 2

- When a person steps out of a rowing boat they push backwards on the boat, and the boat pushes them forwards with an equal but opposite force.
- The friction between the boat and the water is slight and, as the person pushes on the boat, it starts to move backwards reducing the forward motion of the person, who will tend to fall in the water between boat and land.

3 Example 3

- When a bullet is fired from a gun, equal and opposite forces are exerted on the bullet and the gun as the bullet passes down the barrel. Bullet and gun acquire equal *momentum* but in opposite directions.
  mass of bullet x bullet velocity = mass of gun x gun velocity
- Since the mass of the bullet is much less than that of the gun, the bullet will move forward at a much higher velocity than the gun will move backwards.

Newton's third law of motion

1 Example 1

force exacted on the foot by the Earth

force exacted by the foot on the Earth

2 Example 2

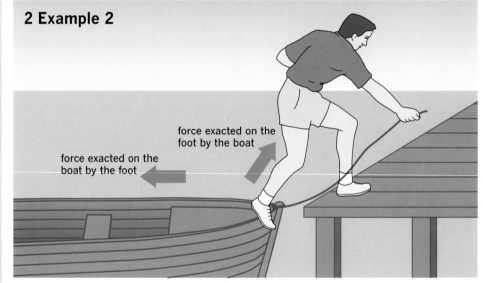

force exacted on the foot by the boat

force exacted on the boat by the foot

3 Example 3

force exacted by the bullet on the gun

force exacted by gun on the bullet

Nature of forces

1 Measuring force applied

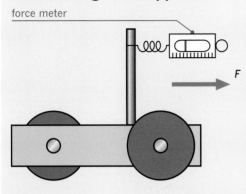

force meter

F

2 Force applied to a trolley

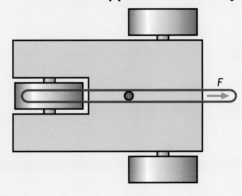

F

3 Opposing forces

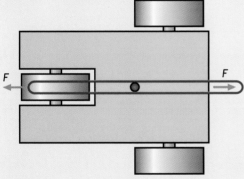

F

F

Equilibrium – no motion or constant motion

4 Vector nature of force

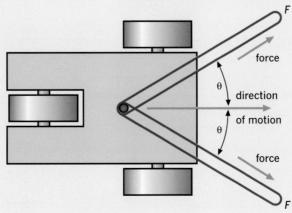

F

force

θ

direction
of motion

θ

force

F

Key words

mass
scalar
vector

Nature of forces

- Force is a *vector*, rather than a *scalar*, quantity—i.e. it has both magnitude and direction.
- Scalar quantities, such as *mass* and length, are added using normal arithmetic but vectors are added geometrically using the parallelogram law (page 12) which considers both their directions and their magnitudes.

1 Measuring force applied

- The force applied to a trolley is measured using a force meter or a newton meter.

2 Force applied to a trolley

- When a force F is applied to the trolley it accelerates in the direction of the force.

3 Opposing forces

- If equal forces are applied to the trolley but in opposite directions, the trolley will remain stationary or, if it is already in motion, it will continue in constant motion.

4 Vector nature of force

- If forces are applied at an angle, the resulting motion is calculated using the parallelogram law.
- In this case, equal forces are applied at equal angles to the trolley's axle and the trolley moves in the direction shown.

1 Adding parallel forces

- Forces are vector quantities, having both magnitude and direction. A force is often represented as an arrow, whose length represents the relative magnitude of the force, and direction indicates the direction in which the force acts.
- A *resultant* force is a single force that produces the same effect as two or more forces.
- *Parallel* forces act in either the same direction or in opposite directions.

2 Adding forces

- Extend the spring by pulling two force meters in different directions. The force exerted by the upper force meter is 6 N, and by the lower force meter, 4 N.
- The spring can be extended by the same amount by pulling a single force meter in a horizontal direction by 8 N.

3 The parallelogram

- Remove the equipment and draw a line 6 cm long representing the 6 N force between c and f, mark the end A.
- To represent the 4 N force draw a line 4 cm long between c and g. Mark end B.
- Complete the parallelogram by making a 4 cm arc centered on A and a 6 cm arc centered on B.
- The diagonal of the parallelogram is 8 cm long, the size of the resultant force in the experiment.

4 Components of weight

- Weight is the force that an object exerts on the ground by virtue of being pulled down by *gravity*. The weight of an object can be resolved into two forces (C_1 and C_2) acting perpendicularly to each other.
- $\cos \theta = C_2/F$ therefore $C_2 = F \cos \theta$
- $\cos \alpha = C_1/F$ therefore $C_1 = F \cos \alpha$ however $\cos \alpha = \sin \theta$ therefore $C_1 = F \sin \theta$.

Adding forces

1 Adding parallel forces

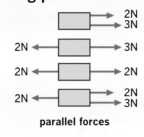

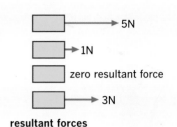

parallel forces　　　　**resultant forces**

2 Adding forces

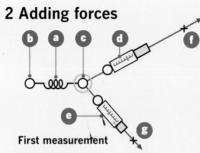

First measurement

a stretched spring
b fixed end
c metal ring with circle drawn round to mark position
d force meter reads 6 N

Second measurement

e force meter reads 4 N
f mark direction of 6 N
g mark direction of 4 N
h stretched spring with same extension
i force meter reads 8 N

3 The parallelogram

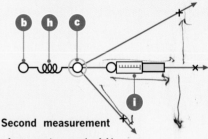

First measurement

j 4 cm line to represent 4 N
k 6 cm line to represent 6 N

Showing how the forces add

l point of arc radius 4 cm centered on **A**
m point of arc radius 6 cm centered on **B**

4 Components of weight

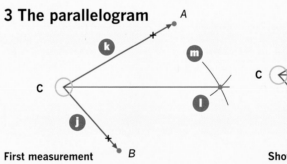

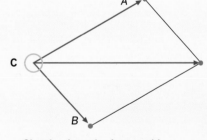

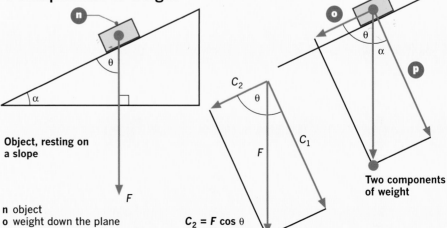

Object, resting on a slope

n object
o weight down the plane
p weight perpendicular to plane

$C_2 = F \cos \theta$
$C_1 = F \sin \theta$

Two components of weight

Turning effect of a force

Key words

equilibrium
lever
moment
torque

1 The moment of a force

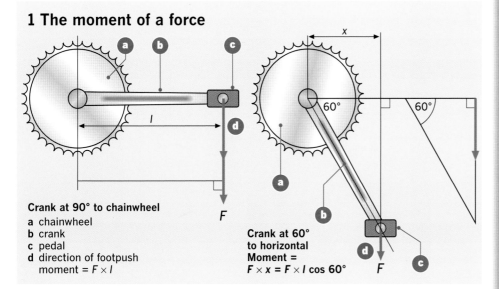

Crank at 90° to chainwheel
a chainwheel
b crank
c pedal
d direction of footpush
  moment = $F \times l$

**Crank at 60°
to horizontal
Moment =**
$F \times x = F \times l \cos 60°$

1 The moment of a force
● The turning effect of a force around a point is called the *moment* or *torque*. The moment of a force is the product of the force and its *perpendicular* distance from the turning point.
● When the crank is *horizontal* the moment = F x l.
● When the crank is 60° to the horizontal the perpendicular distance from the force to the turning point = x = l cos 60˚. The moment in this position is therefore = F x l cos 60˚.

2 The law of moments

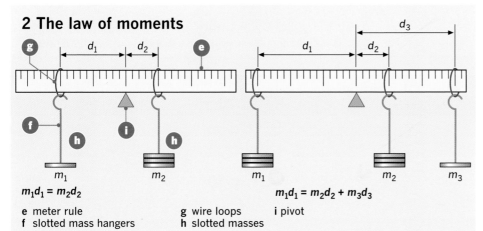

$m_1 d_1 = m_2 d_2$

$m_1 d_1 = m_2 d_2 + m_3 d_3$

e meter rule
f slotted mass hangers
g wire loops
h slotted masses
i pivot

2 The law of moments
● The law of moments (law of the *lever*) states that when a body is in *equilibrium* the sum of the clockwise moments about any point is equal to the sum of the anticlockwise moments about the same point.
● When the meter rule is horizontal $m_1 d_1 = m_2 d_2$. Therefore, if d_1 is twice the distance d_2, m_1 must be half the weight of m_2. A lighter person can counterbalance a heavier person on a seesaw by moving nearer to the pivot.
● Provided that a meter rule is uniform in shape and composition its mass can be thought of as being concentrated at its geometric center. When a meter rule is pivoted at its center, its weight acts at the pivot and produces no moments otherwise the weight of the rule must be taken into account in calculations on moments.

3 Parallel forces in equilibrium

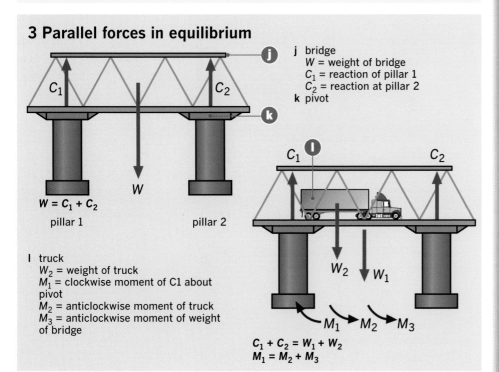

$W = C_1 + C_2$

pillar 1   pillar 2

l truck
  W_2 = weight of truck
  M_1 = clockwise moment of C1 about pivot
  M_2 = anticlockwise moment of truck
  M_3 = anticlockwise moment of weight of bridge

j bridge
  W = weight of bridge
  C_1 = reaction of pillar 1
  C_2 = reaction at pillar 2
k pivot

$C_1 + C_2 = W_1 + W_2$
$M_1 = M_2 + M_3$

3 Parallel forces in equilibrium
● As the truck moves across the bridge from pillar 1 towards pillar 2, the anticlockwise moments about the top of pillar 2 decrease and therefore the magnitude of C_1 decreases.
● Conversely, the clockwise moments acting about the top of pillar 1 increase and therefore the magnitude of C_2 increases.

Key words

momentum
*Newton's laws of
  motion*
vector
velocity

Momentum

- *Momentum*, a *vector* quantity is the product of an object's mass and *velocity*.
- It is measured in kilogram meters per second, kgms^{-1} or Newton seconds.
- Following *Newton's laws of motion*, a system's total momentum is constant unless a net external force acts. This applies in cases of impact and disintegration.

1 Transferred momentum

- The momentum of pendulum A is transferred to pendulum B.

2 Collision of two cars

- If the cars were traveling with equal momentum in opposite directions before impact they would remain at the point of impact as the net momentum would be zero.
- If one car had more momentum than the other the cars would continue to move after impact.

3 Rocket propulsion

- The momentum of the rocket moving in one direction is equal to the momentum of the exhaust gases moving in the opposite direction.

4 Conservation of momentum

- In momentum calculations, movement to the right is considered positive, movement to the left negative.
- When the spring is released the trolleys move apart as shown.
- Since momentum is conserved momentum of trolley A + momentum of trolley B = 0.
- Mass of trolley A = 2m; velocity = $- v_A$. Its momentum = $- 2m \times v_A$. Mass of trolley B = m; velocity v_B. Its momentum = mv_B.
  As momentum is conserved,
  $- 2mv_A + mv_B = 0$; $2mv_A = mv_B$
  Trolley A's velocity is half trolley B's.

Momentum

1 Transferred momentum

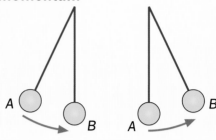

2 Collision of two cars

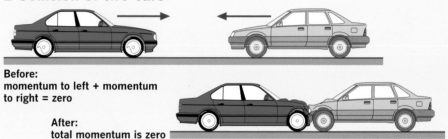

Before:
momentum to left + momentum to right = zero

After:
total momentum is zero

3 Rocket propulsion

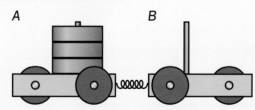

Rate of change of rocket momentum + rate of change of momentum of ejected hot gases

f liquid hydrogen
g liquid oxygen

h combustion chamber
i nozzle
j hot gasses

4 Conservation of momentum

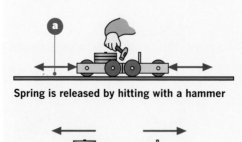

Two mechanics trolleys that can be pushed apart by a compressed spring: mass of trolley A = 2 × mass of trolley B

a trolley runway
b point where trolleys physically separate

Spring is released by hitting with a hammer

Trolleys move apart

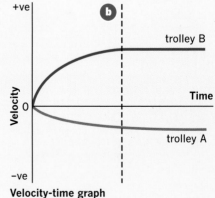

Velocity-time graph

The gravitational force

Key words

Kepler's laws
orbit

1 Kepler's laws

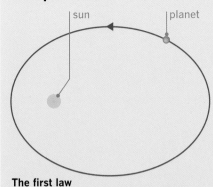

sun   *planet*

The first law

For equal time intervals t_2-t_1 and t_4-t_3
area A = area B

The second law

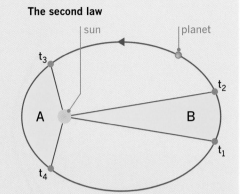

sun   *planet*

t_3 t_2 A B t_1 t_4

1 Kepler's laws

- *Kepler's* first law states that the *orbit* of each planet is an ellipse with the Sun at one focus. The orbits of the planets are often shown as circular.
- Kepler's second law (the law of area) states that the radius vector joining each planet to the Sun covers equal areas in equal times.

2 Sun's gravitational force

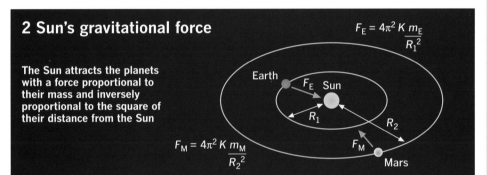

The Sun attracts the planets with a force proportional to their mass and inversely proportional to the square of their distance from the Sun

$$F_E = 4\pi^2 K \frac{m_E}{R_1^2}$$

$$F_M = 4\pi^2 K \frac{m_M}{R_2^2}$$

Earth F_E Sun R_1 R_2 F_M Mars

2 Sun's gravitational force

- The Sun attracts the planets with a force proportional to their mass and inversely proportional to the square of their distance from the Sun.

3 Universal gravitation

m_1 F_{2-1} F_{1-2} m_2

R

$$F_{2-1} = -F_{1-2}$$
$$= \frac{G\, m_1 m_2}{R^2}$$

3 Universal gravitation

- The force of attraction, **F**, between two bodies of mass m_1 and m_2 which are distance R apart is given by

$$F = \frac{g\, m_1\, m_2}{R^2}$$

- **g** is the gravitational constant. Its value is 6.67×10^{-11} N m² kg⁻².

4 Measuring G

- In 1798 Cavendish measured the very small gravitational forces exerted on two large lead spheres by two small gold spheres 5 mm in diameter using a torsion balance. A calibrated wire is twisted with force (**F**).

g is calculated by substituting values for **F**, m_1, m_2 and **R** in the formula

$$F = \frac{g\, m_1\, m_2}{R}$$

where
m_1 is the mass of gold sphere
m_2 is the mass of lead sphere
R is the distance between the centers of m_1 and m_2

4 Measuring G

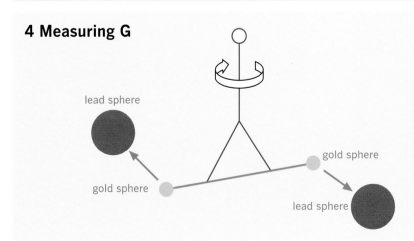

lead sphere

gold sphere

gold sphere

lead sphere

© Diagram Visual Information Ltd.

Key words

acceleration	gravitational field
action at a	mass
distance	terminal velocity
friction	viscosity
gravity	weight

1 Gravity: action at a distance

- The force of *gravity* acts through space and can cause an object which is not in contact with Earth to fall to the ground.
- Earth is surrounded by a *gravitational field* which exerts a force on any object within that field. The strength of a gravitational field is defined as the force acting on unit *mass* in the field.
- Measurements on Earth's surface show that an object of mass 1 kg experiences a force of 9.8 N due to gravity; i.e. its *weight* is 9.8 N.
- The strength of Earth's field is denoted by g and is 9.8 N kg^{-1}. Since N = kg ms^{-2}, g can also be given as 9.8 m s^{-2}, the *acceleration* due to gravity.

2 Free fall and terminal velocity in air

- When an object falls through the air the force of weight acts downwards, pulling it towards the ground while the force of air resistance acts in the opposite opposing this motion.
- Initially, the falling object speeds up however, as it does, air *friction* increases and reduces its acceleration. Eventually, the upward force due to air friction is equal to the weight of the object and the resultant force is zero. The object no longer accelerates but falls at a constant velocity called its *terminal velocity*.

3 Free fall and terminal velocity in a liquid

- Objects moving through *viscous* liquids behave in exactly the same way.
- The ball bearing initially accelerates but as it does the friction acting on it from the oil increases. At some point the ball bearing reaches a constant velocity—its terminal velocity.

Free fall and terminal velocity

1 Gravity: action at a distance

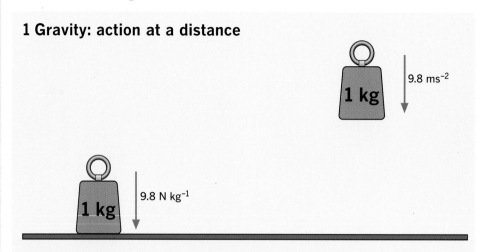

2 Free fall and terminal velocity in air

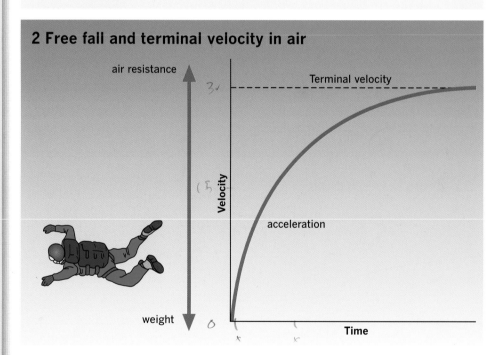

3 Free fall and terminal velocity in a liquid

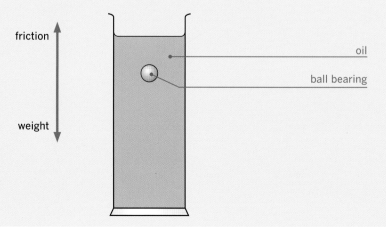

Center of gravity and stability

Key words

center of mass
equilibrium

1 Center of gravity

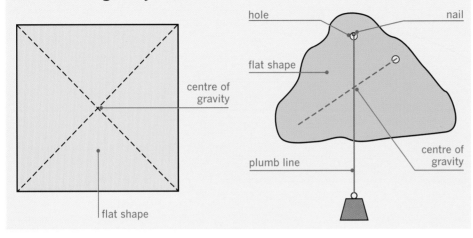

2 Stability

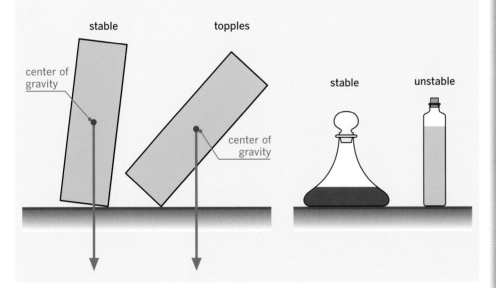

3 Equilibrium

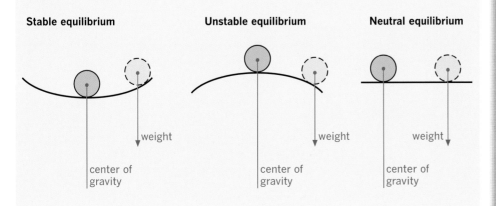

1 Center of gravity

- A body behaves as if its whole weight is concentrated at one point which is called the center of gravity. Since the force of gravity is effectively constant over the small volume of an object on Earth, the center of gravity and *center of mass* are effectively the same point.
- In a regular flat shape, the center of gravity is at the geometric center of the shape.
- In an irregular flat shape the center of gravity is found by suspending the shape on a nail so that it can swing freely, and tying a plumb line (a thread with a weight attached) to the nail. The shape hangs in such a way that its center of gravity is directly below the point from which it is suspended i.e. there is no moment in either direction. The position of the plumb line is marked and the process repeated, suspending the shape from a different place. The center of gravity is where the two lines intersect.

2 Stability

- An object's shape and position affects whether it topples over easily or not.
- An object will topple over if its center of gravity moves outside its base.
- Objects with broad bases are more stable than objects with narrow bases.

3 Equilibrium

- An object is in stable *equilibrium* if, when released after a small displacement (to the position marked with a dotted outline), it moves back to its original position.
- An object is in unstable equilibrium if, when released after a small displacement, it moves further away from its original position.
- An object is in neutral equilibrium if, when released after a small displacement, it remains in the new position.

© Diagram Visual Information Ltd.

Key words

asymptote
gradient
gravitational
* potential*
tangent

Energy and forces

1 Gravitational forces

- The *gravitational potential energy*, **E**, of an object of weight **F** newtons which is **h** meters above the ground is given by **E = F x h**. Rearranging this equation gives **F = E** / **h**

- The *gradient* of the graph at any point is the gradient of the *tangent* at that point. As the curve is uniform, a good approximation is obtained by taking values equidistant from the point and calculating the ratio of the change in energy, **ΔE**, to the change in distance, **Δh**.

- As an object moves further away from Earth, the attraction it experiences as a result of Earth's gravitational field decreases. The curve is *asymptotic* and thus the force never actually becomes zero, but it becomes so small as to be insignificant.

2 Repulsive and attractive forces between atoms

- As atoms move together, their outer electron shells exert a repulsive force on each other.

- At smaller separation distances, however, a force of attraction between atoms increases.

- The attractive and repulsive forces can be combined to give the net force for any separation distance.

- While the attractive force becomes zero for large separations, it decreases less rapidly than does the repulsive force, and there is a separation distance at which the attractive force operates after the repulsive force has become zero.

- At the equilibrium separation distance the repulsive force equals the attractive force and the atoms are stable.

1 Gravitational forces

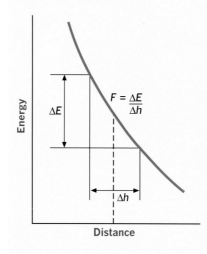

$$F = \frac{\Delta E}{\Delta h}$$

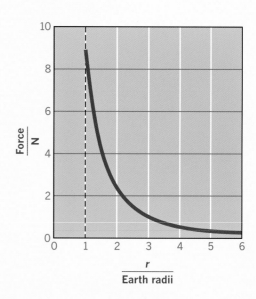

The force of attraction on an object is calculated from the gradient of the energy-distance curve

The force-distance curve

2 Repulsive and attractive forces between atoms

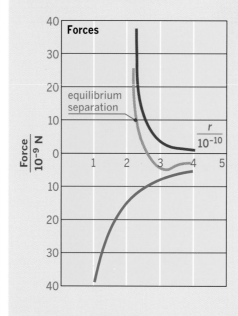

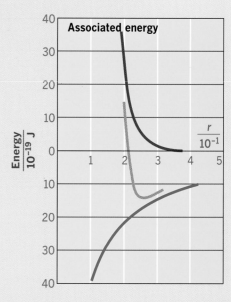

— repulsive force

— net force

— attractive force

Simple machines 1

Key words

force	moment
lever	work
mechanical advantage	

1 First-order levers

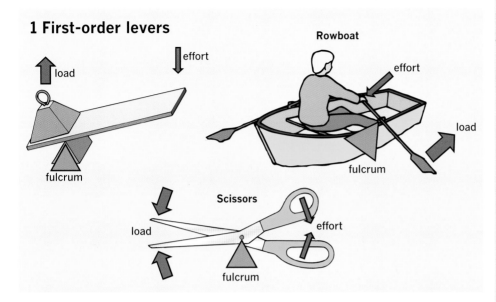

Rowboat

Scissors

2 Second-order levers

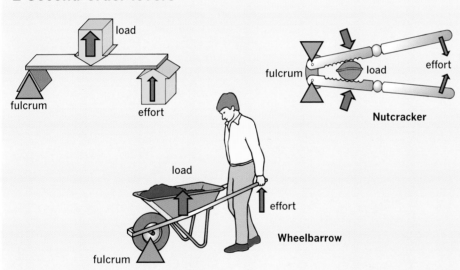

Nutcracker

Wheelbarrow

3 Third-order levers

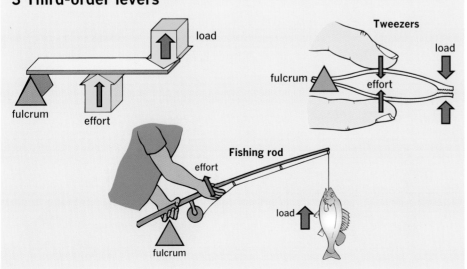

Tweezers

Fishing rod

Simple machines

- A machine is a device in which a *force* applied at one point gives an output force elsewhere.
- The *work* done by a machine, **E**, equals the force applied multiplied by the distance moved, **E = F x d**.
- The force ratio (*mechanical advantage*) of a machine is the ratio of the load to the effort.
  force ratio = load/effort
- The distance ratio (velocity ratio) of a machine is the ratio of the distance moved by the effort to the distance moved by the load.
  distance ratio = distance moved by effort/distance moved by load
- Force multipliers have both a high force ratio and a high distance ratio.
- Distance multipliers have both a low force ratio and a low distance ratio.

Levers

- These simple machines are all based on *levers*. Their action is based on the law of *moments*. A lever may act as a force multiplier or a distance multiplier.
- Crowbars, wheelbarrows, and nutcrackers are force multipliers. A small effort force is applied over a large distance to exert a large force on the load over a small distance.
- The forearm is a distance multiplier. A large effort force is applied over a small distance to exert a small force on the load over a large distance.

1 First-order levers

- A first order lever has the fulcrum between the effort and load.

2 Second-order levers

- A second order lever has the load between the effort and fulcrum.

3 Third-order levers

- A third order lever has the effort between the fulcrum and load.

Key words

efficiency
force
gear wheel
pulley
work

1 Pulley systems

- A simple *pulley* does not magnify the *force* applied but changes the direction that the force acts. Distance ratio is 1.
- In 2- and 4-pulley systems a small effort raises a large load. In a 2-pulley system for every 1 m by which the load is raised the effort is applied for 2 m, thus the distance ratio is 2. In a 4-pulley system the distance ratio is 4.
- If pulley systems were perfect machines they would be frictionless and no energy would be lost thus, using a 4-pulley system, a 40 N load would be raised 1 m by an effort of 10 N moving a distance of 4 m.
- The *efficiency* of a machine is the ratio of useful *work* done, or energy output, to the work or energy input.

$$\text{efficiency} = \frac{\text{work input}}{\text{work output}} \times 100\%$$

or

$$\text{efficiency} = \frac{\text{force ratio}}{\text{distance ratio}} \times 100\%$$

- The efficiency of a machine is always less than 100% as not all of the energy input does useful work.

2 Screw threads

- In a screw thread machine, the thread is usually turned by a handle. Distance ratio equals ratio of the circumference of the circle made by the effort to the pitch of the screw.

3 Water wheels

- Water wheels are driven by flowing water.

4 Gear wheels

- The force ratio and distance ratio of a machine can be changed by *gears*.
- The 15 teeth gear makes two revolutions for each complete revolution of the 30 teeth gear.
- If the effort is applied to the smaller gear to drive the larger gear the distance ratio is 2.

Simple machines 2

1 Pulley systems

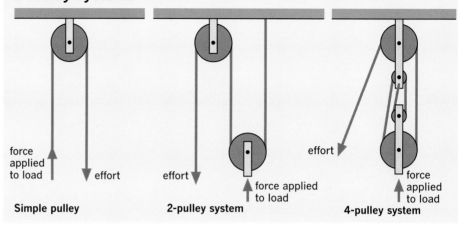

force applied to load | effort
Simple pulley

effort | force applied to load
2-pulley system

effort | force applied to load
4-pulley system

2 Screw threads

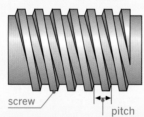

screw | pitch
Screw-thread with a screw

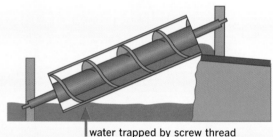

water trapped by screw thread
Raising water with a screw

3 Water wheels

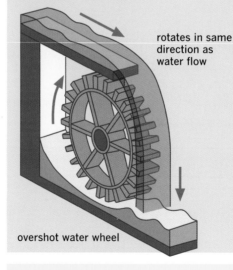

rotates in same direction as water flow

overshot water wheel

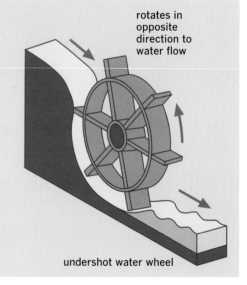

rotates in opposite direction to water flow

undershot water wheel

4 Gear wheels

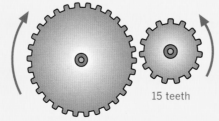

15 teeth

30 teeth

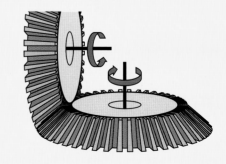

More complicated machines 1

Key words

condense   piston
ignite   pivot
internal
  combustion
  engine

1 Newcomen engine

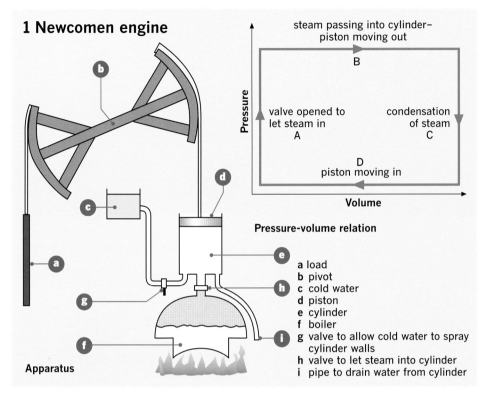

Pressure-volume relation

- steam passing into cylinder–piston moving out
- B
- A valve opened to let steam in
- C condensation of steam
- D piston moving in
- Volume
- Pressure

Apparatus

a load
b pivot
c cold water
d piston
e cylinder
f boiler
g valve to allow cold water to spray cylinder walls
h valve to let steam into cylinder
i pipe to drain water from cylinder

- Newcomen built the first practical engine in the early eighteenth century. Water is heated in the boiler, and turns to steam which is injected into the cylinder under high pressure, forcing the piston upwards. A spray of cold water is injected into the cylinder causing the steam to *condense*, drastically reducing pressure in the cylinder. The *piston* is forced down by atmospheric pressure. Movement is transferred to a load via a *pivot*.
- Pressure volume relation. The pressure in the cylinder rises A) as steam is injected into it and remains constant B) as the piston rises. When a spray of cold water is injected into the cylinder the pressure rapidly falls C) as the steam condenses and remains constant D) as the piston is forced down by atmospheric pressure.

2 Internal combustion

Induction stroke (air and vaporized petrol mixture)

Compression stroke: valves closed

Ignition stroke: valves closed

Exhaust stroke

k piston
l cylinder
m spark plug
n inlet valve open
o outlet valve closed
p ignition
q piston moves down
r exhaust
s intake
t compression

Pressure–volume relation for Otto cycle

- In a four-stroke *internal combustion engine* a mixture of air and petrol burns within the cylinder.
- During the induction stroke the inlet valve opens and the air-petrol mixture passes into the cylinder.
- During the compression stroke both inlet and outlet valves are closed and the air-petrol mixture is compressed.
- During the *ignition* stroke, still with both the inlet and outlet valves closed, the air-petrol mixture is ignited by an electrical discharge from a spark plug. This causes a rapid increase in pressure within the cylinder as the air-petrol mixture is converted to exhaust gases. This increase in pressure forces the piston down.
- During the exhaust stroke the outlet valve opens allowing the exhaust gases to leave the cylinder.
- The pressure volume changes during the cycle are shown on the diagram.

Key words

area	pressure
force	valve
hydraulic jack	
hydraulics	
piston	

More complicated machines 2

- Liquids are almost incompressible and transmit *pressure* applied to them. They are used in *hydraulic* machines.

1 Hydraulic jack

- On the downstroke the *valve* from the fluid reservoir is closed and the valve into the jack cylinder is open. Fluid is forced from the pump cylinder to the jack cylinder by the pump *piston*. This forces up the jack piston.
- On the upstroke the valve leading to the jack cylinder closes. The pressure in the pump cylinder falls and atmospheric pressure forces the valve from the fluid reservoir to open. Atmospheric pressure forces fluid into the pump cylinder.
- Pressure, *force* and *area* are related.

$$\text{pressure} = \frac{\text{force}}{\text{area}}$$

- The pressure exerted by the pump piston equals that exerted on the jack piston. As the area of the jack piston is large, the force exerted on the jack piston is large. However, the pump piston moves down more than the jack piston moves up. The work done by the pump piston equals the work done on the jack piston.

2 Car's hydraulic braking system

- A car braking system consists of a master cylinder and a series of slave cylinders.
- When the brake pedal is depressed pressure is transferred from the master cylinder to each slave cylinder.
- In a disc brake, a pair of brake pads acts on a spinning disc attached to the wheel.
- In a drum brake a drum rotates about a pair of brake shoes, each fitted with a lining.

More complicated machines 2

1 Hydraulic jack

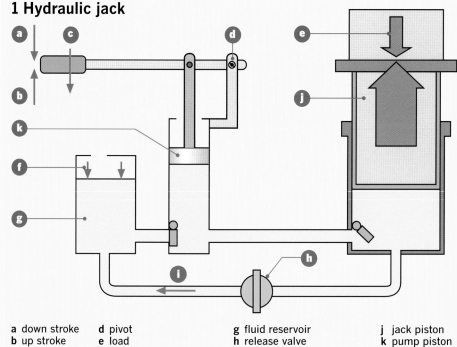

a down stroke	d pivot	g fluid reservoir	j jack piston
b up stroke	e load	h release valve	k pump piston
c effort	f atmospheric pressure	i fluid returns to reservoir	

2 Car's hydraulic braking system

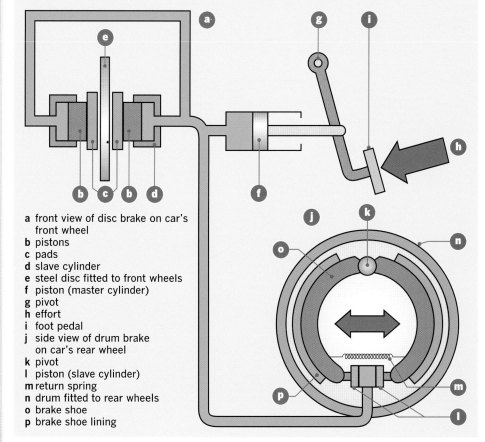

- a front view of disc brake on car's front wheel
- b pistons
- c pads
- d slave cylinder
- e steel disc fitted to front wheels
- f piston (master cylinder)
- g pivot
- h effort
- i foot pedal
- j side view of drum brake on car's rear wheel
- k pivot
- l piston (slave cylinder)
- m return spring
- n drum fitted to rear wheels
- o brake shoe
- p brake shoe lining

Lift pump and force pump

Key words

piston
valve

1 Lift pump

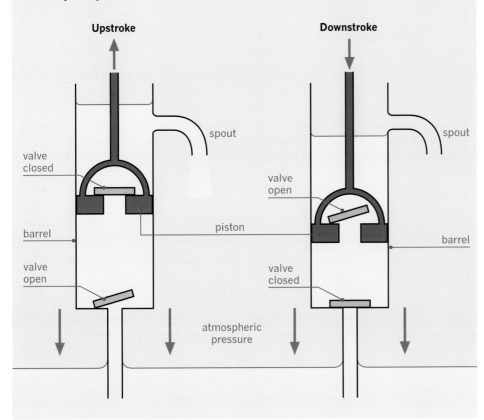

2 Force pump

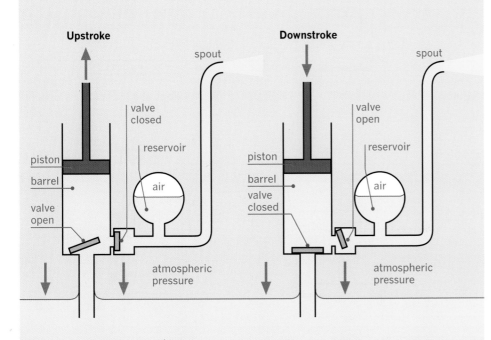

1 Lift pump

- A lift pump must first be primed by pouring water above the *piston* to prevent air leaking past it.
- On the upstroke the piston *valve* closes and the pressure in the barrel falls. Atmospheric pressure acting on the surface of the water forces water up the pipe through the open valve into the barrel. Water above the piston pours out of the barrel through the spout.
- On the downstroke the valve at the base of the barrel closes and the valve in the piston opens. Water passes from below the piston to above it. The barrel above the piston fills, ready for the next upstroke.
- Atmospheric pressure can only support a column of water 10 metres high so this is the maximum theoretical distance there can be between the bottom of the barrel and the surface of the water.

2 Force pump

- On the upstroke the valve leading to the reservoir closes and the valve at the bottom of the barrel opens. This reduces the pressure in the barrel. Atmospheric pressure acting on the surface of the water forces water through the open valve.
- On the downstroke the valve at the bottom of the barrel closes and the valve leading to the reservoir opens. Water is forced into the reservoir and ultimately out through the spout.
- During a downstroke the air in the reservoir is compressed while on an upstroke it expands. This helps to keep a steady flow of water.
- A force pump can raise water more than 10 metres provided the base of the barrel is less than 10 metres from the surface of the water.

Key words

adiabatic	internal energy
change	work
combustion	
energy	
filament	

1 Work

- *Work* is the amount of *energy* transferred from one form into others.
- A suspended weight has potential energy. When it falls, potential energy is transferred to kinetic energy. Kinetic energy does work, resulting in the water being heated.

2 Heat

- A *filament* lamp or fuel *combustion* both release heat energy which can heat water. Work is not done because the energy is not transferred from one form to others; it simply moves from a region of high temperature to a region of low temperature.

3 Adiabatic work

- In an *adiabatic* process no heat enters or escapes a closed system.
- The change in the *internal energy* of a system, ΔU, equals the sum of the energy entering the system by heating, ΔQ, and the energy entering the system through work being done on it, ΔW.
- For an adiabatic process $\Delta Q = 0$ therefore $\Delta U = \Delta W$.
- Any work done is equal to the increase in internal energy.
- Heating: work done by falling weight heats the enclosed system.
- Increasing electrical charge: work done by falling weight charges the electrical cell.
- Magnetization: work done by falling weight magnetizes the iron.
- Compression of a gas: if a gas is compressed in a perfectly insulated cylinder, the work done on the gas equals the increase in internal energy of the gas and the temperature of the gas rises. If the gas is then allowed to expand adiabatically, work is done at the expense of the internal energy and the temperature of the gas falls.

Distinction between heat and work

1 Work

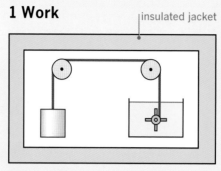
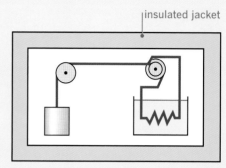

insulated jacket   insulated jacket

Falling weight causes paddle to heat water   **Falling weight drives dynamo to heat water**

2 Heat

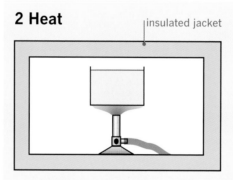
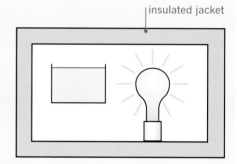

insulated jacket   insulated jacket

3 Adiabatic work

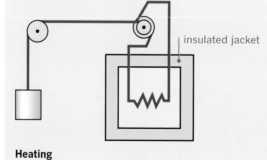

insulated jacket

Heating

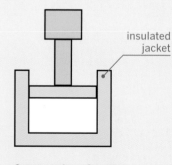

insulated jacket

Compression of a gas

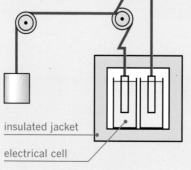

insulated jacket

electrical cell

Increasing electrical charge

insulated jacket

lump of iron

Magnetization

Heat and temperature

1 Zeroth Law: defining temperature

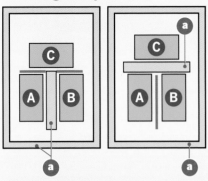

If A and B are each in thermal equilibrium with C then items A and B are in thermal equilibrium with each other

a insulating material

2 Triple point cell

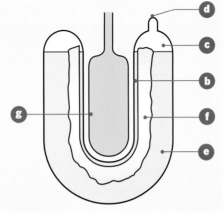

b water layer   e water
c vapor   f ice
d seal-off   g thermometer bulb

3 Constant-volume gas thermometer

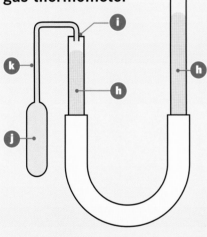

h mercury   j gas
i dead space   k capillary

4 Resistance thermometer

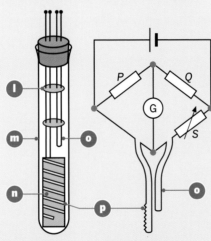

l mica spacers   o dummy leads
m silica tube   p platinum wire
n mica

5 Thermocouple thermometer

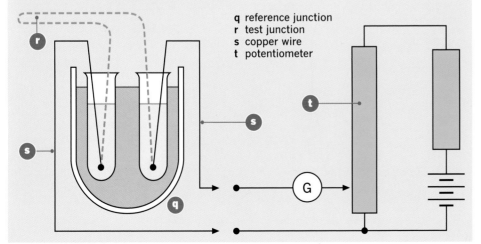

q reference junction
r test junction
s copper wire
t potentiometer

Key words

boiling point   thermocouple
gas law   triple point
melting point   vapor
resistance   Wheatstone
temperature   bridge
thermal equilibrium

1 Zeroth law: defining temperature

- When a hot body and cold body are brought in contact, energy exchange appears to stop after a period of time. The bodies are said to be in *thermal equilibrium*, and *temperature* is the common property they have.

2 Triple point cell

- The *triple point* of water is the temperature (273.16 K and a pressure of 610 Pa) at which ice, water and water *vapor* exist in *equilibrium*.

3 Constant-volume gas thermometer

- To find an unknown temperature, T, firstly find the pressure of the gas at the triple point, P_{TP}, by placing the thermometer bulb in a triple-point cell. The pressure, P_T, at the unknown temperature is determined while keeping the volume of the gas constant.
  Using the universal *gas law*—
  $$P_1V_1/T_1 = P_2V_2/T_2$$
  $$T = 273.16 \times P_T/P_{TP}$$

4 Resistance thermometer

- The electrical *resistance* of pure platinum wire increases significantly between the *melting point* of ice (R_0) and the *boiling point* of water (R_{100}). The thermometer is connected to a *Wheatstone bridge* circuit. If P equals Q then the resistance of the platinum wire R_T at unknown temperature T equals that of S.
  $$T = 100 \times (R_T - R_0)/(R_{100} - R_T)°C.$$

5 Thermocouple thermometer

- If two metals are joined in a circuit with their junctions at different temperatures, a small e.m.f. whose size is related to the temperature difference is produced.

Key words

absolute zero
Celsius
Fahrenheit
Kelvin scale

1 Fahrenheit

- The *Fahrenheit* was devised at the start of the eighteen century. On this scale the ice point is 32° and the steam point 212°. These figures arose because Fahrenheit did not use the ice point and steam fixed points but chose an unspecified ice/salt mixture for the lower fixed point, to which he gave the value 0°, and human body temperature which was given the value 96°.
- The Fahrenheit scale is still sometimes used in the context of weather but is only of historical interest in science.

2 Celsius

- In 1742 the Swedish astronomer Anders *Celsius* proposed a temperature scale in which ice melted at 0° and water boiled at 100°. The Celsius scale is widely used, sometimes being referred to as the centigrade scale since there are 100 degrees between the fixed points. Temperatures on this scale are given in 'degrees Celsius', °C.
- One disadvantage of the Celsius scale is that temperatures below the freezing point of ice are negative.

3 Kelvin

- In 1848 the physicist William Thomson (later Lord Kelvin) suggested a temperature scale which started at the lowest theoretically possible temperature, *absolute zero*. This is known as the absolute or *Kelvin* temperature scale. Degrees on this scale are called kelvins and are denoted by K (not °K). A kelvin is exactly the same size as a Celsius degree i.e. 1 K = 1 °C.

Temperature scales

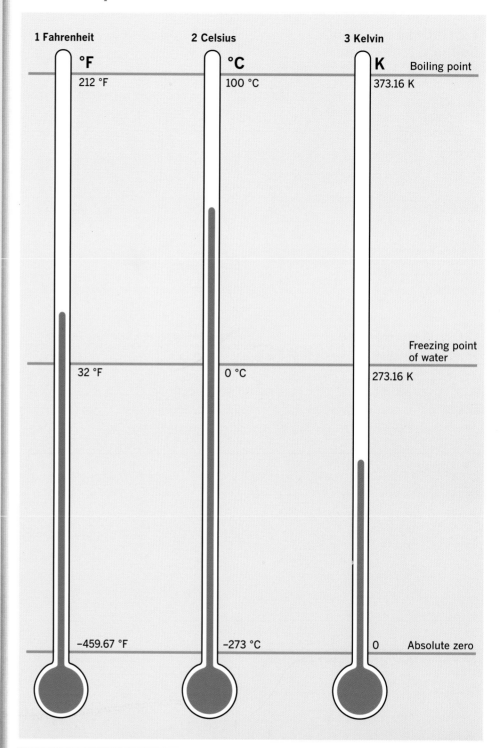

Fahrenheit to Celsius and vice versa

$$°C = (°F - 32) \times \frac{5}{9} \qquad °F = (°C \times \frac{9}{5}) + 32$$

Kelvin to Celsius

$$1 \text{ K} = 1 \text{ °C} \qquad °C = K - 273$$

Thermal conduction 1

1 Different conductors

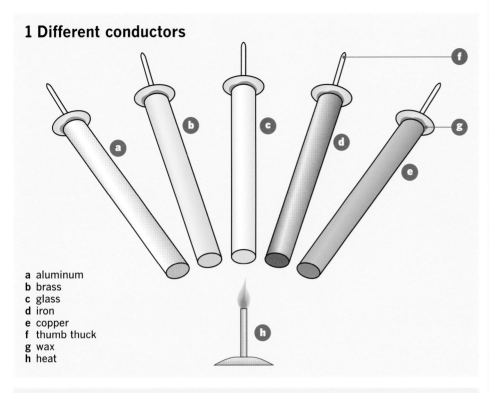

a aluminum
b brass
c glass
d iron
e copper
f thumb thuck
g wax
h heat

2 Water conduction

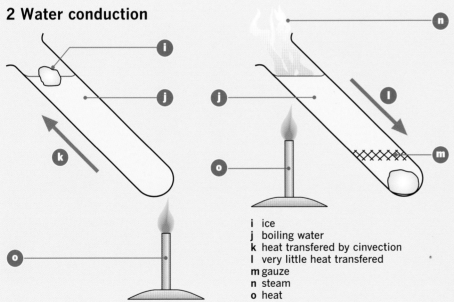

i ice
j boiling water
k heat transfered by cinvection
l very little heat transfered
m gauze
n steam
o heat

3 Air conduction

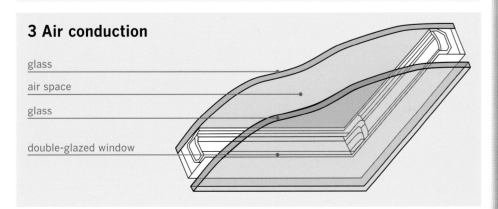

glass

air space

glass

double-glazed window

Thermal conduction

● Thermal *conduction* is the transfer of *internal energy* from particle to particle in matter.
● Metals are good thermal conductors. They contain a 'sea' of free-moving *electrons* that are able to transfer heat quickly from one point to another.
● *Non-metals* are very poor *conductors* of heat and are used for thermal *insulation*. Insulators are used to prevent heat from travelling such as for the handles of pans.

1 Different conductors

● Heat is transferred along the rods by conduction. When the end of the rod heats up the wax melts and the thumb tuck falls. The thumb tack on the copper rod falls first showing that copper is the best thermal conductor. The thumb tack attached to the glass rod takes much longer to fall off as glass is a poor thermal conductor.

2 Water conduction

● Liquids and gases conduct heat but very slowly. Very little heat is transferred through water by conduction.
● When the water at the bottom of a test-tube is heated warm water rises by convection and melts an ice cube on the surface.
● When water at the top of a test-tube is heated it boils before sufficient heat is conducted through the water to melt the ice cube at the bottom of the test-tube.

3 Air conduction

● Air is a very poor thermal conductor. It is for this reason that the air space or cavity between the outer and inner walls of a of a building and the air space between the layers of glass in double glazing help to keep the inside of the building warm in the winter and cool in the summer.

Thermal conduction 2

Key words

conduction	thermal
gradient	conductivity
tangent	
temperature	

1 Temperature gradient

- Some heat conducted through an unlagged bar is lost. The *temperature gradient* along the bar is therefore non-linear. A *tangent* to the curve gives the temperature gradient at that point.
- When the bar is lagged no heat is lost to the surroundings and the temperature gradient along the bar is linear.

2 Coefficient of thermal conductivity

- A thin slab has uniform cross-sectional area **A**, thickness **L**, and a small temperature difference (T_1-T_2) is maintained across. A small quantity of heat, **dQ**, passes through it by conduction in time **t** and its *thermal conductivity* is **k**. $dQ=-k\,A\,t\,(T_1-T_2)/L$ (Negative sign indicating that heat flows towards the lower temperature.) or $k = dQ\,L / A\,t\,(T_2-T_1)$
- Thermal conductivity, **k**, is the rate of heat flow through a material per unit area per unit temperature gradient.

3 Effect on temperature gradient of insulators

- The temperature drop is divided equally over the two thin layers of insulator and the long lagged bar.

4 Measuring k for a good conductor

- Heat should flow through the metal at a measurable rate and the temperature gradient along the metal must be sufficiently steep to measure.

5 Measuring k for a poor conductor

- In order to achieve measurable heat flow the material is in the form of disc a few millimeter thick in a thick metal casing heated by steam.

1 Temperature gradient

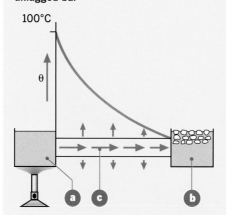
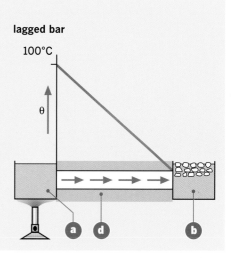

2 Coefficient of thermal conductivity

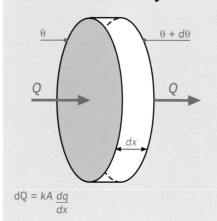

$$dQ = kA \frac{dq}{dx}$$

3 Effect on temperature gradient of insulators

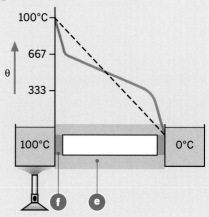
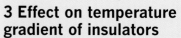

4 Measuring k for a good conductor

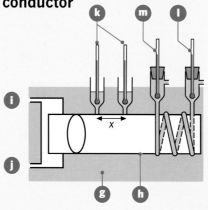

5 Measuring k for a poor conductor

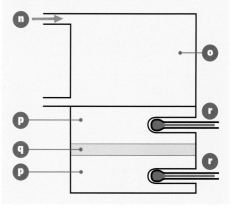

a boiling water
b mixture of ice and water
c unlagged bar
d lagging
e lagged bar
f thin layer of insulating material
g lagging

h copper bar
i steam in
j condensed steam out
k thermometers for measuring temperature gradient along length x of bar
l temperature of water in
m temperature of water out

n steam in
o steam chamber
p heavy metal base
q layer of insulating material
r Thermometers for measuring temperature gradient

Thermal radiation 1

1 Effect of surface on absorption

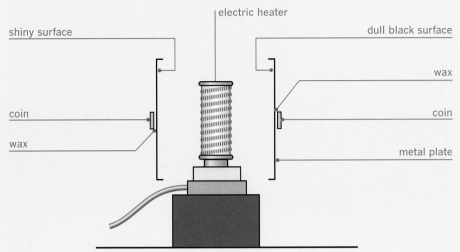

2 Effect of surface on emission

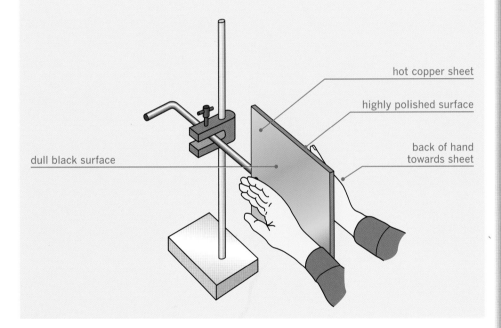

3 Leslie's cube

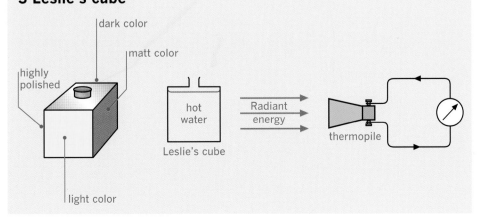

Thermal radiation

- *Thermal radiation* is the transfer of heat in the form of *infrared waves*.
- Bodies above *absolute zero* emit heat *radiation* whose *frequency* is determined by the body's temperature.
- The transfer of heat radiation does not involve matter thus it can pass across a *vacuum*.

1 Effect of surface on absorption

- A coin is attached to each metal plate with wax and an electric heater is placed between the plates ensuring each receives the same amount of radiation. The coin attached to the dull black surface falls first demonstrating that dull black surfaces are better *absorbers* of heat.

2 Effect of surface on emission

- A copper sheet has one side highly polished and the other painted dull black. When the sheet is heated and the backs of the hands placed at equal distances from each side of it the back of the hand facing the dull black surface feels warmer demonstrating that dull black surfaces are better emitters of heat radiation.

3 Leslie's cube

- John Leslie compared the radiating powers of different surfaces using a hollow copper cube filled with hot water. One face was highly polished while the opposite face was made matt black by holding it above a candle flame. The remaining faces were painted in light and dark colors.
- The matt black surface emitted most of radiation, and the highly polished surface least. When comparing the sides painted different colors, the texture of the surface appeared to be more important than the color.

© Diagram Visual Information Ltd.

Key words

electromotive force (e.m.f.)	pyrometer
galvanometer	thermocouple
parabolic reflector	thermopile
	potentiometer

1 Reflection of thermal radiation

- The *parabolic reflector* on a fire is highly polished. The heat radiation emitted by the element is reflected as a series of parallel rays.

2 Differential thermometer

- The bulb painted matt black absorbs heat radiation more quickly. The air in this bulb expands more quickly causing a greater pressure in that side of the U tube.

3 Total radiation pyrometer

- A *pyrometer* measures the temperature of very hot objects using the thermal radiation emitted.
- The radiation emitted by the source is focused onto the blackened foil to which a *thermocouple* is attached. From the *e.m.f.* produced by the thermcouple, the temperature of the source can be calculated.

4 Thermopile

- Heat radiation absorbed by the blackened discs is warms the junctions of the wires attached to them and sets up an e.m.f. which can be measured either by a *potentiometer* or a *galvanometer* connected directly to the *thermopile*.

5 Disappearing filament pyrometer

- Hot bodies emit infrared, visible light and ultraviolet radiation. A disappearing filament optical *pyrometer* responds to light only.
- Light from the hot body and from a tungsten filament lamp pass through a red filter of a known wavelength. The current passing through the filament lamp is adjusted until it appears to be as bright as the light from the source. The temperature is read from the ammeter, calibrated in K.

Thermal radiation 2

1 Reflection of thermal radiation

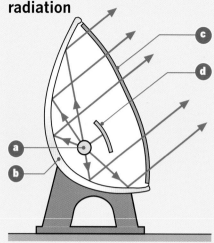

a electrical heating element
b shiny reflecting surface
c protective guard
d shield to cut out direct radiant energy

2 Differential thermometer

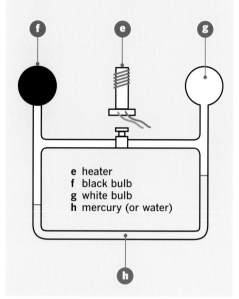

e heater
f black bulb
g white bulb
h mercury (or water)

3 Total radiation pyrometer

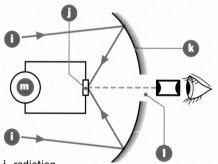

i radiation
j blackened foil and thermocouple at principal focus
k concave mirror
l observation window
m millivoltmeter to measure equilibrium temperature of foil

4 Thermopile

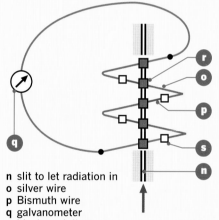

n slit to let radiation in
o silver wire
p Bismuth wire
q galvanometer
r blackened discs
s unblackened discs

5 Disappearing filament pyrometer

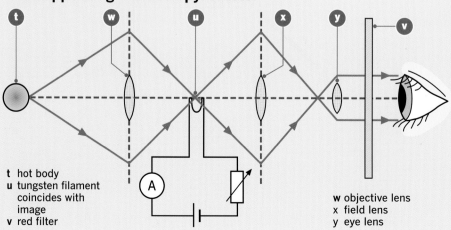

t hot body
u tungsten filament coincides with image
v red filter

w objective lens
x field lens
y eye lens

Convection 1

1 Water circulation

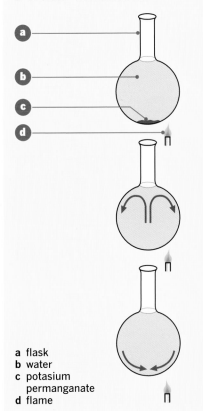

a flask
b water
c potasium permanganate
d flame

2 Domestic water circulation

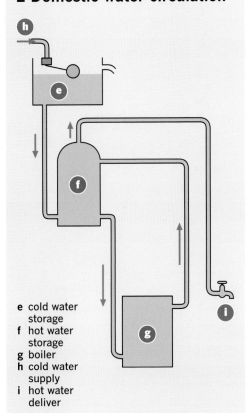

e cold water storage
f hot water storage
g boiler
h cold water supply
i hot water deliver

3 Smoke transference

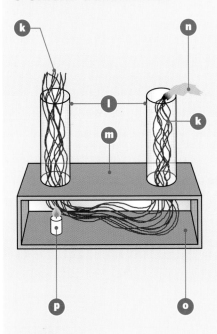

k smoke
l glass chimneys
m box
n smouldering paper
o glass window
p lighted candle

4 Domestic smoke circulation

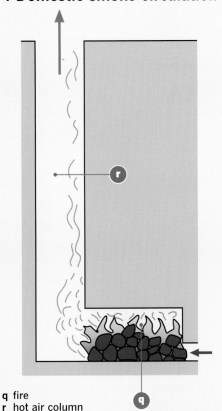

q fire
r hot air column

Convection

- *Convection* is the process by which energy is transferred by the bulk movement of a heated fluid (liquid or gas). When a fluid is heated it *expands* and its *density* becomes less than the surrounding unheated fluid. Less dense fluid rises and is replaced by denser cooler fluid.

1 Water circulation

- Potassium permanganate dissolves in water to give an intense purple solution.
- Heating the water immediately surrounding the potassium permanganate crystals causes it to expand and become less dense. The purple-coloured water rises and is replaced by cooler colorless water.

2 Domestic water circulation

- When the water in the boiler is heated it expands and rises, first to the top of the boiler and then into the top of the hot water cylinder. It is replaced by cooler water passing from the bottom of the hot water cylinder to the bottom of the boiler.
- There is a temperature gradient in the hot water cylinder. Hot water is tapped off from the top while replacement cold water passes into the bottom.

3 Smoke transference

- The air above the candle expands and rises up the chimney to the left. This air is replaced by cooler air passing down the other chimney, drawing smoke down from the smouldering paper. The movement of air is seen by introducing smoke to the box.

4 Domestic smoke circulation

- Air is drawn through a fire in order to replace the hot air from a fire which rises up the chimney.

Key words

absorption	vacuum
conduction	vapor
convection	
Dewar flask	
radiation	

1 Day–night heat exchange

- During the day land heats up more quickly than sea resulting in a cool breeze—a sea breeze.
- During the night land loses heat more quickly resulting in a cool breeze from land to sea—a land breeze.

2 Atmospheric heat exchange

- Differential heating of the atmosphere causes the movement of air we call wind.
- Cold polar air falls as warm tropic air rises forming a polar front. Polar air cools down further as it is pushed north and *convection* currents form, circulating the air. A warm front leads tropic air and a cold front leads polar air.
- Air carries water *vapor* which condenses into tiny droplets forming clouds. When these droplets grow large enough they fall as rain.

3 Dewar flask

- A *Dewar flask* (*vacuum* flask) minimizes the transfer of thermal energy.
- The double-walled vessel is made of glass and the stopper of cork or plastic. These substances are all poor heat *conductors*.
- There is a vacuum between the inner and outer walls of the vessel, preventing convection currents.
- The inner surfaces of the double-walled vessel are silvered, reflecting back heat *radiation* to the contents of the vessel rather than losing it to the surroundings. Similarly, heat radiation from the surroundings is reflected away rather than being *absorbed* by the contents of the vessel.

Convection 2

1 Day-night heat exchange

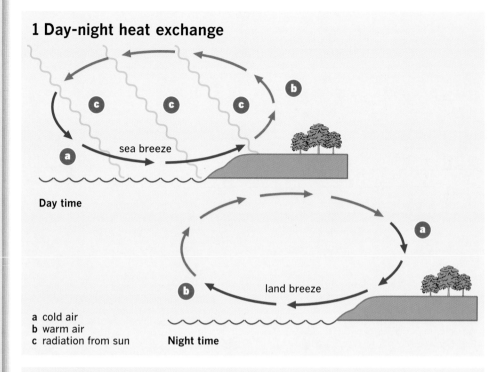

a cold air
b warm air
c radiation from sun

Day time **Night time**

2 Atmospheric heat exchange

Polar air meets tropical air

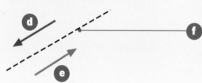

Warm air pushes polar air northward

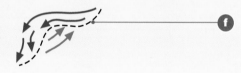

Circulation starts

d polar air	k nimbo-stratus
e tropical air	l alto-stratus
f polar front	m cirro-stratus
g cold front	n cirrus
h warm front	o rain
i cold air	p pressure falling
j warm air	

Section through a depression

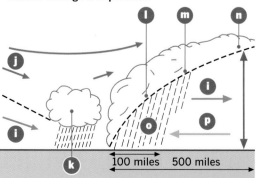

3 Dewar flask

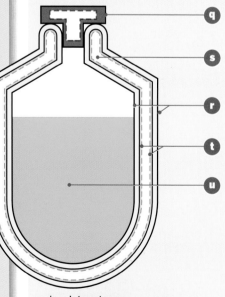

q insulator stopper
r double-walled glass vessel
s vacuum
t silvering facing the vacuum
u hot liquid

Energy changes 1

1 Striking a match

stored CHEMICAL ENERGY in the match

conversion by burning

oxidation

radiant HEAT ENERGY

LIGHT ENERGY

2 Cell lighting a filament lamp

stored CHEMICAL ENERGY in the cell

conversion in the cell

ELECTRICAL ENERGY

conversion in the lamp filament

radiant HEAT ENERGY

LIGHT ENERGY

3 Driving a nail into a block of wood

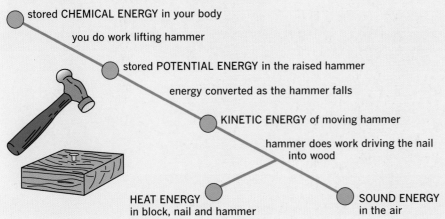

stored CHEMICAL ENERGY in your body

you do work lifting hammer

stored POTENTIAL ENERGY in the raised hammer

energy converted as the hammer falls

KINETIC ENERGY of moving hammer

hammer does work driving the nail into wood

HEAT ENERGY
in block, nail and hammer

SOUND ENERGY
in the air

4 Winding a dynamo's spring to light a lamp

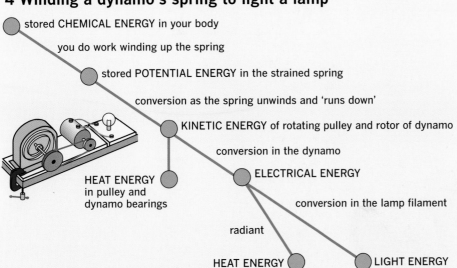

stored CHEMICAL ENERGY in your body

you do work winding up the spring

stored POTENTIAL ENERGY in the strained spring

conversion as the spring unwinds and 'runs down'

KINETIC ENERGY of rotating pulley and rotor of dynamo

conversion in the dynamo

ELECTRICAL ENERGY

HEAT ENERGY
in pulley and
dynamo bearings

conversion in the lamp filament

radiant

HEAT ENERGY

LIGHT ENERGY

Key words

chemical energy
combustion
energy

Energy changes

- The principal of conservation of *energy* states that energy can be neither created nor destroyed but only changes from one form to another.
- In an energy change work done equals the amount of energy changed.
- Energy is measured in joules (J) and kilojoules (kJ).

1 Striking a match

- Chemical energy → Heat energy + Light energy
- *Chemical energy*, stored in fuels such as coal, gas and wood is released in a chemical reaction when fuel combines with oxygen. These are *combustion* reactions.

2 Cell lighting a filament lamp

- Chemical energy → Electrical energy → Heat energy + Light energy
- Chemical energy is stored in cells. Electrical energy results from a chemical reaction in the cell.

3 Driving a nail into a block of wood

- Chemical energy → Potential energy → Kinetic energy → Heat energy + Sound energy
- Potential and kinetic energy are types of mechanical energy. An object's potential energy is the energy it has when above the ground.
- Kinetic energy is the energy possessed by a moving object. It is greater the faster the object moves.

4 Winding a dynamo's spring to light a lamp

- Chemical energy → Potential energy → Kinetic energy → Electrical energy → Heat energy + Light energy
- Energy is always lost in transfers, usually as heat. This is not usually shown in energy flow diagrams.

Key words

battery	exothermic
chemical energy	power
dynamo	
electrical energy	
energy	

Energy changes

- In all *energy* changes, some energy output does not do useful work. No energy change is 100% efficient.
- *Power* is the rate at which energy is transferred from one form to another.

Power = $\dfrac{\text{Work done}}{\text{Time taken}}$

Power is measured in Js^{-1} = watts (W).

1 Electric motor raising a load

- The potential energy of an object relates to its weight and vertical height above the ground.
  Potential energy = Weight x Vertical height above the ground
- *Chemical energy* → *Electrical energy* → Kinetic energy → Potential energy
- The work done raising the load is greater than the potential energy gained because some energy is lost as heat.
- If the raised load is released, gravity pulls it towards the ground. The opposite energy transfers then occur.
  Potential energy → Kinetic energy → Electrical energy → Chemical energy
  The falling weight rotates the belt and pulley. These in turn rotate the motor which now acts as a *dynamo*. The electricity generated recharges the *battery*.

2 Steam engine driving a dynamo

- Combustion is an *exothermic* reaction thus heat is given out.
  fuel + oxygen → products + energy
- Heat produced converts water to steam at raised pressure. This drives a turbine which drives a dynamo. The electricity produced lights a bulb.
- A more powerful steam engine produces more energy per unit time and therefore makes the bulb glow brighter.

Energy changes 2

1 Electric motor raising a load

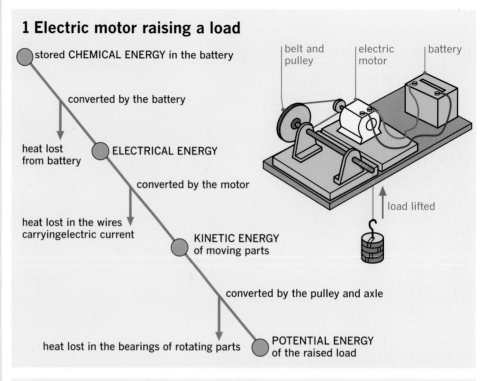

stored CHEMICAL ENERGY in the battery

converted by the battery

heat lost from battery

ELECTRICAL ENERGY

converted by the motor

heat lost in the wires carryingelectric current

KINETIC ENERGY of moving parts

converted by the pulley and axle

heat lost in the bearings of rotating parts

POTENTIAL ENERGY of the raised load

belt and pulley — electric motor — battery — load lifted

2 Steam engine driving a dynamo

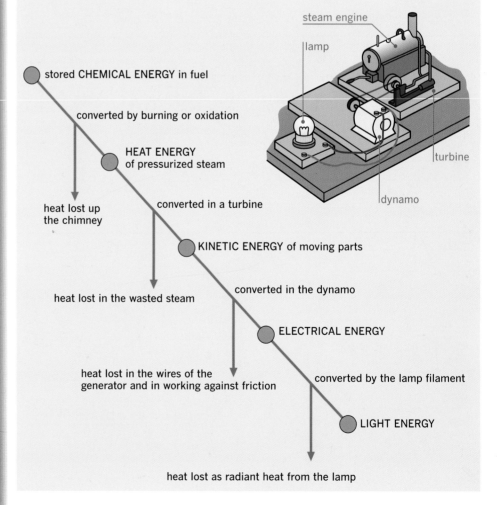

steam engine — lamp — turbine — dynamo

stored CHEMICAL ENERGY in fuel

converted by burning or oxidation

heat lost up the chimney

HEAT ENERGY of pressurized steam

converted in a turbine

heat lost in the wasted steam

KINETIC ENERGY of moving parts

converted in the dynamo

heat lost in the wires of the generator and in working against friction

ELECTRICAL ENERGY

converted by the lamp filament

LIGHT ENERGY

heat lost as radiant heat from the lamp

Energy production and distribution

Key words

basal metabolic
 rate
energy
infrared
respiration

1 Human energy

Energy gains

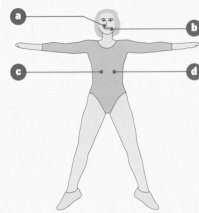

a oxygen
b food input 10 to 20 MJ per day
c energy needed for doing work
d energy lost as heat

e convection losses
f evaporation
g conduction to chair and floor
h infra-red radiation

Typical energy losses from the human body when seated (i.e. not active) (in %)

Energy losses

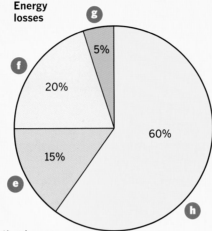

1 Human energy

- Energy is produced in the cells of the body by the process of *respiration*.
  glucose + oxygen →
  carbon dioxide + water + energy
- The *basal metabolic rate* (BMR) is the minimum amount of *energy* needed keep a person alive. It does not remain constant throughout a person's life but changes with growth, development and aging. A new-born baby has a low BMR, typically 100 kJ m^{-2} h^{-1}. This rises to around 220 kJ m^{-2} h^{-1} at the age of one, when body growth is most rapid, and gradually declines to between $150 - 170$ kJ m^{-2} h^{-1} in a young healthy adult. This translates to a total energy requirement per day of $6000 - 7500$ kJ.
- The energy requirement of the body beyond BMR depends upon the level of activity of the person and the ambient temperature of the surroundings.
- The main source of heat loss from the body is heat (*infrared*) radiation.
- Heat is continually being lost in expelled air as this is always saturated with water vapor.

2 Domestic energy

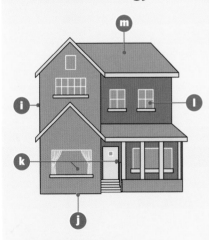

Energy losses from a typical house

i through the walls
j through the floor
k through draughts
l through the window
m through the roof
n central heating
o hot water
p electric lighting and domestic appliances
q cooking

Losses	prevention
the roof	loft insulation
the walls	cavity wall insulation
the windows	double glazing
the floor	carpeting
draughts	draught excluders

Losses

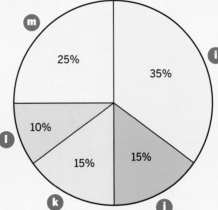

Uses

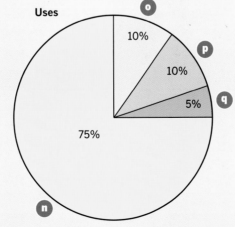

How energy is used in the home

2 Domestic energy

- Buildings in temperate climates are often heated to maintain a higher temperature than the surroundings. Heat is lost from the building to the surroundings in a variety of ways.
- Energy losses can be prevented in a variety of ways.
- The vast majority of energy use in the average home goes on heating the rooms and on providing hot water for bathing. Relatively small amounts are used for lighting and electrical appliances, and for cooking.

Key words

conductor
convection
insulation

1 Roof

- Warm air rises so heat losses through the top of a house are a particular problem.
- In attic *insulation* a layer of an insulating material is laid down between the rafters. Materials used have pockets of air trapped within them. Air is a very poor *conductor* of heat.

2 Wall

- Heat passes from the inside to the outside of a wall by conduction. The air cavity between the inner and outer walls of a house reduces the amount of heat conducted to the outer walls.
- In cavity wall insulation, the cavity is filled with an insulating material. This reduces heat losses by conduction and prevents the formation of *convection* currents which transfer heat from the inner wall.

3 Floor

- Heat passes out of a house into the ground by conduction.
- Underlay and carpets are made of insulating materials which reduce heat losses through the floor.

4 Window

- Double-glazed windows consist of two panes of glass separated by a layer of air. This reduces the amount of heat lost by conduction and also prevents the formation of convection currents which transfer heat from the outer surface of the inner pane of glass.

5 Draughts

- Warm air is able to pass out of, and cold air to pass into a house through badly-fitting doors and windows.
- Draughts are reduced by fitting draught excluders around doors and windows.

Reducing energy losses from houses

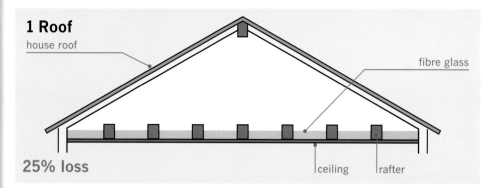

1 Roof

house roof

fibre glass

25% loss

ceiling rafter

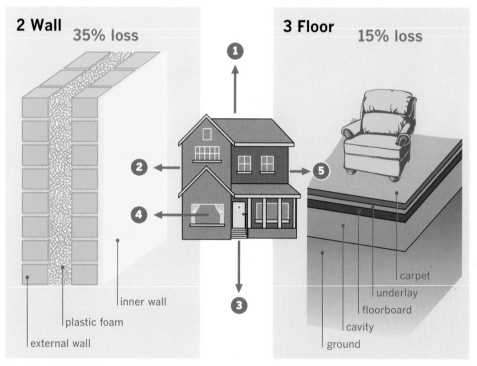

2 Wall   35% loss

inner wall

plastic foam

external wall

3 Floor   15% loss

carpet
underlay
floorboard
cavity
ground

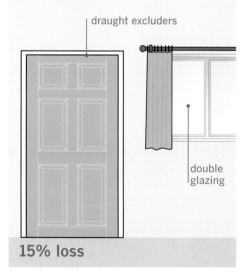

4 Window

10% loss

5 Draughts

draught excluders

double glazing

15% loss

Energy from the Sun

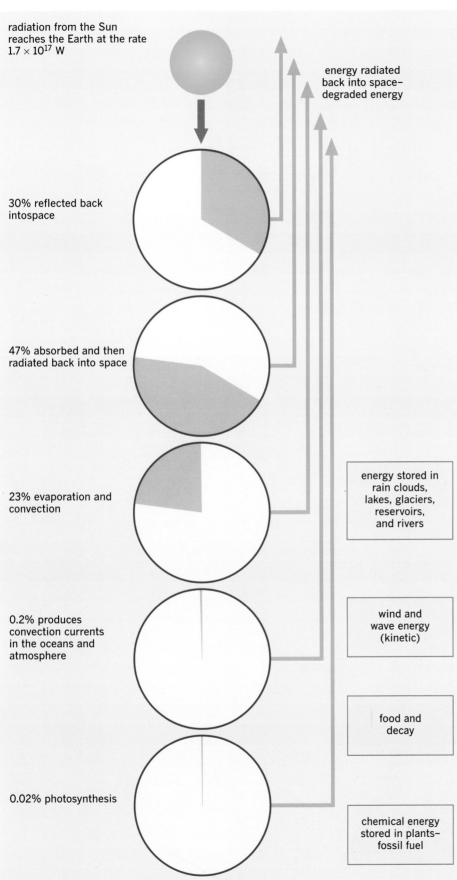

radiation from the Sun
reaches the Earth at the rate
1.7×10^{17} W

energy radiated
back into space–
degraded energy

30% reflected back
intospace

47% absorbed and then
radiated back into space

23% evaporation and
convection

0.2% produces
convection currents
in the oceans and
atmosphere

0.02% photosynthesis

energy stored in
rain clouds,
lakes, glaciers,
reservoirs,
and rivers

wind and
wave energy
(kinetic)

food and
decay

chemical energy
stored in plants–
fossil fuel

Key words

energy
fusion
global warming
mass
normal

Energy from the Sun

- *Energy* is produced on the Sun by nuclear *fusion*. *Mass* is converted to energy according to Einstein's equation $E = mc^2$

  energy = mass x speed of light
  in a vacuum^2

- Every second on the Sun, 700 million tonnes of hydrogen is converted to 695 million tonnes of helium. The remaining 5 million tonnes of mass is converted to energy.

- The mass of the Sun is 2.0×10^{30} kg therefore it could maintain its current rate of energy production for $2.0 \times 10^{30} / 5.0 \times 10^6 = 4.0 \times 10^{23}$ s $\times$ 10^{16} years.

- The solar constant is the solar energy falling per second on a square meter placed *normal* to the Sun's rays at the edge of Earth's atmosphere when Earth is at its average distance from the Sun. Its value is 1.35 kW m^{-2}.

- The actual amount of solar radiation falling at any point on the surface of Earth depends on four factors. The amount of light falling on sunny regions near to the equator is greater than that falling on temperate regions nearer the poles. In temperate regions the amount of light varies with the season. More light falls on a region during the summer and less during the winter. The greater the height of a region above sea level the more light it will receive as less light is absorbed by the atmosphere. The higher the Sun is in the sky the greater the amount of light reaching the ground as less is absorbed by the atmosphere.

- *Global warming* is the result of less of the Sun's energy being reflected and reradiated back into space. Many scientists attribute this to an increase of so called "greenhouse gases," such as carbon dioxide and methane, in the upper atmosphere.

Key words

electron	photovoltaic cell
n-type	satellite
p-type	solar panel
parabolic	
reflector	

1 Solar furnace

- In a solar furnace, a heliostat (a large mirror which tracks the Sun) reflects the Sun's rays onto a *parabolic reflector* formed of a number of plane mirrors. The parabolic reflector focuses the Sun's rays onto a small space, producing a very high temperature.
- At the solar furnace at Odeillo in France around 20,000 small plane mirrors are arranged to form a parabolic reflector of diameter 45 m.
- The furnace generates up to 1 MW with temperatures normally in the range 800–2,500°C.

2 Solar water heating

- Water is pumped through a network of pipes in a panel directed towards the Sun. The pipes are made of copper, a good conductor of heat, and painted matt black to absorb the maximum amount of heat radiation.
- The hot water circulates through a heating coil in a tank where cold water is heated.

3 Solar cells

- *Solar cells* or *photovoltaic cells* convert solar energy directly into electricity.
- These devices are made of layers of *p*– and *n*–*type* silicon. When light falls on the surface the energy frees loosely held *electrons*. This results in an e.m.f. between metal contacts on the top and bottom of the surfaces.
- For practical purposes solar cells are connected together to form solar panels. Such panels have been used widely to power *satellites* in space but their use on Earth has been limited by their high cost.

Solar energy devices

1 Solar furnace

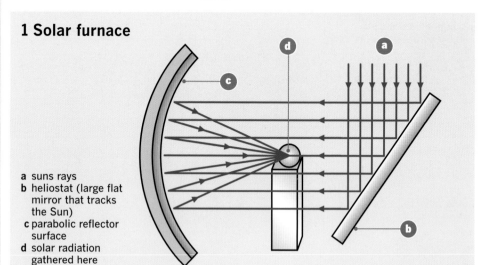

a suns rays
b heliostat (large flat mirror that tracks the Sun)
c parabolic reflector surface
d solar radiation gathered here

2 Solar water heating

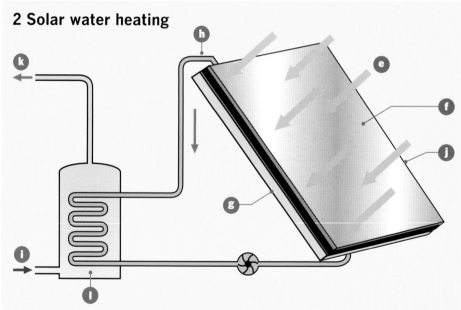

e sunlight
f black heat absorbing surface
g insulation
h hot water
i cold water
j transparent cover
k to domestic hot water system
l panel heat exchange

3 Solar cells

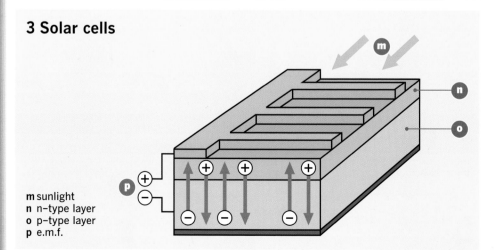

m sunlight
n n–type layer
o p–type layer
p e.m.f.

A typical power station

1 Typical power station

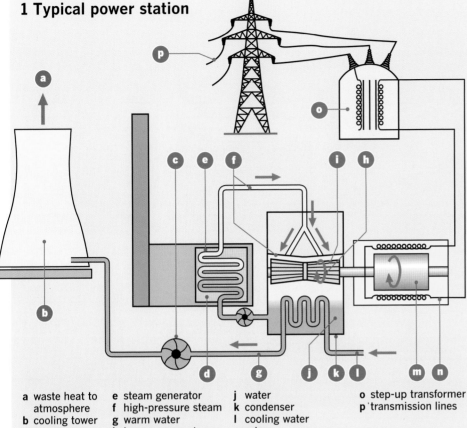

a waste heat to atmosphere
b cooling tower
c pump
d boiler
e steam generator
f high-pressure steam
g warm water
h low pressure steam
i turbine
j water
k condenser
l cooling water
m rotor
n generator stator coils
o step-up transformer
p transmission lines

2 Energy conversions in a power station

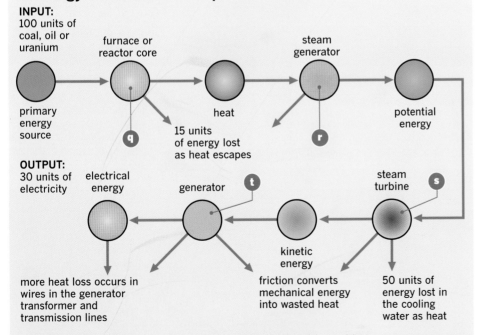

INPUT:
100 units of coal, oil or uranium

furnace or reactor core

steam generator

primary energy source

heat

15 units of energy lost as heat escapes

potential energy

OUTPUT:
30 units of electricity

electrical energy

generator

steam turbine

more heat loss occurs in wires in the generator transformer and transmission lines

kinetic energy

friction converts mechanical energy into wasted heat

50 units of energy lost in the cooling water as heat

q thermal energy produced by burning or nuclear reaction
r thermal energy used to produce steam at high pressure
s steam used to drive turbines
t generator converts mechanical energy into electrical energy

Key words

current	potential
dynamo	difference
energy	power
generator	transformer
magnet	turbine

1 Typical power station

- In a power station heat is used to produce steam at high pressure. High pressure steam drives *turbines* which are connected to a *generator*.
- The generator is essentially a massive *dynamo*. A *magnet* at the center of the generator rotates inducing an electric *current* in the coils of wire which surround it.
- A large power station generates electricity at 25,000 V. If electricity was transmitted at this *potential difference* the losses due to heat as it passed down the lines would be considerable.
- The *energy* lost rises as the square of the current so reducing the current reduces the energy losses considerably.
- Electrical *power* is equal to the product of the current and potential difference.

  power = current x potential difference

- In a step-up *transformer* the current is reduced while potential difference is increased proportionally. The power input and power output remain essentially the same. The resulting output from the step-up transformer has a potential difference of 400,000 V but a much reduced current which reduces energy losses in the lines.

2 Energy conversions in a power station

- Some energy is "lost" during each energy transfer, mainly as low-level heat. The energy is lost in the sense that it doesn't do useful work.
- Efficiency is the ratio of useful output energy to input energy. The overall efficiency of the power station is given by

  efficiency =
  $$\frac{30 \text{ units of electrical energy} \times 100\%}{100 \text{ units of fuel energy}}$$

  = 30%

Key words

energy
fossil fuel
isotope

Non-renewable energy resources

- Non-renewable *energy* sources such as coal, natural gas, crude oil (*fossil fuels*) and uranium (nuclear fuel) are not renewed by natural processes over a short time scale.
- Fossil fuels were formed over many millions of years from plants and animals.

1 Coal

- Drift mines: coal seams run to the surface, coal is easy to remove.
- Open cast mines: coal seams are near the surface. Overlying layers are removed to expose the coal.
- Shaft mines: coal seams lie deep in the ground.

2 Oil and gas

- Oil and natural gas are trapped in porous rock beneath impermeable rock. If rocks are folded by natural processes, oil and gas become concentrated at the peak of the fold.

3 Nuclear

- Although nuclear fuels are non-renewable, amounts used are relatively small compared to fossil fuels and reserves are likely to last much longer.
- The most common fuel is an *isotope* of uranium, uranium U-235. This isotope only forms 0.7% of naturally occurring uranium. For a viable fuel, this percentage is increased to around 2.5% by enrichment.
- The fuel for fast breeder reactors is plutonium. The reactor is surrounded by a blanket of uranium. Neutrons escaping from the core of the reactor convert uranium to plutonium enabling the reactor to breed, or produce more of its own fuel.

Non-renewable energy sources

1 Coal

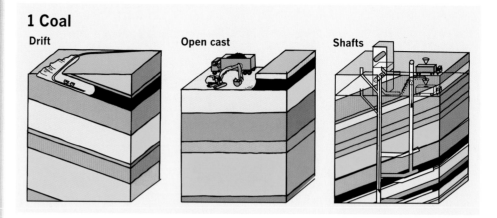

Drift   Open cast   Shafts

2 Oil and gas

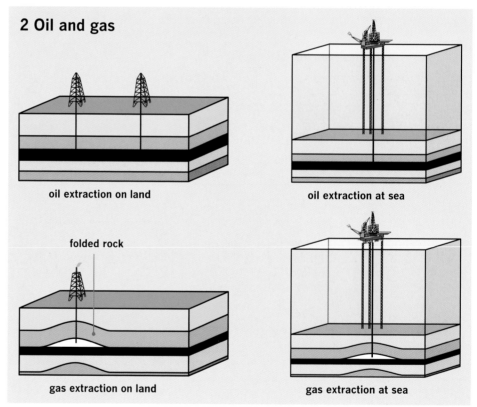

oil extraction on land

oil extraction at sea

folded rock

gas extraction on land

gas extraction at sea

3 Nuclear

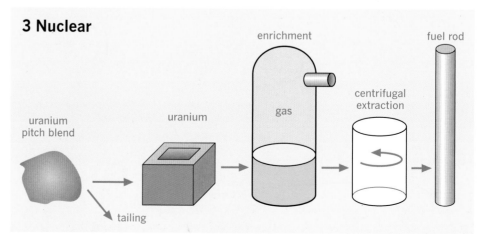

uranium pitch blend

uranium

enrichment

gas

centrifugal extraction

fuel rod

tailing

Renewable energy sources

1 Water

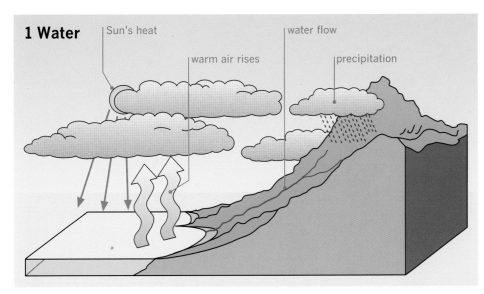

Sun's heat

warm air rises

water flow

precipitation

2 Wind

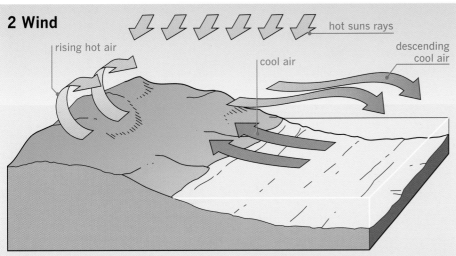

rising hot air

hot suns rays

cool air

descending cool air

3 Tide

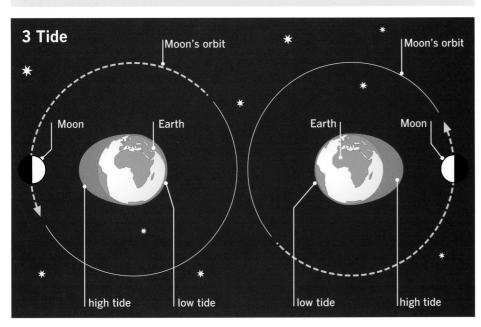

Moon's orbit

Moon's orbit

Moon

Earth

Earth

Moon

high tide

low tide

low tide

high tide

Key words

aquifer	gravity
biogas	hydroelectric
convection	plant
energy	turbine
geothermal	
energy	

Renewable energy sources

● Renewable *energy* sources are those which are renewed by natural sources. They include solar-powered devices, flowing water, tides, waves, wind, *geothermal aquifers*, geothermal hot dry rock structures and *biogas* generators.

1 Water

● The continuous movement of water between Earth and the atmosphere gives rise to the water cycle.

● Water that falls on high ground has potential energy. As the water flows down towards the sea the energy can be used in a variety of ways including generating electricity in *hydroelectric plants*.

2 Wind

● Heat is transferred through the atmosphere by *convection* currents.

● When air is warmed it expands, becomes less dense and rises, creating a region of low pressure on Earth's surface. In turn, cooler air falls to take its place creating an area of high pressure.

● Wind is air that moves from regions of high pressure to regions of low pressure. Wind has kinetic energy which can be used to drive windmills and wind *turbines*.

3 Tide

● The *gravitational* attraction of the Moon pulls on that part of Earth's surface which is closest to it. This causes a slight distortion in the land mass but the main effect is pulling the oceans out in a bulge in the direction of the Moon and in the opposite direction on the far side of Earth.

● The result is high and low tides. Water at high tide has potential energy which can be used to generate electricity.

Key words

condenser
energy
generator
turbine
vaporization

1 Wind energy

- Modern wind technology led to the construction of wind *turbines* which are specially designed to generate electricity from the kinetic *energy* of the wind.
- To operate successfully, wind turbines must be placed in areas where the wind often blows and the average wind speed is high.

2 Ocean thermal energy conversion

- Tropical seas absorb huge amounts of solar radiation. Ocean Thermal Energy Conversion (OTEC) uses this energy to generate electricity.
- OTEC makes use of the difference between the warm surface of the ocean and the cold water at depths below 600 metres. Provided there is a minimum temperature difference of around 20°C net power can be generated.
- In a closed-cycle system heat from warm surface sea water causes a working fluid (such as ammonia) to boil and become a gas. The resulting increase in pressure drives a turbine attached to a *generator*. Cold sea water passes through a *condenser* converting ammonia gas back to liquid which is then recycled through the system.
- In an open-cycle system the warm water itself is the working fluid. Water at the surface *vaporizes* in a near vacuum providing the pressure increase needed to drive a turbine. The vapor is condensed by cold sea water. The fresh water produced can be used for drinking, irrigation or aquaculture.

3 Hydroelectric

- In a hydroelectric plant the kinetic energy of flowing water turns a turbine which is connected to a generator and electricity is produced.

Alternative energy sources 1

1 Wind energy

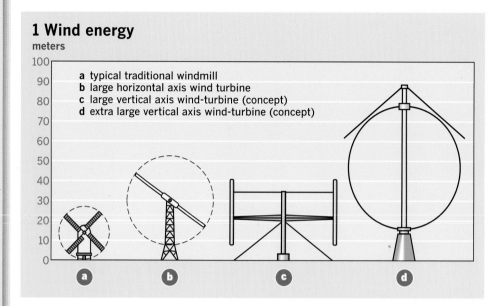

meters

a typical traditional windmill
b large horizontal axis wind turbine
c large vertical axis wind-turbine (concept)
d extra large vertical axis wind-turbine (concept)

2 Ocean thermal energy conversion (OTEC)

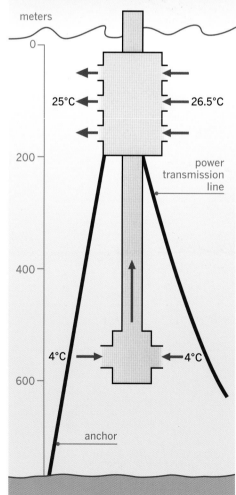

meters

25°C   26.5°C

power
transmission
line

4°C   4°C

anchor

3 Hydroelectric

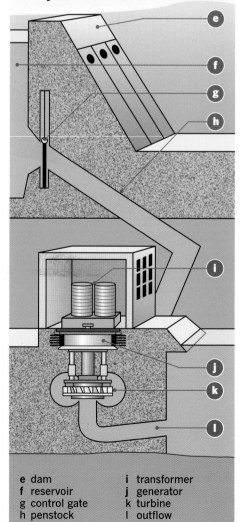

e dam
f reservoir
g control gate
h penstock
i transformer
j generator
k turbine
l outflow

Alternative energy sources 2

Key words
energy
generator
pressure
tidal energy
turbine

1 Tidal energy

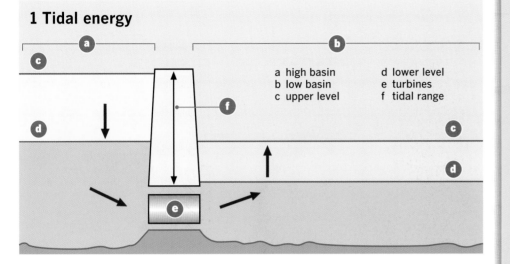

a high basin   d lower level
b low basin   e turbines
c upper level   f tidal range

2 Wave energy

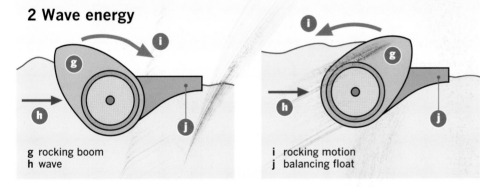

g rocking boom
h wave

i rocking motion
j balancing float

3 Tidal swell

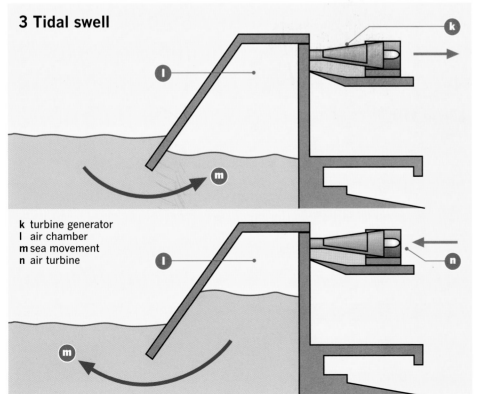

k turbine generator
l air chamber
m sea movement
n air turbine

1 Tidal energy

- The first and, to date, the world's only large-scale tidal barrage was built between 1961 and 1966 across the estuary of the Rance river in France.
- Tides rise and fall and different times of the day. As a tide rises, the level of water in the high basin rises. At high tide all gates are closed trapping the sea water behind the barrage.
- At low tide the water level in the high basin is higher than the water level in the low basin. The water trapped in the high basin has potential *energy*. It is allowed to flow out through *turbine generators* which are driven by the moving water to produce electricity.

2 Wave energy

- Rocking booms are strung offshore where they are kept in continual motion by the waves. As the waves rise and fall the boom is rocked up and down and this motion is used to generate electricity.

3 Tidal swell

- The wave-driven device is built in a natural rock gulley on the coast so that the waves are channelled into it.
- As the wave rolls in, the water level inside the chamber rises and air is forced upwards and out through the turbine generator.
- As the water level falls, the air *pressure* inside the chamber drops and, due to atmospheric pressure, air is forced in through the turbine generator.
- The turbine is a special design called a Wells turbine which can extract energy from the air stream no matter in which direction it flows so electricity is generated both as the water level rises and falls.

Key words

absorption	fermentation
aquifer	geothermal
biogas	energy
energy	heat pump
evaporation	

Alternative energy sources 3

1 Geothermal energy

- In some parts of the world there are very hot rocks quite near to the surface. When rain permeates down into the rocks it is heated and forms a *geothermal aquifer*.
- Heat *energy* is also extracted from geothermal hot rock structures which lie deeper in the ground. Two wells are drilled into the rocks terminating several hundred meters apart. Cold water is piped down one of the wells and is heated as it passes through the hot rocks. The resulting hot water rises to the surface through the second well.

2 Domestic heat pump

- Refrigerators and air conditioning units are basically *heat pumps* which transfer heat energy from one place to another. Heat pumps can be used both for cooling and for heating.
- A heat pump consists of a closed system containing a volatile substance which changes phase between being a liquid and a gas.
- The compressor pump compresses the gas, converting it to a liquid as it passes into the house. This change of state releases energy that warms the inside of the house. When the liquid passes back out of the house it *evaporates* to become a gas. This change of state requires energy that is *absorbed* from the surroundings. The net effect transfers heat energy from outside to inside the house.

3 Biogas unit

- In a *biogas* unit, a slurry of animal manure and water is *fermented* to release biogas. The main constituent of biogas is methane which is used as a fuel for cooking and heating. The residue which remains provides a useful fertiliser for improving plant growth.

1 Geothermal energy unit

a expansion tank
b flow control valve
c heat exchange
d cold water
e hot water
f permeable rock
g cold water down
h hot water up

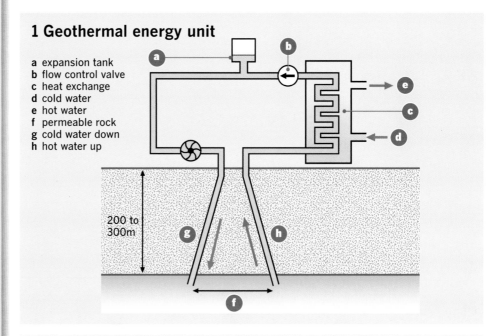

200 to 300m

2 Domestic heat pump

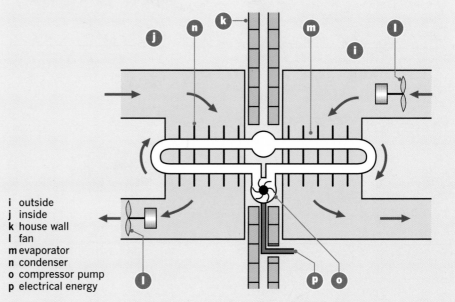

i outside
j inside
k house wall
l fan
m evaporator
n condenser
o compressor pump
p electrical energy

3 Biogas unit

q manure and water
r manure slurry
s stirrer
t methane
u fertilizer

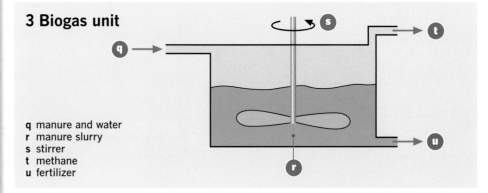

Nuclear energy

© Diagram Visual Information Ltd.

Key words

chain reaction	nuclear energy
control rod	nuclide
fission	
moderator	
neutron	

1 Nuclear fission

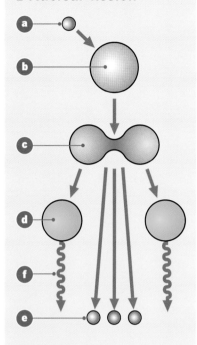

a neutron
b uranium nucleus
c unstable nucleus
d fission fragments, eg krypton and barium
e neutrons
f gamma–radiation

3 Chain reaction

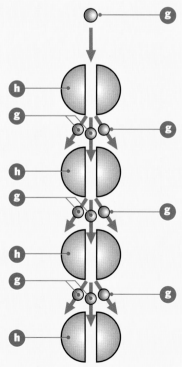

g neutron
h fission of uranium nucleus

2 Controlling a chain reaction

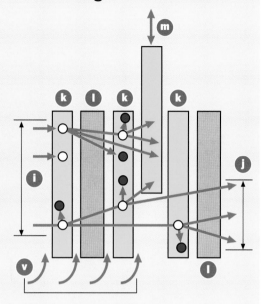

i thermal neutrons from another fuel rod
j thermal neutrons to another fuel rod
k fuel rod
l moderator (eg graphite)
m control rod which can be raised or lowered

4 Advanced gas-cooled reactor

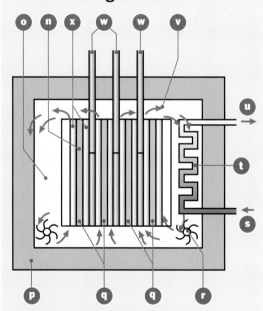

n Reactor core up to 1500°C
o CO_2 coolant
p concrete pressure and radiation shield
q 15000 graphite bricks locked together
r gas circulating pumps
s water
t steam generator
u steam at 650°C and 40 atm pressure
v flow of coolant
w boron steel control rods
x uranium fuel rods

1 Nuclear fission

- *Nuclear energy* results from nuclear *fission* of large unstable *nuclides* like uranium-235.
- Uranium-235 undergoes spontaneous fission, but in a nuclear power station the fission occurs by bombarding the uranium nuclei with *neutrons*. When hit by a slow-moving neutron, the unstable nucleus breaks into two smaller nuclei of similar size and three neutrons are released. The combined mass of the products is slightly less than the reactants; some mass is converted to energy.

2 Chain reaction

- The three neutrons released can cause the fission of three more uranium-235 nuclei releasing nine neutrons. These, in turn, can cause the fission of nine more uranium-235 nuclei and so on. This *chain reaction* is controlled in a nuclear reactor by limiting the number of neutrons

3 Controlling a chain reaction

- In order to increase the chances that neutrons will cause the fission of uranium-235 nuclei they are slowed by a *moderator*.
- *Control rods*, suspended between the fuel rods, can be raised or lowered as needed to control the nuclear reaction. They are made of alloys such as boron steel that absorb neutrons. When they are lowered more neutrons are absorbed, slowing the chain reaction.

4 Advanced gas–cooled reactor

- Temperature is controlled in an advanced gas-cooled reactor by circulating carbon dioxide gas. Heat is removed in heat exchangers which convert water into high-pressure steam.

Key words

compression	wavelength
longitudinal wave	
rarefaction	
transverse wave	
wave	

Waves

- *Waves* may be classified as transverse or longitudinal depending on the direction of displacement. Both types of wave can conveniently be shown using a slinky spring.

1 Transverse waves

- In a *transverse wave* the displacement is at right angles to the direction in which the wave is traveling.
- A transverse wave produces a series of crests and troughs as the wave form is repeated in a regular cycle. The *wavelength* of the wave, denoted by the symbol λ, is the horizontal distance from any point on the cycle to the analogous point on the next cycle. This is often conveniently taken as the distance from one crest to the next. Altering the size of the crests and troughs does not alter the wavelength of the wave.
- Light is an example of a transverse wave form.

2 Longitudinal waves

- In a *longitudinal wave* the displacement is in the same direction as the direction in which the wave is traveling.
- A longitudinal wave produces a series of *rarefactions* and *compressions* as the wave causes particles to move closer together or further apart in a regular cycle. The wavelength of the wave (λ) is the horizontal distance from any point on the cycle to the analogous point on the next cycle. This is often conveniently taken as the distance from one compression to the next.
- Sound is an example of a longitudinal wave form.

Describing waves

1 Transverse waves

Vibration and direction of the wave

vibration of source producing the wave

direction of travel of the wave

Demonstrating a transverse wave in a slinky spring

hand moved side to side | slinky spring

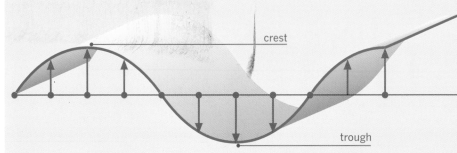

Displacement of the particles if the wave is transverse

crest

trough

Graphical plot λ = wavelength

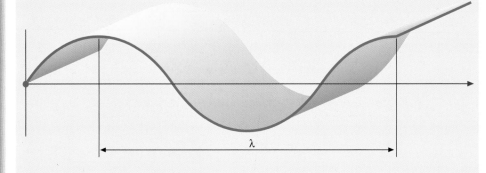

λ

2 Longitudinal waves

Vibration and direction of the wave

direction of travel of the wave

vibration of source producing the wave

Demonstrating a longitudinal wave in a slinky spring

slinky spring | compression of the spring

hand gives spring a pulse

Displacement of the particles if the wave is longitudinal

rarefaction | compression | rarefaction | compression

λ

Huygen's construction 1

Key words

phase
tangent
wave

1 Relationship between wave fronts and waves

Spherical wave fronts from a point source S

ray

ray · · · ray

S

direction of wave

ray

wave fronts

Plane wavefronts from a broad source

wave front

ray · direction of wave

wave fronts

2 Huygen's construction for a plane progressive wave

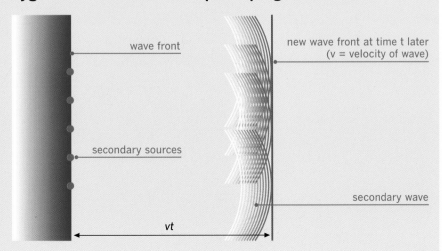

wave front

secondary sources

new wave front at time t later
(v = velocity of wave)

secondary wave

vt

1 Relationship between wave fronts and waves

- A *wave* front is a line or a surface in which all points are in the same *phase*.
- A point source generates circular wave fronts while a line source generates straight wave fronts. The distance between adjacent wave fronts corresponds with the wavelength. A line at right angles to a wave front which indicates its direction of travel is called a ray.

2 Huygen's construction for a plane progressive wave

- Huygens proposed a construction which can be used to explain reflection, refraction and dispersion of waves.
- This proposal was based on the idea that every point on a wave front could be regarded as a source of secondary waves which would spread out with the same velocity as the wave itself.
- A new wave front could therefore be considered to be the common *tangent* of a set of secondary waves. Since all the secondary waves travel at the same speed, this tangent would be parallel to the original wave.
- This construction implies that waves should also travel in the opposite direction i.e. backwards. This does not occur in practice. The assumption is made that the amplitude of the secondary waves varies from a maximum in the direction of travel to zero in the opposite direction.

Huygen's construction 2

© Diagram Visual Information Ltd.

Key words

angle of incidence	refractive index
normal	tangent
radius	wave
reflection	wavelength

1 Reflection

- *Wave* front **AB** approaches the reflecting surface obliquely. A touches at A, B at B'.
- Draw an arc (*radius* BB') centered on A; draw the *tangent* to this arc from B' touching the arc at A'. A is *reflected* in the direction AA'.
- In triangles AA'B' and ABB' angle AA'B' = angle ABB' = 90°; AB' is a common side; AA' = BB'.
- As the triangles are congruent, the angles made by the incident wave front and the reflected wave front with the reflecting surface are the same— angle BAB' = angle A'B'A.
- Wave front is at right angles to its associated ray so *angle of incidence*, i, equals angle of reflection, r.

2 Refraction

- Wave front **AB** approaches the boundary between two media. Velocity in 1 is v_1; in 2, v_2. After **t** seconds, wave front is at A'B'.
- If $v_1 > v_2$ the *refracted* ray is bent towards the *normal* as shown. If $v_1 < v_2$ the refracted ray is bent away from the normal.
- In the triangles BAB' and A'AB' $\sin i_1/\sin i_2 = \sin BAB'/\sin A'B'A = BB'/AB' \div AA'/AB' = BB' / AA' = v_1 t / v_2 t$. Therefore $\sin i_1/\sin i_2 = v_1/v_2$. As v_1 and v_2 are constant for given media and wavelength, $\sin i_1/\sin i_2$ is also constant. Angle i_2 (angle of refraction) is normally represented by r. $\sin i /\sin r =$ **refractive index**. (constant, depending on media)

3 Optical dispersion

- The value of v_1/v_2 differs for different *wavelengths* (colors).
- White light is a mixture of different wavelengths. When passing between mediums, each wavelength is refracted by a different amount, dispersing into separate colors.

1 Reflection

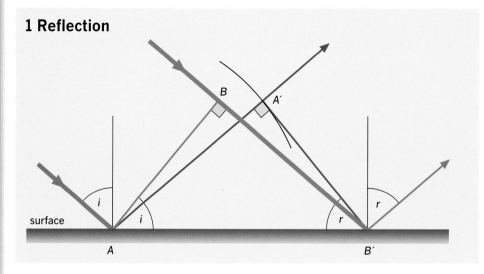

surface

2 Refraction

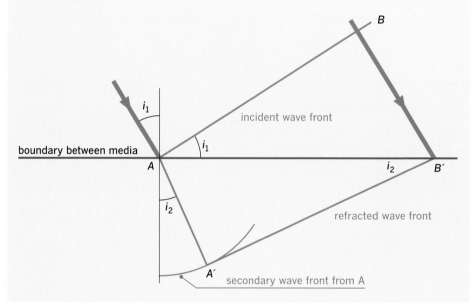

incident wave front

boundary between media

refracted wave front

secondary wave front from A

3 Optical dispersion

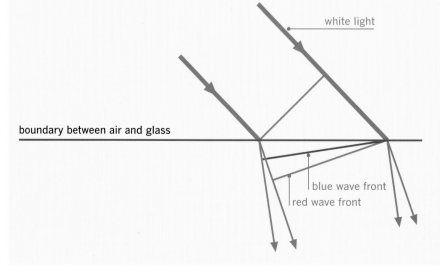

white light

boundary between air and glass

blue wave front
red wave front

The principle of superposition 1

Key words

interference
phase
principle of
  superposition
wave

1 Reinforcement

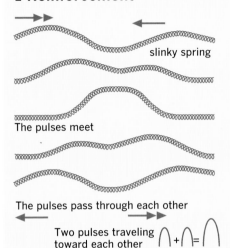

slinky spring

The pulses meet

The pulses pass through each other

Two pulses traveling toward each other

2 Cancellation

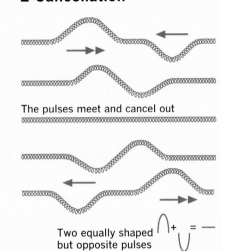

The pulses meet and cancel out

Two equally shaped but opposite pulses

3 Addition of two waves

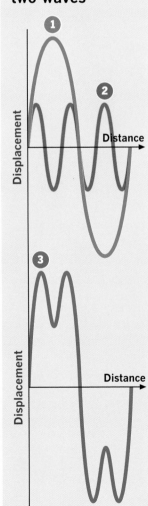

Displacement

Distance

Displacement

Distance

4 Interference

A lines joining points of destructive interference

B lines joining points of constructive interference

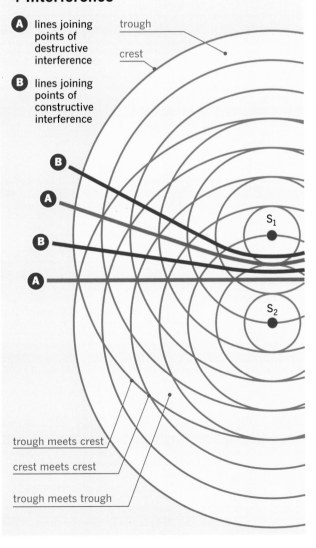

trough

crest

B
A
B
A

S_1

S_2

trough meets crest

crest meets crest

trough meets trough

Superposition
- A slinky spring is used to show how *waves* affect each other.

1 Reinforcement
- When the crest of one wave coincides with another, they reinforce each other—they are in *phase*. The resulting single crest is the sum of the two crests.

2 Cancellation
- When the crest of one wave coincides with the trough of the other, they are out of phase and cancel each other out. The result is a straight line if the crest and the trough are of equal sizes.

3 Addition of two waves
- A wave's upward displacement is regarded as positive, downward as negative. When adding two waves (1 and 2) the displacement at any point (3) is the sum of the displacements of the two waves at that point.

4 Interference
- An *interference* pattern forms when peaks and troughs of circular waves formed by point sources (such as S1 and S2) combine.
- Constructive interference occurs where the waves are in phase with each other. The waves reinforce each other forming peaks which are the sum of the peaks of the waves, and troughs which are sum of the troughs.
- Destructive interference occurs where the two waves are out of phase with each other. The peak of one wave coincides with the trough of another, canceling both out.
- Lines connecting points of constructive interference (B) and points of destructive interference (A) form an alternating sequence in the interference pattern.

Key words

amplitude	principle of
cathode ray	superposition
oscilloscope	simple harmonic
frequency	motion
Lissajous figures	sine wave
phase	
potential	
difference	

The principle of superposition 2

1 Addition of sine waves with perpendicular axes

- The effect of combining two sinusoidal waves of the same *frequency* and *amplitude* can be observed by applying two sinusoidal *potential differences* to the X-plates and Y-plates of a *cathode ray oscilloscope*.
- The electron beam is thus subjected to two mutually perpendicular *simple harmonic motions* and the shape of the trace produced on the screen depends on the *phase* difference between the potential differences.
- In general the resulting trace is an ellipse except when the phase difference is 0°, 90° and 180°.
- When two potential differences of different frequencies are applied to the X-plates and Y-plates more complex figures, known as *Lissajous figures*, are obtained.

2 How sine waves add to form an ellipse

- The 3-dimensional structures of the *sine waves* combine to give a 2-dimensional elliptical shape.

1 Addition of sine waves with perpendicular axes

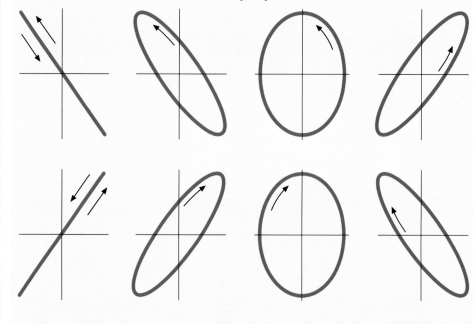

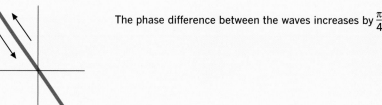

The phase difference between the waves increases by $\frac{\pi}{4}$

2 How sine waves add to form an ellipse

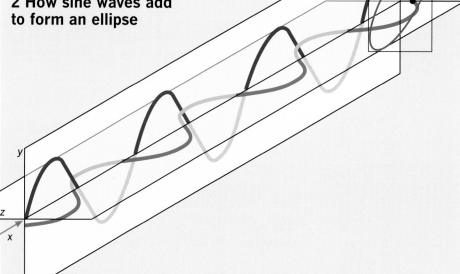

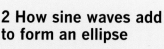

The principle of superposition 3

Key words

amplitude   wave
frequency
phase
principle of
  superposition

Formation of complex wave forms by addition of two or more waves (resulting wave shown in green)

1 First example

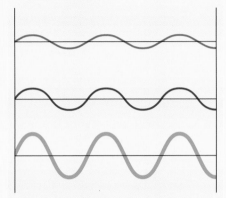

Two waves, same frequency, different amplitude

2 Second example

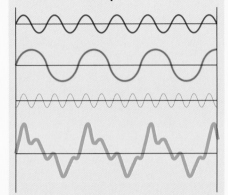

Three waves of different frequencies, amplitudes and phases

3 Third example

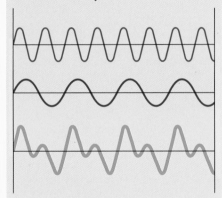

Two waves, same amplitude, frequency in ratio 2:1

4 Fourth example

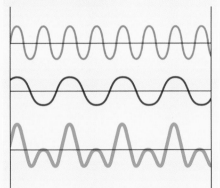

Two waves, same amplitude, frequency in ratio 2:1, but different phase

5 Fifth example

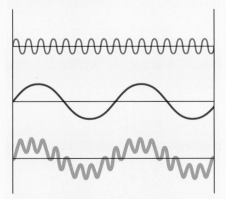

Two waves, high frequency and low frequency

6 Sixth example

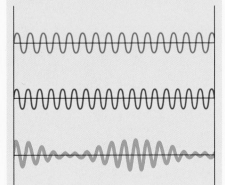

Two waves of very nearly the same frequency

Formation of complex wave forms

● The superposition of two or more waves results from combining the *amplitudes* of *waves* at each point.

1 First example

● When two waves of the same *frequency* are combined in *phase* the resultant wave has a larger amplitude than either of the contributing waves.

2 Second example

● Mixtures of waves of different frequencies and wavelengths result in complex wave patterns.

3 Third example

● When two waves of the same amplitude whose frequencies are in the ratio 2:1 are combined, a stepped wave corresponding to the two frequencies is formed.

4 Fourth example

● If the phase of the waves is changed the overall wave pattern also changes however, the contribution of each wave can still be seen.

5 Fifth example

● When two waves, one of high frequency and one of low frequency, are combined the resulting wave has the low frequency wave structure with the high frequency wave pattern superimposed on it in place of the smooth curve.

6 Sixth example

● Combining two similar waves of the same frequency which are only slightly out of phase forms a wave showing a regular pattern of changing amplitude which gradually changes between maximum and minimum values.

Key words

amplitude	stroboscope
harmonic	transverse wave
node	
oscillation	
stationary wave	

1 Apparatus to produce stationary waves

- When one end of a rubber cord is fixed and the other is moved up and down at regular intervals, using an electrical vibrator, two progressive trains of *transverse waves* travel along the cord in opposite directions.

2 "Stroboscopic" view of stationary waves

- If the frequency with which the cord is moved up and down is slowly increased at certain frequencies one or more high amplitude vibrating loops is formed. These are called standing waves or *stationary waves*—wave form appears to be frozen and does not move along the spring in either direction.
- Points on the stationary wave where displacement is zero are called *nodes* and denoted by N.
- Within one loop all particles *oscillate* in phase but with different *amplitudes*. Points on the stationary wave where there is maximum displacement are called antinodes and denoted by A.
- The frequency of the stationary wave and the progressive wave is the same and the wavelength is twice the distance between successive nodes or antinodes.
- Increasing the number of nodes and antinodes by one each time provides a series of *harmonics*.

3 Formation of stationary waves

- When the trains of waves are completely in phase the result is a stationary wave with maximum amplitude equal to twice the amplitude of the progressive wave.
- When the trains of waves are completely out of phase (anti-phase) the result is a stationary wave of zero amplitude at all i.e. a straight line.

Stationary waves

1 Apparatus to produce stationary waves

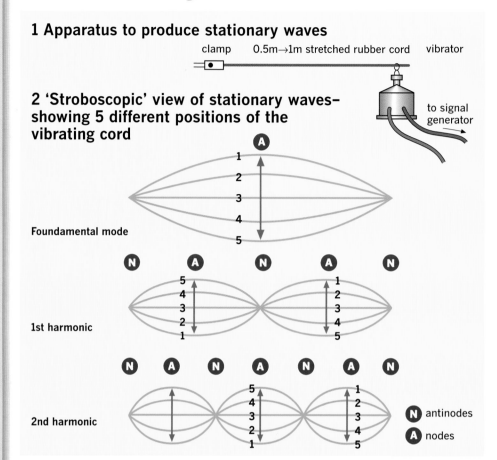

clamp   0.5m→1m stretched rubber cord   vibrator

to signal generator

2 'Stroboscopic' view of stationary waves– showing 5 different positions of the vibrating cord

Foundamental mode

1st harmonic

2nd harmonic

N antinodes

A nodes

3 Formation of stationary waves

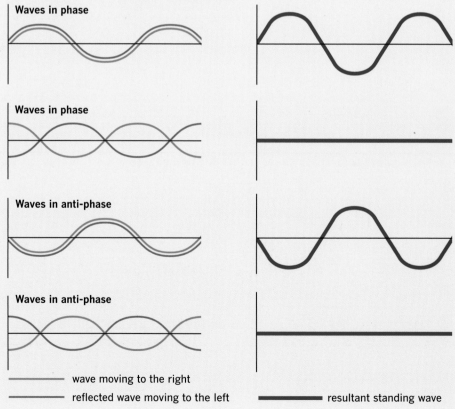

Waves in phase

Waves in phase

Waves in anti-phase

Waves in anti-phase

—— wave moving to the right

—— reflected wave moving to the left

—— resultant standing wave

Sound waves 1

1 Production of a sound wave

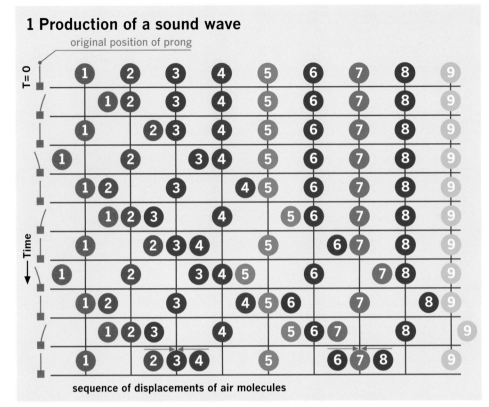

sequence of displacements of air molecules

2 Displacement of air molecules forming a wave

3 Pressure changes

4 Displacement of individual air molecule

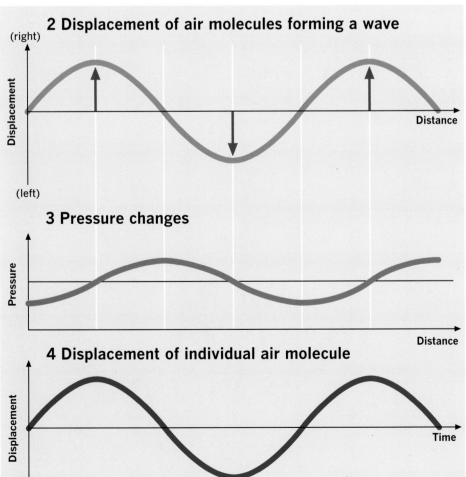

Key words

longitudinal wave
molecule
transverse wave
vacuum

Sound waves

● Sound is a *longitudinal wave* form which can travel through solids, liquids, and gases, but not through a *vacuum*. It travels fastest through solids and slowest through gases and its speed depends on temperature.

material	speed of sound (m/s at 0°C)
air	331.5
water	1437
steel	5000
Temperature (°C)	Speed of sound in air (m/s)
0	331.5
20	344.0
40	356.2

1 Production of a sound wave

● A vibrating prong displaces adjacent air *molecules*, which transfer the motion to others, forming regular regions of compression and rarefaction which creates a sound wave which passes through the air.

2 Displacement of air molecules forming a wave

● Sound is represented as a *transverse wave* whose displacement is perpendicular to the its direction of motion.

3 Pressure changes

● Pressure increases where air molecules crowd together in regions of compression. Pressure decreases in regions of rarefaction.

4 Displacement of individual air molecule

● As a wave passes, air molecules are displaced in one direction and then in the other. A graph of this displacement against time forms a regular transverse wave form.

Key words

amplitude	principle of
beat	superposition
frequency	resonance
longitudinal wave	stationary wave
node	

1 Demonstrating rarefaction and compression regions

- *Stationary* sound waves can be obtained in air using Kundt's tube—a calibrated tube sealed at one end with a small loudspeaker at the other end.
- The speaker produces progressive *longitudinal waves* which travel the length of the tube. These waves are reflected back in the opposite direction and interfere with the incident waves.
- The *frequency* of the sound is varied until it equals the natural frequency of vibration of the air column in the tube; *resonance* occurs as a standing wave forms in the tube. This is displayed using lycopodium powder, which swirls away from the antinodes, where the air particles are vibrating most strongly and forms heaps at the *nodes*.

2 Displacement and pressure graphs

- In a stationary longitudinal wave the maximum pressure variation occurs at a displacement node and is zero at a displacement antinode—i.e. displacement nodes correspond with pressure antinodes and vice versa.

3 Formation of beats

- *Beats* occur when two notes of slightly different frequencies but similar *amplitude* sound together. Beat frequency is the difference in frequency between the two notes. Beat period is its reciprocal.
- Superposition of the waves can explain beats. Sound is loudest when the waves are almost completely in phase, and quietest when the waves are almost completely out of phase.

Sound waves 2

1 Demonstrating rarefaction and compression regions in a stationary sound wave

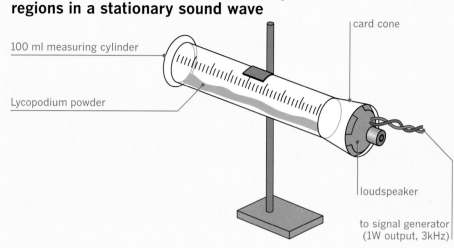

card cone
100 ml measuring cylinder
Lycopodium powder
loudspeaker
to signal generator (1W output, 3kHz)

2 Displacement and pressure graphs for a stationary sound wave

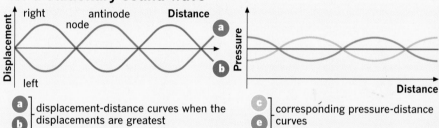

right
antinode
node
Distance
left
Displacement
Pressure
Distance

a, b] displacement-distance curves when the displacements are greatest

c, e] corresponding pressure-distance curves

d] line of normal pressure

3 Formation of beats

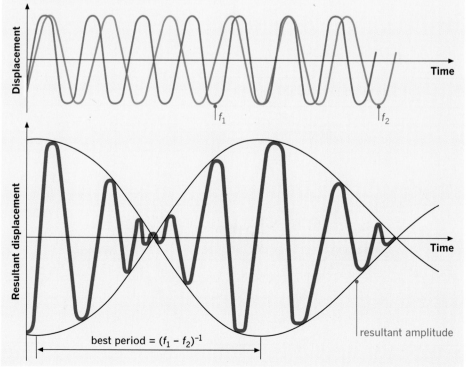

Displacement
Time
f_1
f_2

Resultant displacement
Time

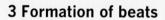

best period = $(f_1 - f_2)^{-1}$

resultant amplitude

Sound waves 3

1 Tuning fork

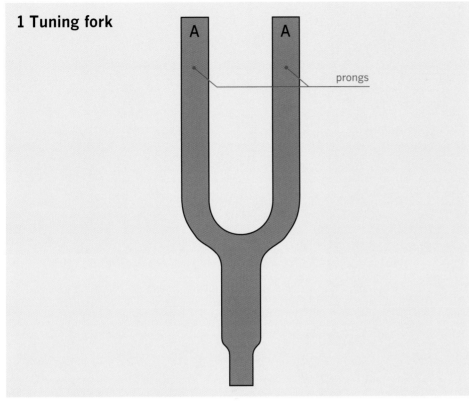

prongs

2 Spread of sound from a vibrating tuning fork

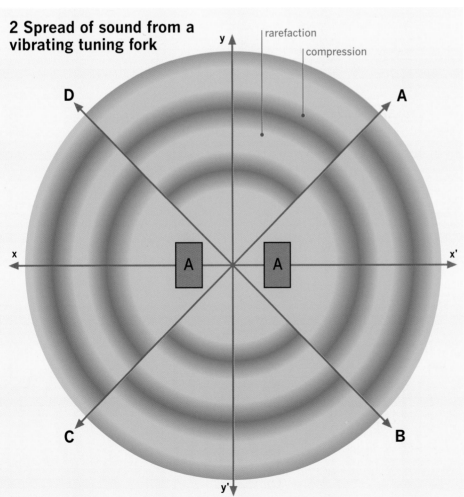

Key words

frequency
phase
principle of
  superposition
wave

1 Tuning fork

- When a tuning fork is struck the prongs vibrate at a fixed predetermined *frequency*. The simultaneous vibrations produced by the prongs can be used to demonstrate how waves superimpose.

2 Spread of sound from a vibrating tuning fork

- When the prongs are moving away from each other a rarefaction is produced in the air particles between them. This rarefaction travels in the direction Y and Y'. Simultaneously, compressions are produced outside the prongs and these travel in the directions X and X'.
- When the prongs are moving towards each other a compression is produced in the air particles between them. This compression travels in the direction Y and Y'. Simultaneously, rarefactions are produced outside the prongs and these travel in the directions X and X'.
- Whenever a rarefaction or compression occurs in the directions Y and Y', the opposite occurs in the directions X and X'. The rarefactions and compressions spread out from the tuning fork as spherical *waves* and destructive interference occurs along the lines A, B, C and D.
- If the tuning fork is held upright close to the ear and slowly rotated about a vertical axis, the sound is lost four times in each revolution. This corresponds to when the tuning fork is in positions A, B, C and D, where the two waves are out of *phase* and cancel each other out.

Key words

angle of	phase
incidence	reflection
diffraction	refraction
frequency	stroboscope
interference	wave

1 Ripple tank

- *Wave* behavior can be studied by observing water waves in a ripple tank—a shallow tank of water. Regular vibrations are produced using a low voltage motor attached to a wooden beam. The beam can make straight waves and, by attaching dippers, curved waves.
- The wave patterns can be "frozen" using a *stroboscopic* light so they can be observed and measured more easily.

2 Reflected straight waves

- Straight waves are reflected by a barrier. The *angle of incidence* equals the angle of *reflection*. The *frequency* of the incident and reflected waves is the same.

3 Reflected curved waves

- The curvature of curved waves is reversed on reflection by a straight barrier, their frequency is unchanged.

4 Refracted waves

- When water waves pass into shallower water they are *refracted*.

5 Interference

- *Interference* patterns can be formed using a pair of dippers to produce circular waves of the same frequency simultaneously. The pattern shows regions of constructive interference, where the waves are completely in *phase*, and regions of destructive interference where the waves are completely out of phase.

6 Diffraction

- Waves spread on passing through an opening or around an object. This is called *diffraction*.
- Maximum diffraction occurs when waves pass through a gap whose size equals the *wavelength* of the waves.

Water waves

1 Ripple tank

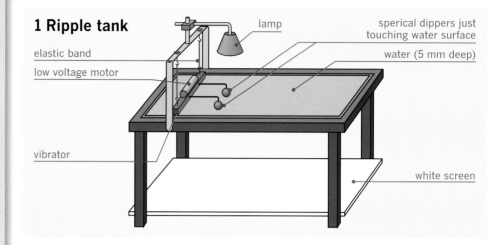

lamp
sperical dippers just touching water surface
water (5 mm deep)
elastic band
low voltage motor
vibrator
white screen

2 Reflected straight waves

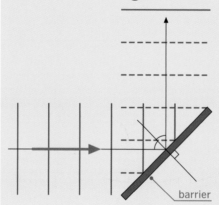

barrier

3 Reflected curved waves

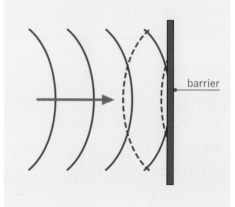

barrier

4 Refracted waves

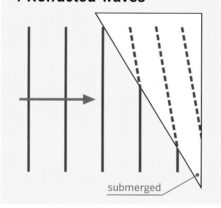

submerged

5 Interference

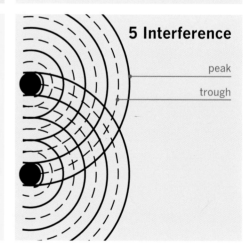

peak
trough

6 Diffraction

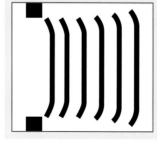
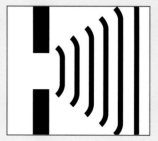

Seismic waves 1

1 P wave

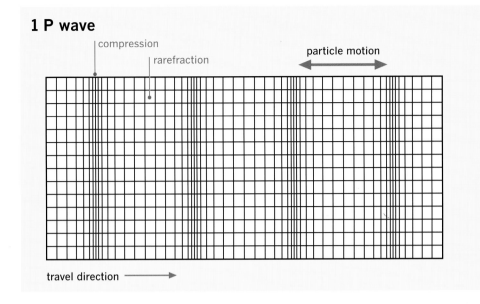

compression

rarefraction

particle motion

travel direction

2 S wave

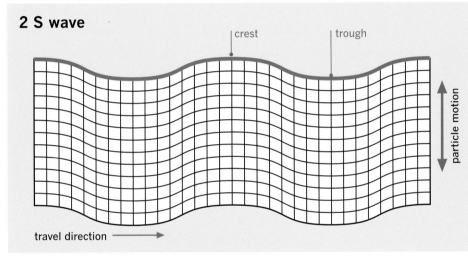

crest

trough

particle motion

travel direction

3 Seismograph

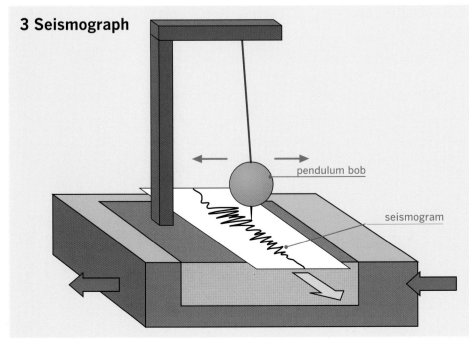

pendulum bob

seismogram

Key words

longitudinal wave	seismic wave
pendulum	transverse wave
Richter scale	

Seismic waves

- Seismic waves are vibrations caused by movement inside Earth which manifests itself as an earthquake. There are two types of seismic waves.

1 P wave

- P (primary) waves are *longitudinal waves* which shake the ground in the direction that the wave is traveling. Their speed depends on the nature of the rock through which they are traveling. A typical value is 6 km/s.

2 S wave

- S (shear) waves are *transverse waves* which shake the ground in directions perpendicular to the direction of travel. S waves travel more slowly than P waves. A typical value is 4 km/s.

3 Seismograph

- Earthquakes are recorded on a seismograph. When the ground shakes the base and frame of the instrument move with it, but the *pendulum* bob, due to its high inertia, does not. Movement is recorded as seismogram.
- Earthquake severity is measured on the logarithmic *Richter scale*. A magnitude 5 earthquake is thus ten times more severe than a magnitude 4 earthquake.

Richter scale	Comment
<3.5	Recorded by seismograms, not usually felt
3.5–5.5	Felt, little structural damage
5.6–6.0	Causes slight to moderate damage to buildings over a small area.
6.1–7.0	Some destruction in areas up to 100 km from the earthquake center
7.1–7.9	Major damage over a large area extending beyond 100 km from earthquake center
>8.0	Severe damage over area several hundred km from earthquake center

Seismic waves 2

1 Estimating distance from earthquake's epicenter

- The ratio between the average speed of a **P** wave and its following **S** wave is reasonably constant. It enables seismologists to estimate the distance to an earthquake from an observation station.
- The further an observation post is from the *epicenter* of an earthquake, the longer the time gap between the arrival of **P** waves and then **S** waves.
- Taking typical values of 6 km/s for **P** waves and 4 km/s for **S** waves, the distance from an observation station to the epicenter is given by:

Distance (km) = time between the arrival of P waves and S waves x 12

- The distance to the epicenter can also be estimated from a graph of time difference against distance.

2 Estimating position of earthquake's epicenter

- The time gap between the arrival of **P** waves and **S** waves at an observation station indicates that the epicenter of an earthquake is at a distance **d** kilometers from station but gives no information about its direction. The epicenter of the earthquake could lie anywhere on a circle *radius* d from the observation station.
- In order to fix the position of the epicenter of an earthquake it is necessary to use information from three observation stations. If a circle is drawn from each observation station at a radius corresponding to the distance from the epicenter its position is at the point where the circles intersect.

1 Estimating distance from earthquake's epicenter

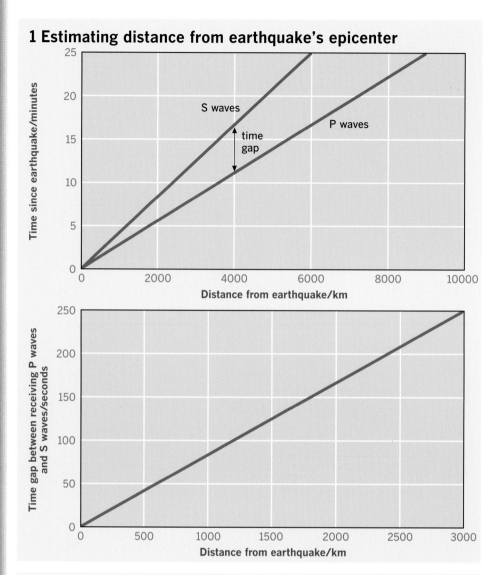

2 Estimating position of earthquake's epicenter

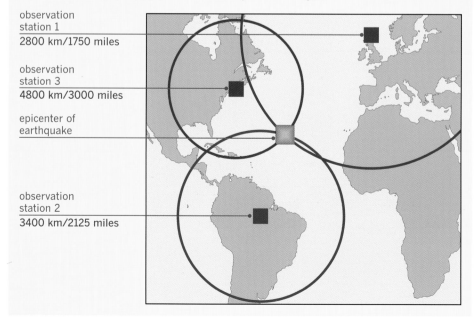

observation station 1
2800 km/1750 miles

observation station 3
4800 km/3000 miles

epicenter of earthquake

observation station 2
3400 km/2125 miles

Musical notes

1 Waveform

Key words

amplitude
frequency
fundamental
harmonic

1 Waveform

- Musical instruments produce a range of notes, often due to vibrating strings or vibrating columns of air. The same note played on different musical instruments sounds different because, unlike a tuning fork, musical instruments do not produce pure notes.
- A musical instrument produces a *fundamental frequency* together with a series of overtones at lower amplitudes. The fundamental has the lowest frequency and the overtones have frequencies that are multiples of this fundamental.
- The number and *amplitudes* of the overtones determine the quality of the sound and are typical of the particular musical instrument thus middle "C" on a violin sounds different from the same note played on a piano.
- The fundamental frequency is also called the first *harmonic*. If this is equal to f then the overtones have frequencies of 2f, 3f, 4f, etc. They are called the second harmonic, third harmonic, fourth harmonic and so on.

2 Waveform of 440 Hz note

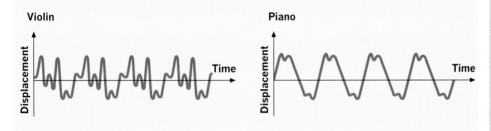

Violin — Displacement / Time
Piano — Displacement / Time

2 Waveform of 440 Hz note

- It is possible to analyse the frequencies and amplitudes of the harmonics which combine to produce a note on a musical instrument.
- When a note of frequency 440 Hz is played on a violin and a piano the mixture of harmonics is very different.

3 Frequency spectrum of 440 Hz note

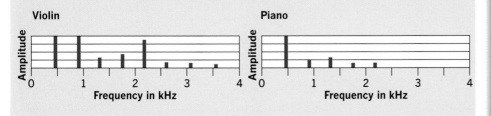

Violin — Amplitude / Frequency in kHz
Piano — Amplitude / Frequency in kHz

3 Frequency spectrum of 440 Hz note

- The amplitude of the second and fifth harmonics on the violin is much higher than the corresponding harmonics on the piano. This difference contributes significantly to the different sound of this note on the two instruments.

Key words

amplitude	node
frequency	stationary wave
fundamental	transverse wave
harmonic	wavelength
longitudinal wave	

1 Stringed instruments

- These produce sound forming *longitudinal waves* as their strings are plucked, stroked or struck, causing them to vibrate.
- Progressive *transverse waves* travel from both fixed ends of the string, so reflected waves meet incident waves. A *stationary wave* forms when the stationary wave pattern fits the length of the string in terms of *wavelengths*.
- A progressive longitudinal sound wave of the same *frequency* forms in air surrounding the stationary transverse wave on the string.
- The sound produced by vibrating strings has low *amplitude*. It is transmitted by the strings to the hollow body of the instrument (cello, guitar) or to the sounding board (piano) where it is amplified by causing vibration in a surrounding air.

2 First harmonic

- The fixed ends of a string are displacement *nodes*, N.
- The simplest stationary wave occurs whith one displacement antinode between the fixed ends. This happens when the string is plucked at its center.
- The distance between the nodes is half a wavelength ($\lambda/2$).
- The vibration creates the *fundamental* frequency, or first *harmonic*.
- The frequency of a note, $f = n/\lambda$, (n is the speed of the transverse wave along the string).

3 Second harmonic

- The string can vibrate in two parts if plucked one quarter along its length—there are two half wavelengths. This is the second harmonic.

4 Third harmonic

- The next harmonic is obtained when the string vibrates in three parts—there are three half wavelengths. This is the third harmonic.

Vibrating strings

1 Stringed instruments

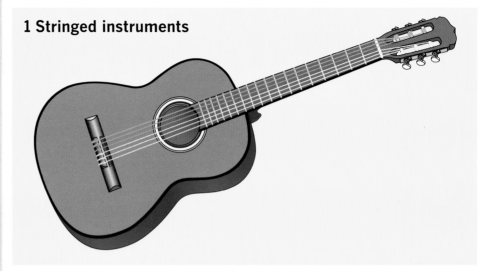

2 First harmonic

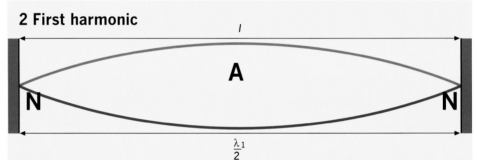

λ_1 is the wavelength of the stationary wave.
$\lambda_1 = 2l$
$f_1 = n/\lambda_1$ therefore $f_1 = n/2l$

3 Second harmonic

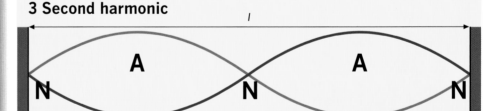

λ_2 is the wavelength of the stationary wave.
$\lambda_2 = l$
$f_2 = n/\lambda_2$ therefore $f_2 = n/l$

4 Third harmonic

λ_3 is the wavelength of the stationary wave.
$\lambda_3 = 2l/3$
$f_3 = n/\lambda_3$ therefore $f_3 = 3n/2l$

Vibrating columns of air

1 Harmonics produced by a closed pipe

Fundamental
(First harmonic) $\lambda_1 = 4l$
$f_1 = n/\lambda_1$
$f_1 = n/4l$

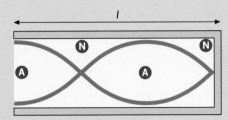

Second harmonic $\lambda_2 = \dfrac{4l}{3}$
$f_2 = n/\lambda_2$
$f_2 = 3n/4l$

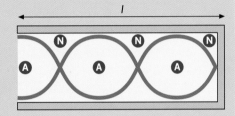

Third harmonic $\lambda_3 = \dfrac{4l}{5}$
$f_3 = n/\lambda_3$
$f_3 = 5n/4l$

2 Harmonics produced in an open pipe

First harmonic $\lambda_1 = 2l$
$f_1 = n/\lambda_1$
$f_1 = n/2l$

Second harmonic $\lambda_2 = l$
$f_2 = n/\lambda_2$
$f_2 = n/l$

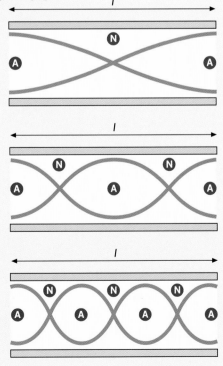

Third harmonic $\lambda_3 = \dfrac{2l}{3}$
$f_3 = n/\lambda_3$
$f_3 = 3n/2l$

(N) antinodes
(A) nodes

Key words

frequency	stationary wave
fundamental	wavelength
harmonic	
longitudinal wave	
node	

Vibrating columns of air

- Sound is produced in wind instruments by stationary *longitudinal waves* formed in air columns inside pipes.
- Vibration starts with a disturbance at one end of the pipe, the other end of the pipe may be closed or open.

1 Harmonics produced by a closed pipe

- The simplest *stationary wave* in a closed pipe has a displacement *node* (N) at the closed end and an antinode (A) at the open end.
- The distance between the node and antinode is ¼ the *wavelength*, λ_1, of the stationary wave.
- The *frequency*; f, of a **note** = n/λ (n is the speed of sound in air).
- If the pipe is of length, *l*, then $\lambda_1 = 4l$; $f_1 = n/4l$. This is the *fundamental* frequency or first *harmonic*.
- The next stationary wave occurs when another node and antinode are added. For this note $\lambda_2 = 4l/3$; $f_2 = 3n/4l$. This is the second *harmonic*.
- For the next stationary wave $\lambda_3 = 4l/5$; $f_3 = 5n/4l$. This is the third harmonic.
- Closed pipes give only odd-numbered harmonics.

2 Harmonics produced by an open pipe

- The simplest stationary wave in an open pipe has a displacement node (N) in the center and an antinode (A) at each end.
- If the pipe is of length *l*, then $\lambda_1 = 2l$; $f_1 = n/2l$. This is the fundamental frequency or first harmonic.
- The next stationary wave occurs when another node and antinode are added. For this note $\lambda_2 = l$; $f_2 = n/l$. This is the second harmonic.
- For the next stationary wave $\lambda_3 = 2l/3$; $f_3 = 3n/2l$. This is the third harmonic.

Key words

amplitude
frequency
pendulum
resonance

Resonance

● All objects have a natural *frequency* at which they vibrate. The vibration can be started and increased by another object vibrating at the same frequency. This effect is called *resonance*.

1 Pendulum resonance

● A heavy metal ball is set swinging as a *pendulum* forcing the lighter weights to swing. The light weight whose length matches the pendulum's has a much greater *amplitude* than the rest. This weight resonates with the pendulum.

2 Wire resonance

● The length of a stretched wire is altered until it vibrates at the same frequency as the tuning fork. At this frequency the amplitude of the wire's vibrations increase dislodging the paper rider. The wire resonates with the tuning fork.

3 Air resonance

● The length of the air column is altered by moving the tube up and down until it vibrates with the same frequency as the tuning fork, and the sound of the vibrating fork is amplified. The air column resonates with the tuning fork.

4 Destructive resonance

● If large structures such as tall towers and suspended bridges start to vibrate at their natural frequencies the results can be disastrous.
● The collapse of the Tacoma Narrows Bridge, USA in 1940 is well-known. It is thought that the bridge began to resonate due to a cross wind of a particular frequency. This caused the bridge to shake itself apart.
● Models of large structures are tested in wind tunnels to ensure that their natural vibrating frequencies are outside the range of vibrations caused by winds.

Resonance

1 Pendulum resonance

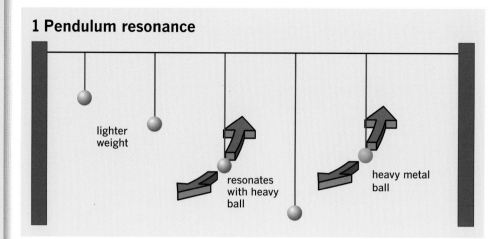

lighter weight

resonates with heavy ball

heavy metal ball

2 Wire resonance

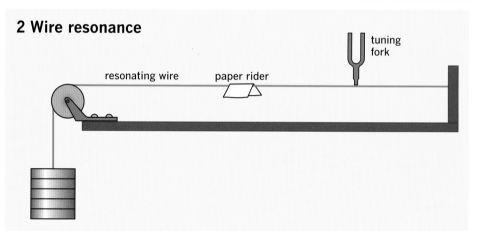

resonating wire   paper rider   tuning fork

3 Air resonance

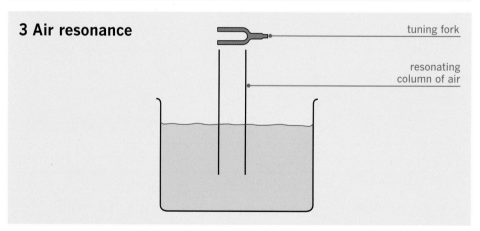

tuning fork

resonating column of air

4 Destructive resonance

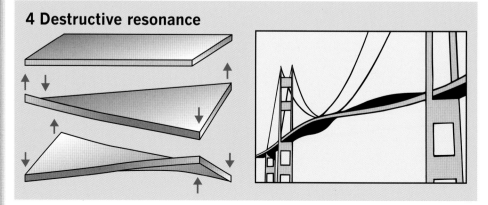

Scales

1 Keyboard scale

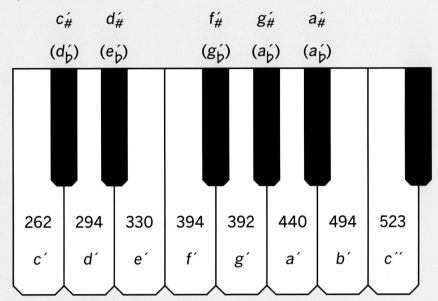

Frequency ratio between each of the 13 notes and the next is 1.0595 (chromatic semitone)

Keyboard scale (equally tempered) A compromise with diatonic scale

Tonic sol-fa notation

2 Frequencies (scientific)

	256	288	320	341	384	427	480	512
Intervals	$\frac{9}{8}$	$\frac{10}{9}$	$\frac{16}{15}$	$\frac{9}{8}$	$\frac{10}{9}$	$\frac{9}{8}$	$\frac{16}{15}$	
ITones	Major	Minor	Semi	Major	Minor	Major	Semitone	

Key words

diatonic scale
frequency
octave

Scales

- As music developed it became obvious that some combinations of notes of certain frequencies gave pleasing results while others did not. The results of these observations gave rise to musical scales.

1 Keyboard scale

- Music evolved along different lines in different parts of the world and scales were adopted accordingly. In Europe, music came to be based on the *diatonic scale*. This consists of eight notes and can be shown in a variety of ways.
- For scientific purposes the diatonic scale has been standardised as a sequence of notes between middle C (c′) and upper C (c″). Middle C has the *frequency* 256 Hz while upper C has the frequency 512 Hz. Scientific tuning forks pitched at these two notes are however, not suitable for tuning musical instruments.
- As far as music is concerned the ratio of the pitches of the various notes on the scale is more important than the actual pitch of the notes. In the eighteenth century it would be unlikely to find two organs, for example, with middle C pipes of exactly the same pitch but this did not create a problem provided the ratios between the notes was the same for all instruments.
- In 1939 an international committee agreed to standardise absolute pitch based on the note middle A at 440 Hz.

2 Frequencies (scientific)

- Certain intervals have been given specific names. A ratio of 9:8 is a major tone, 10:9 is a minor tone and 16:15 a semitone. The interval between the top and bottom notes of a scale is 2:1 and is called an *octave*.

Key words

auditory nerve
cochlea
Eustachian tube
ossicles
pharynx

1 Ear

- The outer ear consists of the pinna and the outer ear canal which collect and channel sound to the tympanic membrane (eardrum) causing it to vibrate in and out.
- The middle ear, separated from the outer ear by the tympanic membrane and from the inner ear by the oval window and round window, contains tiny bones or *ossicles* called the malleus (hammer), incus (anvil) and stapes (stirrup). These are the smallest bones in the body and are held in place by muscle and ligament. The ossicles transfer and magnify sound from the tympanic membrane to the oval window.
- The *eustachian* tube connects the middle ear to the *pharynx*. It ensures equal air pressure on both sides of the tympanic membrane.
- The outer and middle ear are air-filled. The inner ear is fluid-filled and contains the semicircular canals, concerned with balance and the cochlea, concerned with hearing.

2 Cochlea

- The *cochlea* consists of three parallel canals separated by membranes. The basilar membrane separates the middle and tympanic canals. The tectorial membrane runs parallel with the basilar membrane the full length of the cochlea.

3 Receptor cells

- There is a series of receptor cells between the tectorial and basilar membranes. A sensory hair on one end of each cell touches the tectorial membrane while the other end is connected to a nerve fiber.
- Movement of the basilar membrane causes distortions of the receptor cells, resulting in impulses being sent to the brain along the *auditory nerves*.

The human ear

1 Ear

outer ear	middle ear	inner ear
filled with air	filled with air	filled with fluid

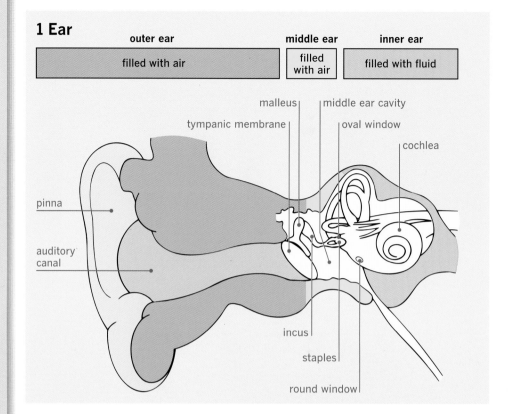

2 Cochlea

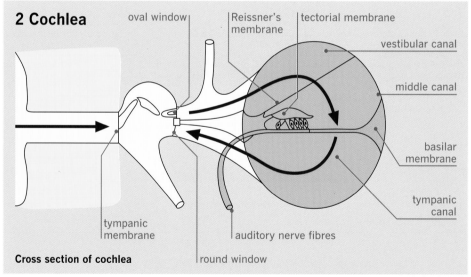

Cross section of cochlea

3 Receptor cells

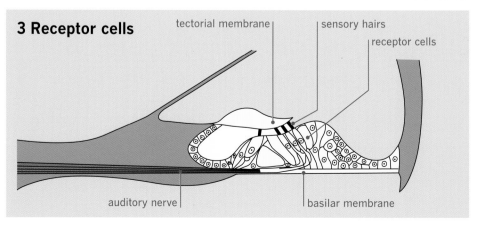

Audio range

1 Audio range comparison

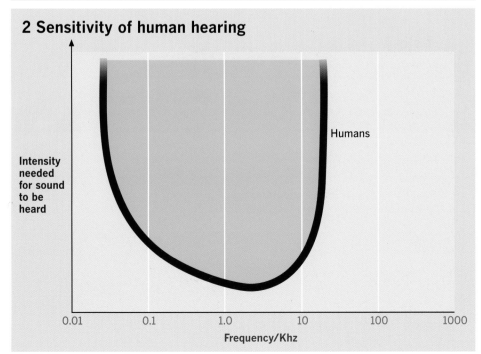

Humans

Bats

Grasshoppers

Rodents

Whales

Tenrecs

highly sensitive

less sensitive

Frequency/Khz

0.01   0.1   1.0   10   100   1000

2 Sensitivity of human hearing

Intensity needed for sound to be heard

Humans

Frequency/Khz

0.01   0.1   1.0   10   100   1000

Key words

frequency
infrasound
ultrasound

1 Audio range comparison

● Human beings can only hear sounds in the range 20–20,000 Hz. These are called the limits of audibility and decrease with age. Humans usually lose the ability to hear sounds at the high-*frequency* end of the range as they grow older.

● Many animals hear sound over a different range than humans. For example, bats are able to detect sounds at much higher frequencies than humans. They use short bursts of high-pitched sound to locate flying insects.

2 Sensitivity of human hearing

● Although the limits of audibility for a human are 20–20,000 Hz this does not mean that the human ear can detect sound equally well at all frequencies over the whole range. The human ear is most sensitive in the range 1000–10,000 Hz.

● Sounds below the lower limit of audibility i.e. <20 Hz, are called *infrasound*. Such sounds are too low to be detected by the ear but the vibrations might still be detected by the body.

● Sounds above upper limit of audibility i.e. > 20,000 Hz, are called *ultrasound*. Ultrasound has a variety of uses in industry and in medicine.

Key words

frequency
infrasound
sonar
ultrasound

Infrasound and ultrasound

1 Infrasound

- The *frequency* of *infrasound* (typically 20 Hz down to 0.001 Hz) is too low to be detected by the human ear. It can cover long distances and negotiate obstacles with little dissipation.
- Infrasound may result from natural phenomena—ocean waves, avalanches, earthquakes, volcanoes, and meteors—and be detected by seismographs. Infrasound is also generated by some man-made processes such as explosions.
- Some animals use infrasound to communicate over varying distances of up to many miles. Migrating birds may use naturally generated infrasound, from sources such as turbulent airflow over mountain ranges, as a navigational aid.

2 Sonar

- The frequency of *ultrasound* (greater than 20,000 Hz). is too high to be detected by the human ear. *Sonar* uses ultrasound to build up a "picture" of the surroundings.

3 Animal sonar

- Animals such as bats, whales and dolphins also use ultrasound for navigation.

4 Medical ultrasound

- Ultrasound travels at a different speeds in different substances. Some is reflected when passing from one substance to another, and it can be detected. The bigger the speed difference, the greater the reflection.
- Ultrasound is used in hospitals to produce pictures of the inside of the body. Such scans are often performed to observe the unborn baby.
- Saline gel prevents the formation of a layer of air between probe and skin, allowing more ultrasound to enter the body without reflection. This allows formation of a good image.

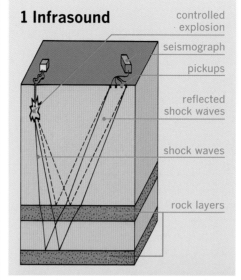

1 Infrasound

controlled explosion
seismograph
pickups
reflected shock waves
shock waves
rock layers

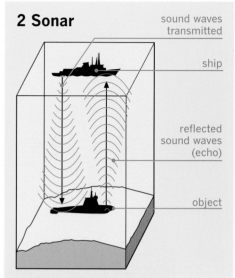

2 Sonar

sound waves transmitted
ship
reflected sound waves (echo)
object

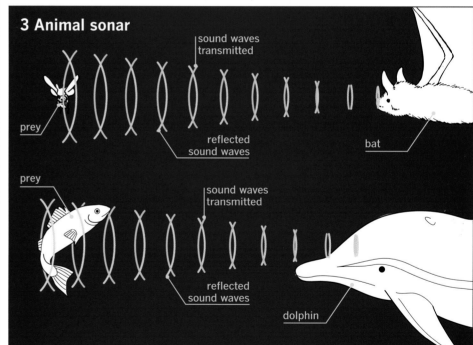

3 Animal sonar

sound waves transmitted
prey
reflected sound waves
bat
prey
sound waves transmitted
reflected sound waves
dolphin

4 Medical ultrasound

Substance	Speed of ultrasound (m/s)
Air	334
Bone	3360
Fat	1476
Muscle	1540
Saline gel	1515

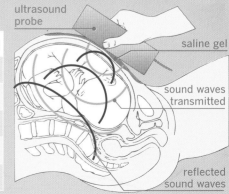

ultrasound probe
saline gel
sound waves transmitted
reflected sound waves

Noise and decibel ratings

Noise		Distance		Decibel rating
		m	ft	db
a	Whisper	5	15	30
b	Inside an urban home	–	–	50
c	Light traffic	15	50	55
d	Normal conversation	1	3	60
e	Pneumatic drill	15	50	85
f	Heavy traffic	15	50	90
g	Loud shout	15	50	100
h	Jet taking off	600	2000	105
i	Disco at full volume	–	–	117
j	Jet taking off	60	200	120

Noises rated at 120–130 dB cause pain; above 140 dB
can cause permanent ear damage

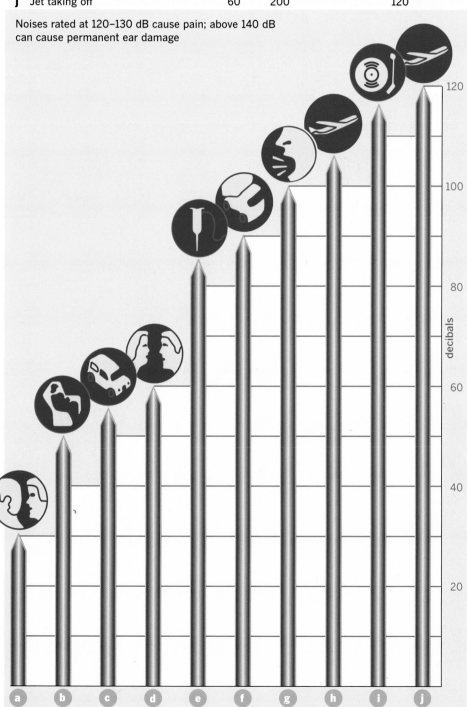

decibals

Key words

cochlea
decibel (dB)
frequency

Noise and decibel ratings

- The human ear responds to the ratio of the power of sounds rather than the difference in power. To the ear, a change of loudness from 0.1 W to 1 W is the same as from 1 W to 10 therefore the logarithm to base 10 ($\log_{10}$) of these changes is the same.
- The unit used to measure change in power is the bel, B. If the power of sound changes from P_1 to P_2 then **number of bels change = $\log_{10}(P_2/P_1)$**
- The bel is too large for practical use so in practice the *decibel* is used. **number of decibels change = $10 \log_{10}(P_2/P_1)$**
- The decibel scale is logarithmic, thus an increase from 10 dB to 20 dB corresponds to a tenfold increase in the power of the sound.
- Noise-induced hearing loss may result from a single very loud noise or frequent exposure to loud noise.
- Loud noise damages the sensory hairs in the *cochlea* either temporarily or permanently depending on the loudness of the noise and the amount of exposure.
- Sounds less than 80 dB are unlikely to cause permanent hearing loss. Regular exposure to noise above 85 dB will cause a gradual hearing loss and louder noises accelerate this loss.
- For unprotected ears, allowed exposure time decreases by one-half for each 5 dB increase in average noise level. Exposure time is limited to 8 hours at 90 dB, 4 hours at 95 dB, and 2 hours at 100 dB. The highest permissible noise exposure for the unprotected ear is 115 dB for 15 minutes each day.
- Sound *frequency* is measured in hertz, Hz. The human ear can detect sound in the range 20–20,000 Hz. Human speech is in the range 300–4000 Hz. When a person becomes deaf, higher frequency sounds are lost first.

Key words

frequency	transverse wave
fundamental	wavelength
resonance	
sonometer	
tension	

Measurement of the speed of sound 1

1 Relation between wave velocity and tension in a wire

- A tuning fork vibrates when struck. If a tuning fork's base is placed on the wire of a *sonometer*, the wire vibrates.
- The vibrating wire's *frequency* depends on its length, which is varied by moving the bridge until it equals the tuning fork's frequency.
- *Resonance* occurs between the tuning fork and the string and the paper rider is thrown off the string.
- The speed of a *transverse wave* traveling along a stretched wire, $n = \sqrt{(T/m)}$ where T = tension and m = mass per unit length.
- For a vibrating wire of length l, the frequency of the *fundamental* note, $f = n/2l$, it follows that $f = \sqrt{(T/m)} / 2l$
- f is therefore inversely proportional to l when T and m are constant. f is also proportional to the square root of T when l and m are constant.

2 Speed of sound measurement

- A tuning fork is struck and held over a tube standing in a large glass jar which is slowly raised and lowered until the note's sound is loudest, showing resonance between the tuning fork and the air column in the tube. The stationary wave in the air column is one quarter of the note's *wavelength*. Therefore $l_1 + x = \lambda/4$ (l_1 is the length of the tube above the water level; x is the end correction).
- When the tube is raised further using the same tuning fork a second resonance position is found, corresponding to an air column three quarters of a wavelength. $l_2 + x = 3\lambda/4$.
- Thus $l_2 - l_1 = \lambda/2$. The frequency, f, of the tuning fork is known, the speed of sound in air, $n = f\lambda$.

1 Relation between wave velocity and tension in a wire

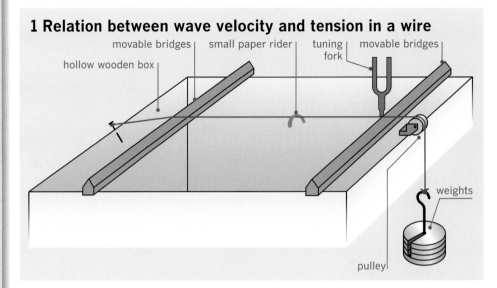

movable bridges   small paper rider   tuning fork   movable bridges

hollow wooden box

weights

pulley

2 Speed of sound measurement

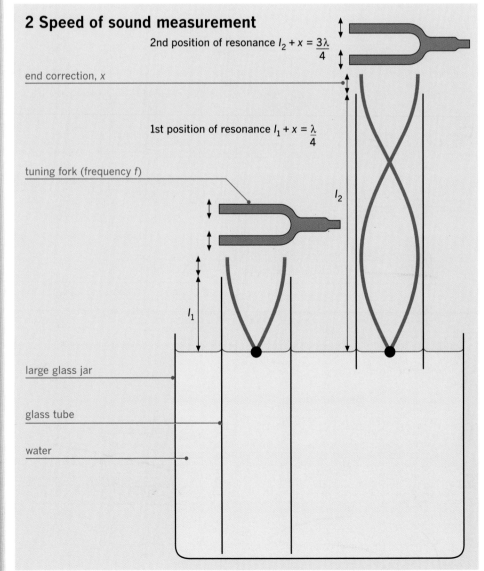

2nd position of resonance $l_2 + x = \dfrac{3\lambda}{4}$

end correction, x

1st position of resonance $l_1 + x = \dfrac{\lambda}{4}$

tuning fork (frequency f)

l_2

l_1

large glass jar

glass tube

water

Measurement of the speed of sound 2

Key words

cathode ray
  oscilloscope
compression
frequency
rarefaction

1 Speed of sound in a metal rod

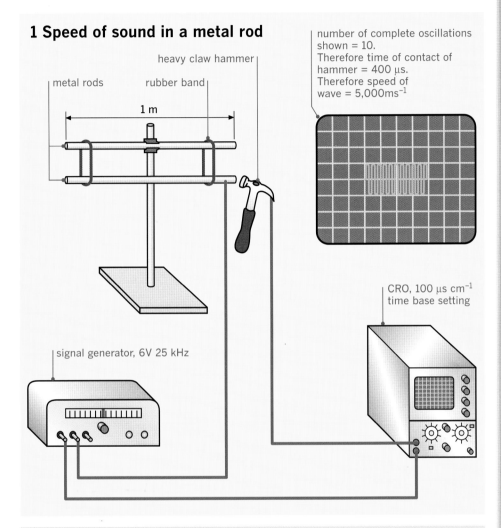

metal rods   rubber band   heavy claw hammer

1 m

number of complete oscillations shown = 10.
Therefore time of contact of hammer = 400 μs.
Therefore speed of wave = 5,000ms⁻¹

CRO, 100 μs cm⁻¹ time base setting

signal generator, 6V 25 kHz

1 Speed of sound in a metal rod

- The method provides an approximate value for the speed of sound as it passes through steel.
- The output from a signal generator becomes the input of a *cathode ray oscilloscope* (CRO) when the hammer strikes the lower rod.
- A *compression* pulse passes along the rod and is reflected at the left end of the steel rod as a *rarefaction* pulse. This wave passes back towards the right end of the steel rod where it breaks the contact between the rod and the hammer.
- If the *frequency* of the signal is 25,000 Hz and there are 10 complete oscillations on the CRO it follows that the steel bar and the hammer must have been in contact for $10/25,000 = 4 \times 10^{-4}$ s = **400 ms**. During this time the wave has traveled twice the length of the steel bar which is 2 m. The speed of sound in steel is therefore $2 / 4 \times 10^{-4} = 5,000$ ms⁻¹.

2 Speed of a mechanical wave

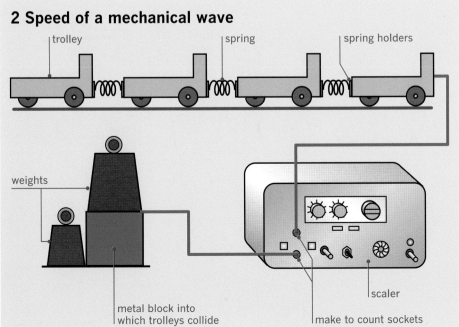

trolley   spring   spring holders

weights

metal block into which trolleys collide

scaler

make to count sockets

2 Speed of a mechanical wave

- The trolleys are linked by springs.
- The trolleys are pushed together towards the metal block. The left-most trolley stops when it hits the metal block, completing the circuit. The compression pulse passes from trolley to trolley as each spring in turn is compressed. The right-most trolley then starts to move to the right initiating an expansion pulse. Each spring expands in turn until the left-most trolley moves and the circuit is broken.
- The scaler records the length of time taken for the pulse to pass twice the distance from the front of the left-most trolley to the back of the right-most trolley. If this distance is measured the speed of the mechanical wave can be calculated.

1 Diffraction of waves at a small aperture

● Ends of *waves* passing through a narrow aperture curve on diffraction. Curvature is greatest when the gap is similar in size to the *wavelength*.

2 Young's double-slit experiment

● A wave passing through two slits produces two coherent waves of the same *frequency*, equal or similar magnitude and a constant *phase* difference. An *interference* pattern forms when coherent waves cross.

3 Observing interference fringes

● *Monochromatic light* from a narrow slit falling on two slits (close together and parallel to the first slit) forms two coherent light sources. *Diffraction* occurs if the pair of slits is sufficiently narrow. A pattern of equally alternate bright and dark vertical bands, or interference fringes forms. Bright bands indicate where the waves are in phase and hence at maximum amplitude. Dark bands indicate where the waves are out of phase and amplitude is zero.

4 Path difference in Young's experiment

● A bright fringe occurs if the path difference from the slits equals a whole number of wavelengths (apart from the central bright fringe).

● The first bright fringe occurs at **k**, a distance **x** above the central bright fringe. The path difference of light reaching **k** from S_1 and S_2 is S_2A. $\sin \theta^1 = S_2A/d$. $\sin \theta = x/D$. As **d** is very small relative to **D**, $\theta^1 = \theta$. A bright fringe appears when the path difference is $n\lambda$. Therefore, for the first fringe (n=1), $\lambda/d = x/D$; $\lambda = xd/D$

Interference of two beams of light 1

1 Diffraction of waves at a small aperture

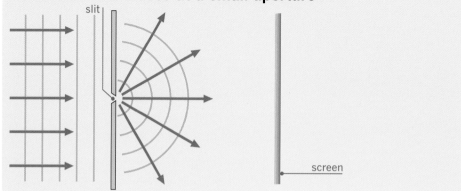

slit

screen

2 Young's double-slit experiment

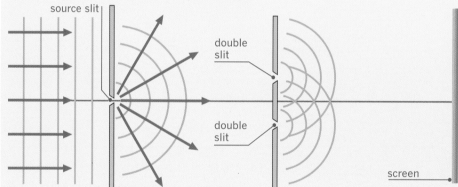

source slit

double slit

double slit

screen

3 Observing interference fringes

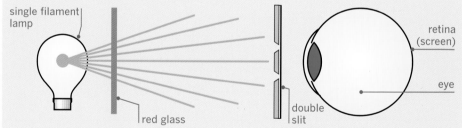

single filament lamp

retina (screen)

eye

red glass

double slit

4 Path difference in Young's experiment

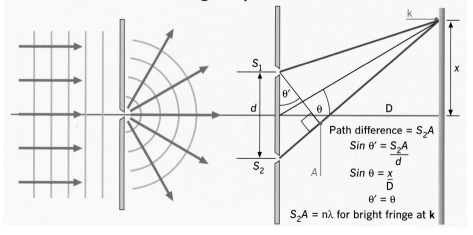

k

S_1

θ'

d

θ

D

x

S_2

A

Path difference = S_2A

$\sin \theta' = \dfrac{S_2A}{d}$

$\sin \theta = \dfrac{x}{D}$

$\theta' = \theta$

$S_2A = n\lambda$ for bright fringe at **k**

Interference of two beams of light 2

Key words

interference	prism
interference	virtual image
fringes	
monochromatic	
light	

1 Fresnel's biprism

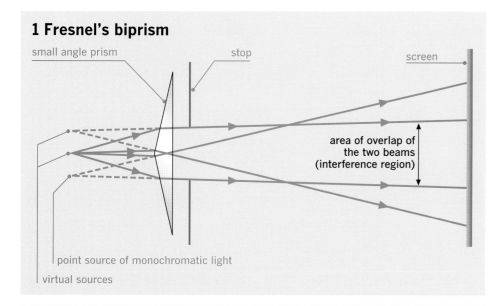

small angle prism

stop

screen

area of overlap of the two beams (interference region)

point source of monochromatic light

virtual sources

2 Fresnel's mirrors

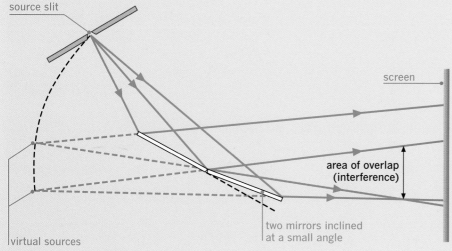

source slit

screen

area of overlap (interference)

virtual sources

two mirrors inclined at a small angle

3 Lloyd's mirror

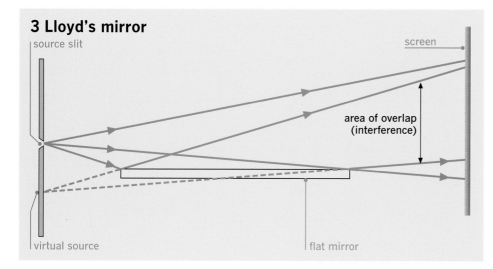

source slit

screen

area of overlap (interference)

virtual source

flat mirror

1 Fresnel's biprism

- When *monochromatic light* falls on a small-angled *prism* two *virtual images* are formed by *refraction* at each half of the prism. This gives the effect of three light sources, one real and two imaginary. These act as coherent sources which are close together due to the small refracting angle.
- An *interference* pattern, similar to that from a double slit but brighter, is obtained where the two refracted beams overlap. The pattern can conveniently observed using a traveling eyepiece focused on the fringes.

2 Fresnel's mirrors

- When two mirrors are inclined at a very small angle to each other they produce two virtual sources of light from one real monochromatic source. The light from the two virtual sources is coherent.
- The two reflected beams appear to come from two closely-spaced virtual sources. They interfere with each other and producing an interference pattern of bright and dark fringes.

3 Lloyd's mirror

- Lloyd's mirror may also be used to demonstrate interference. Light from a monochromatic slit source reflects from a glass surface set at a small angle from the horizontal. The result is that light also appears to come from a second virtual source. The light from the real and virtual sources is coherent and an interference pattern of fringes is formed.

Key words

interference
interference
  fringes
lens
monochromatic
  light

reflection
refractive index
wave

Interference involving multiple reflections

1 Multiple reflections in a plane parallel film

- When *monochromatic light* strikes a parallel film some is *reflected* at the upper surface and some, transmitted through the film, is reflected at the lower surface, resulting in a series of coherent *waves* which *interfere* when brought together.

2 Path difference between two consecutive rays

- *Refractive index* of the film μ = speed of light in air/speed of light in film.
- Path length difference between rays, 1 and 2 = μ (AF + FB) −AD = 2 μd cos θ' = $n\lambda$.
- The waves are coherent and *interference fringes* are formed.

3 Interference fringes in a wedge film

- Interference fringes are produced by a thin wedge of air.
- When monochromatic light shines onto the glass plates some is reflected up by the lower surface of the top plate and some, transmitted through the air, is reflected up by the upper surface of the bottom plate. Both waves originate from the same point, they are coherent and interfere when brought together.

4 Newton's rings

- Monochromatic light is reflected by a glass slide and falls on the film of air between a plano-convex *lens* and an optical flat. To each side of the center of the lens there is a wedge of air gradually increasing in thickness from zero moving outwards.
- Light reflected by the lower surface of the lens and by the upper surface of the optical flat create interference fringes which take the form of rings. As their radii increase, the spacing between them decreases.

1 Multiple reflections in a plane parallel film

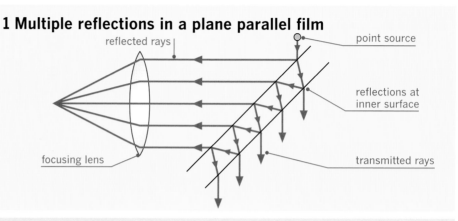

point source

reflected rays

reflections at inner surface

focusing lens

transmitted rays

2 Path difference between two consecutive rays

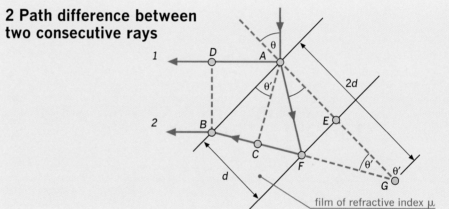

film of refractive index μ

3 Interference fringes in a wedge film

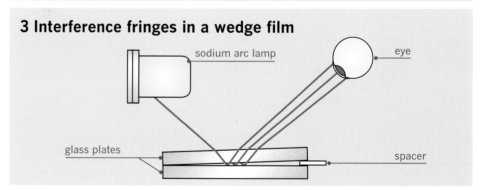

sodium arc lamp

eye

glass plates

spacer

4 Newton's rings

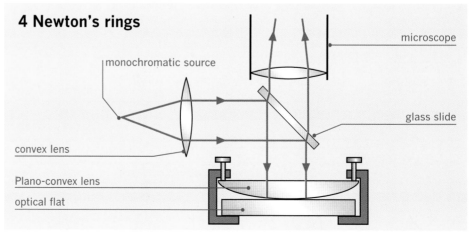

microscope

monochromatic source

glass slide

convex lens

Plano-convex lens

optical flat

Diffraction at a single slit

1 Diffraction pattern

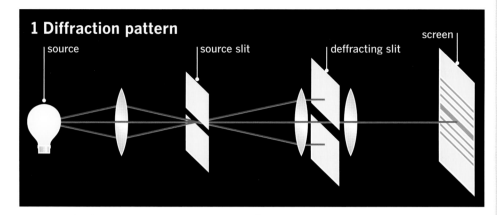

source · source slit · deffracting slit · screen

Key words

diffraction	principle of
interference	superposition
monochromatic	wave
light	wavelength

2 Wave fronts and interference

points of maximum interference

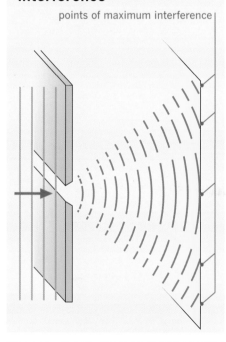

3 Angular width of central maximum

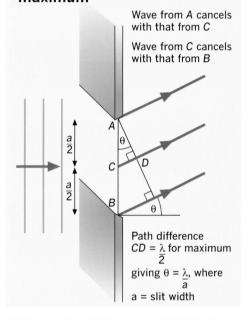

Wave from A cancels with that from C

Wave from C cancels with that from B

Path difference $CD = \frac{\lambda}{2}$ for maximum

giving $\theta = \frac{\lambda}{a}$, where

a = slit width

5 Intensity distribution

4 Position of next minimum

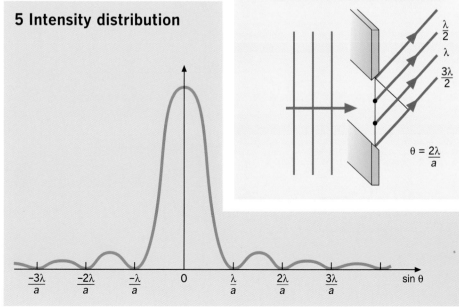

$\frac{\lambda}{2}$

λ

$\frac{3\lambda}{2}$

$\theta = \frac{2\lambda}{a}$

$\frac{-3\lambda}{a}$ $\frac{-2\lambda}{a}$ $\frac{-\lambda}{a}$ 0 $\frac{\lambda}{a}$ $\frac{2\lambda}{a}$ $\frac{3\lambda}{a}$ sin θ

1 Diffraction pattern

- *Diffraction* results from superposition of waves from different parts of the same *wave* front, while *interference* results from superposition of waves on two different wave fronts.
- *Monochromatic light* passes through a horizontal source slit and then a horizontal diffracting slit. A diffraction pattern is formed on the screen.

2 Wave fronts and interference

- A horizontal slit can be thought of a series of vertical strips, each being a source of secondary wavelets. The wavelets can be added using the *principle of superposition*.

3 Angular width of central maximum

- First dark band forms at θ° to incident beam, if path difference for secondary wavelets from strip C, immediately below A is λ/2. Destructive interference occurs between these wavelets, causing darkness in direction θ when CD = λ/2.
- Since sin θ = 2CD / a, sin θ = λ/a.

4 Position of next minimum

- sin θ = nλ /a where n = ±1, ±2, etc. corresponding to pairs of dark bands on either side of the original direction of the incident beam.

5 Intensity distribution

- From sin θ = λ/a, if a (slit width) is much larger than λ (*wavelength*), angle θ is very small and the dark bands will be very close to the central maximum. Most of the emergent light from the slit will be in the direction of the incident light and minimal diffraction occurs.
  If a = λ; sin θ = 1; therefore θ = 90°. The width of the central band is twice that of any other bright band.

Key words

diffraction
interference
interference
  fringes
lens

wavelength

Diffraction at a double slit

1 Observing diffraction from a double slit

- If slits are sufficiently narrow, *diffraction* occurs and each slit acts as a source of secondary wavelets which superimpose on each other. In some directions there is constructive *interference* resulting in bright bands while in others there is destructive interference resulting in dark bands.
- In addition to interference occurring between wavelets from different slits, it also occurs between wavelets produced by the same slit. The wavelets formed at each slit each form a diffraction pattern. These patterns are similar in nature and traveling in the same direction so they will coincide if focused by a *lens*.

2 Intensity pattern

- Interference produces a regular pattern of dark and bright bands of similar intensity.
- Diffraction at one slit produces a central bright band which is twice the width of the series of other less bright bands on either side of it.
- The two patterns come together to form a resultant intensity distribution.

3 Altering slit width

- The number of *interference fringes* formed depends on the amount of diffraction that occurs at each slit which, in turn, depends on the width of the slits. The narrower the slits the greater the number of fringes due to increased diffraction. However, since the slits are narrow, less light gets through and the fringes become fainter.
- In practice, in order to generate fringes which are easily seen, it is necessary to have slits which are many *wavelengths* wide.

1 Observing diffraction from a double slit

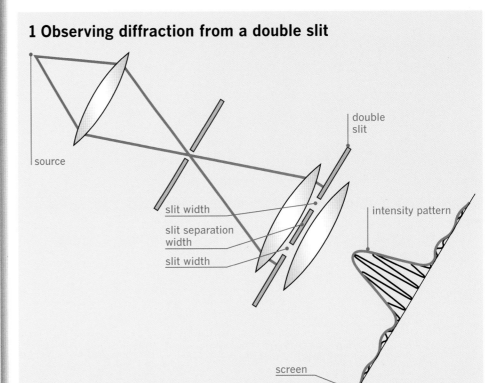

source

slit width
slit separation width
slit width

double slit

intensity pattern

screen

2 Intensity pattern

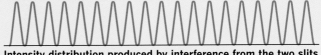

Intensity distribution produced by interference from the two slits

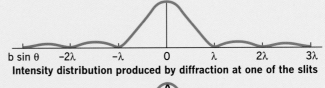

b sin θ   −2λ   −λ   0   λ   2λ   3λ

Intensity distribution produced by diffraction at one of the slits

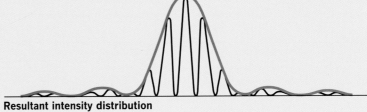

Resultant intensity distribution

3 Altering slit width

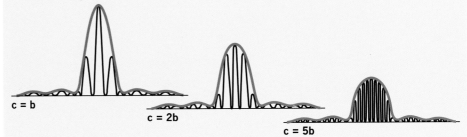

c = b

c = 2b

c = 5b

Diffraction grating

Key words

diffraction	monochromatic
diffraction grating	light
interference	prism
interference	spectrum
fringes	wavelength

1 Diffraction and construction of intensity pattern

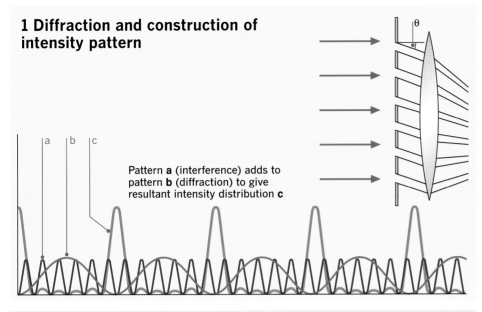

Pattern **a** (interference) adds to pattern **b** (diffraction) to give resultant intensity distribution **c**

2 Intensity pattern

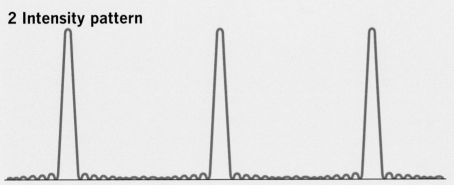

3 Formation of spectral lines by a grating

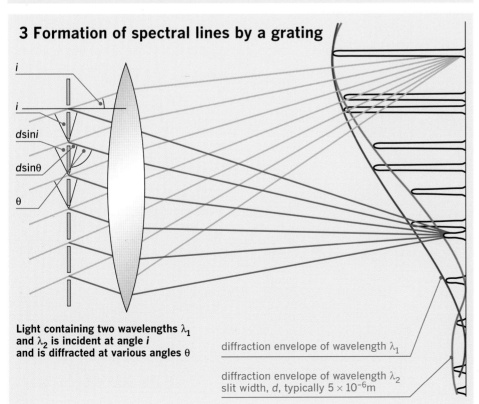

Light containing two wavelengths λ_1 and λ_2 is incident at angle i and is diffracted at various angles θ

diffraction envelope of wavelength λ_1

diffraction envelope of wavelength λ_2
slit width, d, typically 5×10^{-6}m

1 Diffraction and construction of intensity pattern

- A *diffraction grating* consists of many evenly spaced equally sized fine parallel slits. A series of light and dark *interference fringes* forms when *monochromatic light* falls on the grating. A diffraction pattern also forms at each slit.

2 Intensity pattern

- Light and dark bands formed by *interference* and *diffraction* combine forming an intensity pattern.

3 Formation of spectral lines by a grating

- Diffraction gratings are used to produce spectra for very accurate measurement of *wavelength*. They are frequently preferred to *prisms* because they give very sharp spectra.
- Consider plane waves of monochromatic light, wavelength λ, falling on a diffraction grating, whose slits are separated by distance, d, (grating spacing). For wavelets coming from two adjacent slits and traveling at angle θ to the direction of the incident light, the path difference between them corresponding to one wavelength will be $d \sin \theta$. This is true of corresponding pairs of adjacent slits. In the general case for all such waves $d \sin \theta = n \lambda$, where n gives the order of the *spectrum*, and reinforcement of diffracted wavelets occurs in direction θ. Intensity is greatest when the wavelets are focused by a lens.
- If light of mixed wavelengths falls onto the diffraction grating θ is different for each, corresponding to the difference in wavelength. The angle at which reinforcement of diffracted wavelets occurs is different for each wavelength, thus light of different wavelengths is separated.

Key words

aperture
diffraction
Rayleigh criterion
resolving power
wavelength

Resolution

● Resolution is the ability of an optical
system to form distinct separate
images of objects that are close
together. *Resolving power* depends on
the size of hole or slit through which
objects are viewed and the color of the
light. It is easier to resolve an object
which is illuminated by short
wavelength light (blue) than by long
wavelength light (red).

1 Formation of diffraction images

● Resolving power also depends on the
distance between objects. When two
slit sources form *diffraction* images
resolution depends on the angle
subtended by the sources at the slit.

2 Diffraction images of two slit sources

● As the angle subtended at the slit by
the two sources decreases so does the
resolution of their diffraction images.

● Rayleigh suggested objects should be
considered to be just resolved when
the first minimum of one image
coincides with the central maximum of
the other image. If slit width equals **b**
then $\alpha = \lambda/b$. As the wavelength of
light decreases so α decreases.

● Assuming the pupil of the human eye
is 2×10^{-3} m and the average
wavelength of white light is 6×10^{-7} m
the resolving power of the eye is
$6 \times 10^{-7} / 2 \times 10^{-3} = 3 \times 10^{-4}$ radians.

3 Resolving power of a microscope

● In a microscope the lens acts as a
circular *aperture*.

● The *Rayleigh criterion* for a circular
aperture is $\sin \alpha = 1.22 \lambda / d$ where α
is the angle subtended by the images,
λ is the wavelength of light and **d** is
the diameter of the aperture.

Resolving power

1 Formation of diffraction images

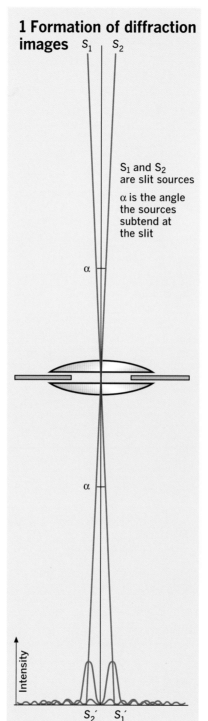

S_1 and S_2
are slit sources

α is the angle
the sources
subtend at
the slit

2 Diffraction images of two slit sources

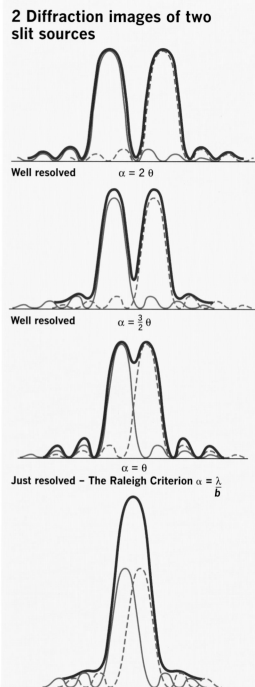

Well resolved $\alpha = 2\,\theta$

Well resolved $\alpha = \frac{3}{2}\,\theta$

Just resolved – The Raleigh Criterion $\alpha = \dfrac{\lambda}{b}$

Not resolved $\alpha = \frac{1}{2}\,\theta$

3 Resolving power of a microscope

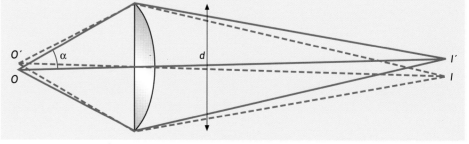

Polarization 1

Key words

Nicol prism
Polaroid
polarization
reflection
refraction

1 Demonstration

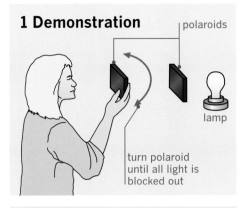

polaroids

turn polaroid until all light is blocked out

lamp

2 Analogy

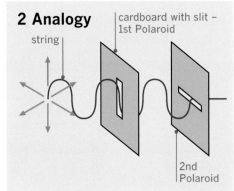

cardboard with slit – 1st Polaroid

string

2nd Polaroid

3 Nicol prism

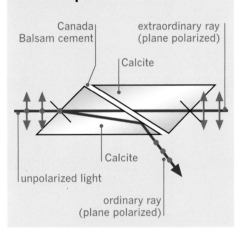

Canada Balsam cement

extraordinary ray (plane polarized)

Calcite

Calcite

unpolarized light

ordinary ray (plane polarized)

4 Polarization by reflection

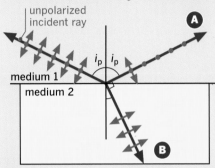

unpolarized incident ray

i_p i_p

A

medium 1

medium 2

B

Since angle between **A** and **B** = 90° for polarization then $\mu = \tan i_p$ where the refractive index of the second medium with respect to the first is denoted by μ

5 Sheets of glass

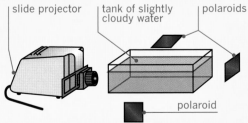

plane polarized reflected light

unpolarized incident light

partially polarized transmitted light

6 Scattering

slide projector   tank of slightly cloudy water   polaroids

polaroid

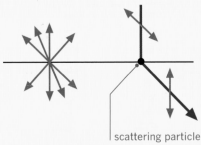

scattering particle

Polarization produced by scattering   **Illustrating scattering**

1 Demonstration

- *Polarization* shows that light waves are transverse in character.
- A lamp viewed through a *Polaroid* appears normal although dimmer. Rotating the Polaroid has no effect.
- If the lamp is viewed through two Polaroids and one is slowly rotated, a position is reached where light is completely blocked off. If the rotation is continued the light is restored.

2 Analogy

- Vibrations in light waves occur in all directions perpendicular to the direction of travel.
- A Polaroid acts like a slit, allowing only waves vibrating in one direction to pass. No waves pass if a second slit is placed perpendicular to the first.

3 Nicol prism

- A *Nicol prism* consists of Icelandic spar, a form of calcite.
- An unpolarized ray of light passing through a Nicol prism splits into an ordinary and an extraordinary ray— polarized at right angles to each other. The extraordinary ray is transmitted.

4 Polarization by reflection

- Light *reflected* by glass or water is partially plane polarized. At the polarizing angle, i_p, an unpolarized ray of light splits into two plane polarized rays. One is reflected, the other is *refracted*.

5 Sheets of glass

- When light falls on glass plates, separated by thin layers of air, the reflected light rays are plane polarized transmitted rays are partly polarized.

6 Scattering

- Light rays are scattered by collisions with particles in cloudy water, this results in rays of plane polarized light.

Polarization 2

Key words

absorption
electromagnetic
  spectrum
microwaves
Nicol prism
Polaroid
polarization

1 Light rays resolved into two planes of vibration

- Many sources produce unpolarized light. Rays vibrate perpendicularly to the direction traveled by the ray.
- Unpolarized light can be represented by arrows whose direction corresponds to the direction of vibration. Dots represent arrows going into and out of the page.
- Any vibration can be resolved into two perpendicular components.

2 Light and electromagnetism

- Visible light is part of the *electromagnetic spectrum*. It is regarded as a combination of varying electric and magnetic fields at right angles to each other.
- Light vibrations are taken to be variations of the electric field.
- *Polaroid* consists of tiny crystals aligned in the same direction on a nitrocellulose sheet. The crystals polarize light by selective *absorption*.
- The effect is similar to the *polarization* of *microwaves* by a grid of wires.

3 Parallel and crossed tourmaline crystals

- The mineral tourmaline also polarizes light by selective absorption. Two wafers placed in parallel produce polarized light. If one of the wafers is rotated through 90° no light passes.

4 Nicol prisms used as polarizer and analyzer

- When *Nicol prisms* are placed in parallel, polarized light is transmitted through them. When the same prisms are placed in the "crossed" position the polarized light transmitted by the first is absorbed by the second and there is no overall transmission.

1 Light rays resolved into two planes of vibration

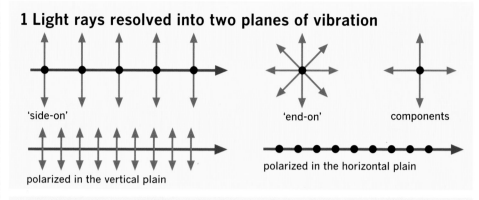

'side-on'

'end-on'

components

polarized in the vertical plain

polarized in the horizontal plain

2 Light and electromagnetism

Light as an electronmagnetic wave

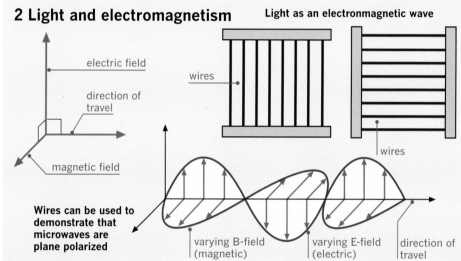

electric field

direction of travel

magnetic field

wires

wires

Wires can be used to demonstrate that microwaves are plane polarized

varying B-field (magnetic)

varying E-field (electric)

direction of travel

3 Parallel and crossed tourmaline crystals

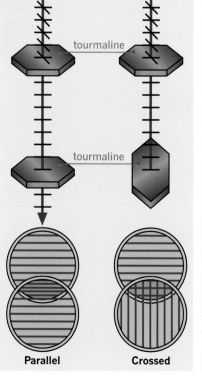

tourmaline

tourmaline

Parallel

Crossed

4 Nicol prisms used as polarizer and analyzer

Parallel nicols – E ray transmitted

Crossed nicols – no transmission

Parallel nicols – E ray transmitted

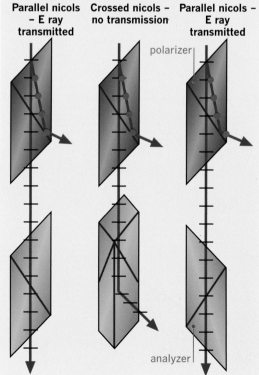

polarizer

analyzer

Measurement of the velocity of light

Key words

concave	speed of
plane	electromagnetic
prism	waves
reflection	

1 Fizeau's rotating wheel

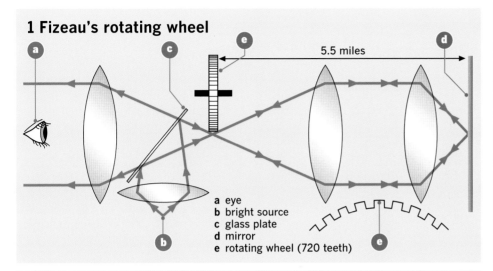

- a eye
- b bright source
- c glass plate
- d mirror
- e rotating wheel (720 teeth)

5.5 miles

2 Michelson's rotating prism

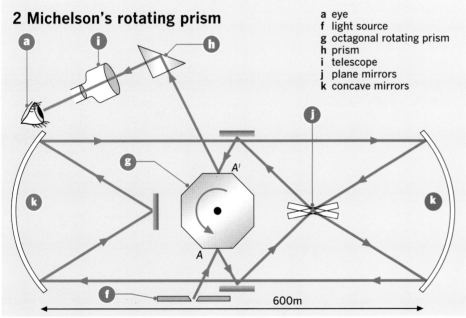

- a eye
- f light source
- g octagonal rotating prism
- h prism
- i telescope
- j plane mirrors
- k concave mirrors

600m

3 Foucault's method

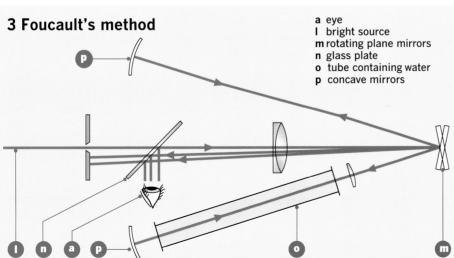

- a eye
- l bright source
- m rotating plane mirrors
- n glass plate
- o tube containing water
- p concave mirrors

1 Fizeau's rotating wheel

- A ray of light is reflected by a glass plate, passes between the teeth of the wheel to a distant mirror and is reflected back. When the wheel is rotating slowly the light returns in time to pass through the opening through which it was transmitted. As the speed of rotation increases, the light is blocked when the wheel has advanced half the distance between adjacent gaps. As the speed increases, the wheel advances the whole distance between adjacent gaps and the light will again pass through.
- As the distances, the wheel's speed of rotation when light was transmitted, and its speed when light was blocked were known, Fizeau could calculate the speed of light.

2 Michelson's rotating prism

- Light passes through a slit and is reflected by one side of a *prism*. After reflection by a *plane* mirror, it is reflected between a pair of *concave* mirrors. The returning beam is *reflected* at the opposite side of the prism and, after reflection, viewed.
- When the prism is stationary, the image is seen by light reflected from surface A'. As the prism rotates, the image disappears, but it reappears when the rotation speed increases, and is seen in the same position as when the prism is stationary. Light reflected from A now arrives at A' in the time taken by the prism to rotate through 45° or ⅛ of a revolution.

3 Foucault's method

- Light is reflected by rotating plane mirrors onto a pair of concave mirrors set an equal distance away. The difference in the speed of light in air and in water is shown by the different time taken for the light beams to be reflected back to the eyepiece.

Electromagnetic spectrum 1

Key words

diffraction	interference
electromagnetic	vacuum
spectrum	wave
frequency	wavelength
gamma radiation	

1 Electromagnetic radiation

- The *electromagnetic spectrum* consists of a series of *wave*-like radiations which carry energy and exhibit *interference* and *diffraction*.
- Because of their electrical origin and ability to travel in a *vacuum*, they are regarded as a combination of electric and magnetic forces (hence the name) directed at right angles to each other and to the direction of travel.

2 Electromagnetic spectrum

- The electromagnetic spectrum is divided into a series of regions on the basis of *wavelength* or *frequency*.
- For all electromagnetic radiation:
  speed in a vacuum =
  wavelength x frequency
  $c = \lambda \upsilon$
- Since speed in a vacuum is constant, the frequency of electromagnetic radiation increases as wavelength decreases and vice versa.
- The energy of electromagnetic radiation increases with its frequency thus *gamma rays* are the most energetic and able to pass through thick layers of solid materials.

3 Light waves

- The visible spectrum of light is part of the electromagnetic spectrum. The colors of the spectrum correspond to the colors of the rainbow: red, orange, yellow, green, blue, indigo and violet, although there is some dispute over whether indigo and violet are sufficiently different in appearance to justify being regarded as different colors.
- What makes light of one color different from light of another color is its wavelength. Red light has the longest wavelength (and therefore the lowest frequency) while violet light has the shortest wavelength (and highest frequency).

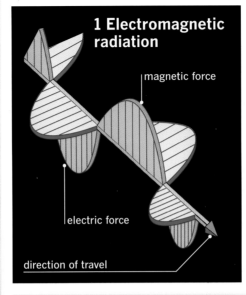

1 Electromagnetic radiation

magnetic force

electric force

direction of travel

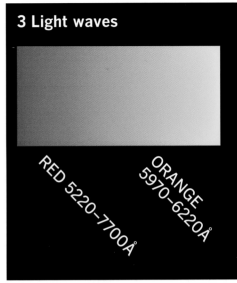

3 Light waves

RED 5220–7700Å

ORANGE 5970–6220Å

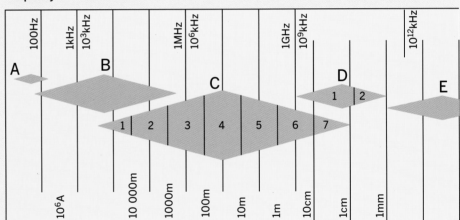

2 Electromagnetic spectrum

Frequency

100Hz · 1kHz · 10^3kHz · 1MHz · 10^6kHz · 1GHz · 10^9kHz · 10^{12}kHz

A B C D 1 2 E

1 2 3 4 5 6 7

10^6Å · 10 000m · 1000m · 100m · 10m · 1m · 10cm · 1cm · 1mm

Wavelength

ENERGY DECREASE

1 km · 1 m · 1 cm · 0.01 mm

A	B	C₂	C₄	D₁	D₂
Generated electricity	Induction heating	Radio waves	Radio waves	Micro waves	Micro waves

Electromagnetic spectrum 2

Key words

flourescence	X-rays
infrared	
microwaves	
radioactivity	
radio waves	
ultraviolet light	

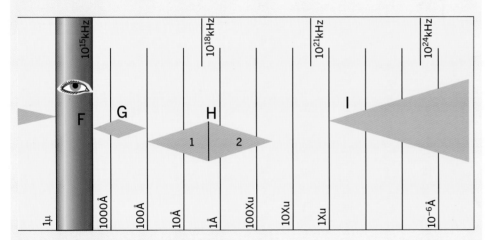

Tests indicate that, according to average judgement, names for the pure spectral colors should be applied to light of the following wavelenghts

YELLOW 5770–5970Å

GREEN 4920–5770Å

BLUE 4550–4920Å

VIOLET 3900–4550Å

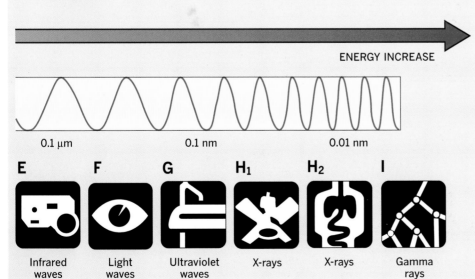

ENERGY INCREASE

0.1 μm   0.1 nm   0.01 nm

E	F	G	H₁	H₂	I
Infrared waves	Light waves	Ultraviolet waves	X-rays	X-rays	Gamma rays

Gamma rays

- Gamma radiation is emitted as a result of radioactive decay. Gamma rays have high energy and are the most penetrating and least *ionising* of the three radiations emitted in *radioactivity*.

X-rays

- *X-rays* are produced in X-ray tubes by the impact of high speed electrons on metal targets.
- High frequency X-rays can penetrate solid objects. Longer wavelength X-rays can penetrate flesh but not bone. They are used to obtain "pictures" of bones and teeth inside the body.

Ultraviolet waves

- *Ultraviolet* radiation is emitted by white-hot objects (such as the Sun) and from certain gas discharges.
- This radiation gives rise to *fluorescence* and *photoelectric effects*. It causes the skin to tan and is used in the formation of vitamin D.

Infrared waves

- *Infrared* radiation is thermal radiation (heat). All bodies emit infrared radiation and it is one means of transferring heat.
- Infrared is used to transfer data between IT equipment without cables.

Microwaves

- *Microwave* sources include tubes called klystrons.
- Microwaves are used in radar and in microwave ovens to cook food.

Radio waves

- *Radio waves* are important in communication. Information is added to the wave before transmisson. At the receiver the information is separated from the carrier wave and amplified.

Key words

black body	thermistor
bolometer	thermocouple
infrared	thermopile
prism	wheatstone
radiation	bridge
spectrum	

1 Intensity of filament lamp

- Light sources emit both light and heat. When *radiation* from a filament lamp is dispersed by a *prism*, *infrared* radiation is refracted less than visible light and can be detected beyond the red end of the *spectrum*.

2 The thermopile

- When two different metals are joined in a circuit with their junctions kept at different temperatures, a small e.m.f. is produced and a current flows.
- Several *thermocouples* connected in series form a *thermopile*.
- Hot junctions of a thermopile are painted dull black to increase heat absorption, while the cold junctions are shielded from the heat radiation.

3 The bolometer

- A small temperature change causes a large change in the electrical resistance of a *thermistor*.
- A *bolometer* contains one active and one compensating thermistor in a *Wheatstone bridge* circuit. Change in temperature alters the active thermistor's resistance, unbalancing the potential difference. The required rebalancing relates to the size of the temperature change.

4 Black body radiation

- A *black body* theoretically absorbs all the radiation falling on it. It is a standard to judge other bodies by.
- A cylinder with dull black interior surfaces and a small hole through which radiation enters approximates to a black body. Radiation entering is absorbed before exiting.
- Wien's displacement law states that at a temperature, the wavelength of the majority of the energy radiated has a particular wavelength λ_{max}. This wavelength decreases with rising temperature $\lambda_{max}T = $ constant.

Infrared

1 Intensity of a filament lamp

a 12 V 24 W filament lamp   c prism   e phototransistor   g 1.5 V battery
b lens   d white screen   f milliameter

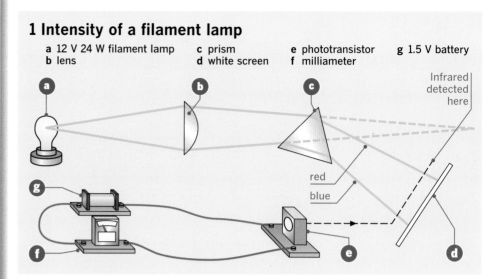

2 The thermopile

h thermocouple wires   k galvanometer   m horn
i cold junction   l incident radiation   n to galvanometer
j hot junction

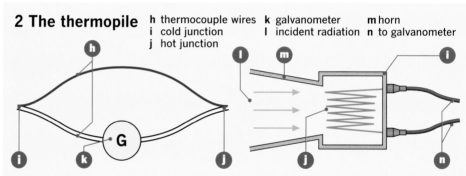

3 The bolometer

o active thermistor
p compensating thermistor
q bridge circuit and connections to bolometer

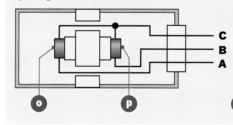

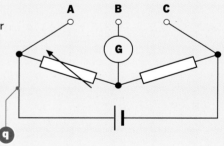

4 Black body radiation

Producing a black body

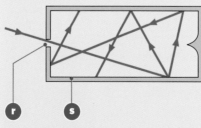

r small hole
s dull black surface
t visible region

Black body radiation spectrum

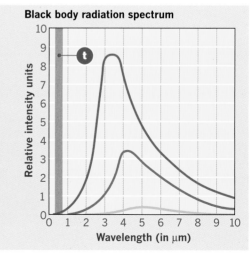

Relative intensity units vs Wavelength (in μm)

Absorption and scattering

Key words

absorption	wavelength
Rayleigh's	
scattering law	
reflection	
spectrograph	

1 Scattering by particles

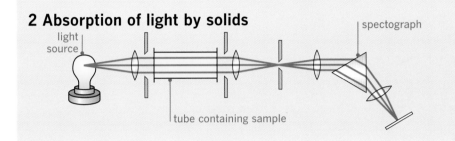

$I_o - I = I_s$

2 Absorption of light by solids

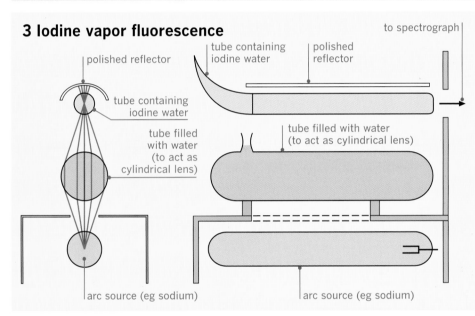

light source

spectrograph

tube containing sample

3 Iodine vapor fluorescence

to spectrograph

polished reflector

tube containing
iodine water

polished
reflector

tube containing
iodine water

tube filled
with water
(to act as
cylindrical lens)

tube filled with water
(to act as cylindrical lens)

arc source (eg sodium)

arc source (eg sodium)

4 Reflection and scattering

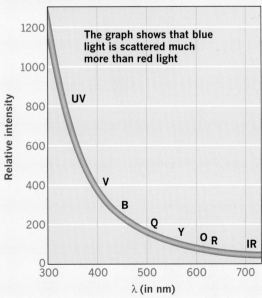

Reflection

Scattering

5 Rayleigh scattering

The graph shows that blue
light is scattered much
more than red light

UV

V

B

Q

Y

O R

IR

Relative intensity

1200

1000

800

600

400

200

0

300   400   500   600   700

λ (in nm)

1 Scattering by particles

- Some light passing through a tube containing particles collides and is *reflected* in several directions, whilst the remainder passes straight through.

2 Absorption of light by solids

- Different substances *absorb* light of different *wavelengths*.
- Light which has passed through a sample can be separated into a series of rays of different wavelengths by diffraction and be displayed as a *spectrograph*.

3 Iodine vapor fluorescence

- A spectrograph records the wavelengths of light absorbed by iodine vapor.

4 Reflection and scattering

- The nature of scattering depends on the size of the particles involved.

5 Rayleigh scattering

- *Rayleigh scattering* is the effect where light is scattered by particles smaller than the wavelength of light. It is most prominent in gases.
- Such particles scatter more short than long wavelength light. The wavelength of blue light is around 400 nm, red light around 700 nm.
- Nitrogen and oxygen molecules cause Rayleigh scattering. Blue light is scattered about 10 times more than red. When the sun is overhead blue light is scattered many times before it reaches our eyes so the sky appears uniformly blue. Red light is scattered relatively little and so appears to be coming only from the sun.
- At sunrise and sunset, sunlight travels through a thicker atmospheric layer causing increased scattering of red light which can make the sky appear redder.

Key words

chirp	frequency
dispersion	prism
electromagnetic	refraction
radiation	refractive index
electromagnetic	wavelength
spectrum	

Dispersion

1 Dispersion curves

- The *refractive index*, μ, of a medium is the ratio of the speed of light in that medium to the speed of light in a second medium (often air).
- The change in speed of *electromagnetic radiation* passing from one medium into another depends on its *wavelength*. When a mixture of radiations of different wavelengths, such as white light, passes from air into a glass *prism* it separates into its component wavelengths.

2 Anomalous dispersion of sodium vapor

- Sodium vapor is formed by heating sodium metal in a sealed tube. Light is polarised using a horizontal slit before passing through the vapor.
- A sequence of images of the horizontal slit separated by gaps forms. The radiation bands are detected by a spectroscope.

3 Anomalous dispersion of quartz in infrared

- Over a short range of wavelengths quartz absorbs all radiation and *refracts* none.

4 Dispersion curve for material transparent to light

- *Dispersion* occurs in all regions of the *electromagnetic spectrum*.
- Higher *frequency* components of light passing through a normally dispersive medium travel slower than lower frequency components. The light becomes positively *chirped*, or up-chirped, increasing in frequency with time. Higher frequency components of light passing through an anomalously dispersive medium travel faster than low ones, the pulse becomes negatively chirped, or down chirped, decreasing in frequency with time.

1 Dispersion curves

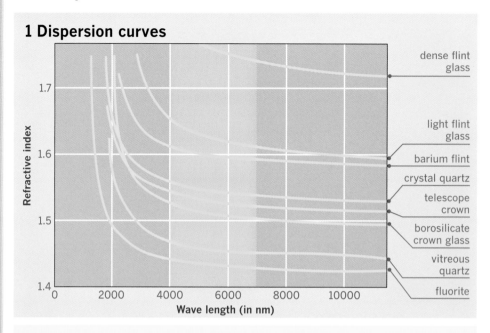

2 Anomalous dispersion of sodium vapor

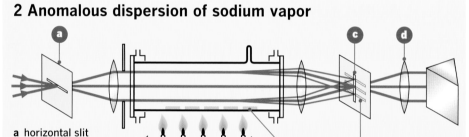

a horizontal slit
b sodium
c vertical slite

3 Anomalous dispersion of quartz in infrared

a visible region
b absorption band

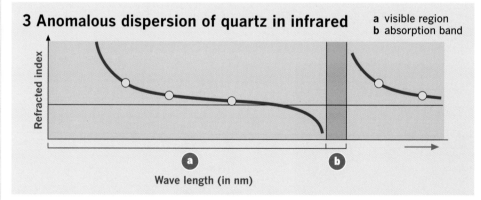

Wave length (in nm)

4 Dispersion curve for material transparent to light

a X-rays
b far ultraviolet
c near ultraviolet
d visible
e near infra-red
f far infra-red
g radio waves

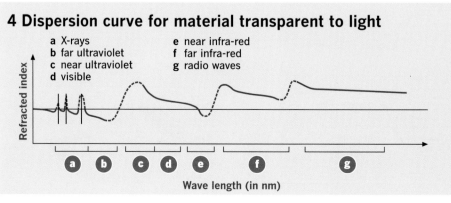

Wave length (in nm)

Reflection 1

1 Reflection of light rays from polished surface

incident ray
reflected ray
polished surface

2 Reflection of light rays from rough surface

rough surface

3 Verifying law of reflection

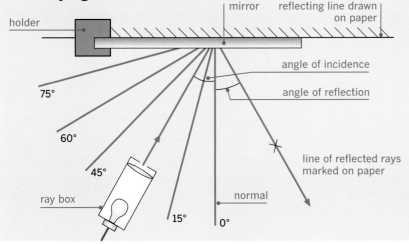

holder
mirror
reflecting line drawn on paper
angle of incidence
angle of reflection
75°
60°
line of reflected rays marked on paper
45°
ray box
normal
15°
0°

4 Ray diagram to find image position

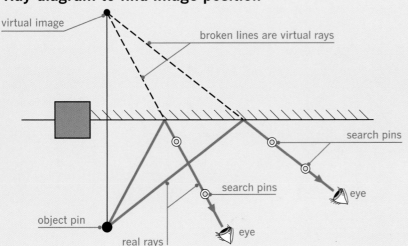

virtual image
broken lines are virtual rays
search pins
search pins
eye
object pin
real rays
eye

Key words

angle of incidence
virtual image
laws of reflection
normal
reflection

1 Reflection of light rays from polished surface

- When parallel light rays fall on a highly polished surface they are reflected as a parallel beam. This is described as regular *reflection*. The angle of reflection of each ray equals the *angle of incidence*.

2 Reflection of light rays from rough surface

- Most surfaces are not totally smooth, therefore light is reflected in many different directions. This is diffuse reflection. Although light rays are reflected in different directions each individual ray obeys the laws of reflection; its angle of reflection equals its angle of incidence.

3 Verifying law of reflection

- The angle of incidence is the angle between the incident light ray and the normal. The angle of reflection is the angle between the reflected ray and the *normal*.
- The first law of reflection states that the angle of reflection equals the angle of incidence.
- The second *law of reflection* states that the angle of incidence, the angle of reflection and the normal all lie in the same plane.

4 Ray diagram to find image position

- An object's image seen in a mirror is located by aligning two pins with the image from two different positions. The image is at the point where the lines of the pairs of pins intersect.
- The image of an object in a mirror is upright, same size and *virtual*. Its position is at an equal perpendicular distance behind the mirror as the object is in front of it.
- When an object is viewed in a mirror its image is laterally inverted.

Key words

angle of	plane
incidence	reflection
concave	virtual ray
convex	
focus	

1 Action of the periscope

- When a mirror is set at an angle of 45° to the horizontal (or vertical) the *angle of incidence* of a ray of light parallel to the horizontal is 45° and the angle of *reflection* is also 45°. The result is that the direction of the ray of light changes by 90° or a right angle.
- In a periscope two mirrors arranged at 45° are aligned in such a way that the observer can see above or around an object. The first mirror alters the direction of light by a right angle and the second mirror restores the light to its original direction.

2 Kaleidoscope

- In a kaleidoscope two *plane* mirrors are set at an angle of 60° with an object between them. The object is often a small number of coloured glass or plastic shapes.
- The mirrors provide a series of multiple images which form a symmetrical pattern at the end of the kaleidoscope.

3 Action of a concave mirror

- A *concave* mirror is also called a converging mirror. It reflects parallel rays of light to a single point or *focus*. The focus of a concave mirror lies in front of the mirror and is real.

4 Action of a convex mirror

- A *convex* mirror is also called a diverging mirror. It reflects parallel rays of light away from the mirror in such a way that they appear to be coming from a single point or focus. The focus of a convex mirror lies behind the mirror and is therefore *virtual*.

Reflection 2

1 Action of the periscope

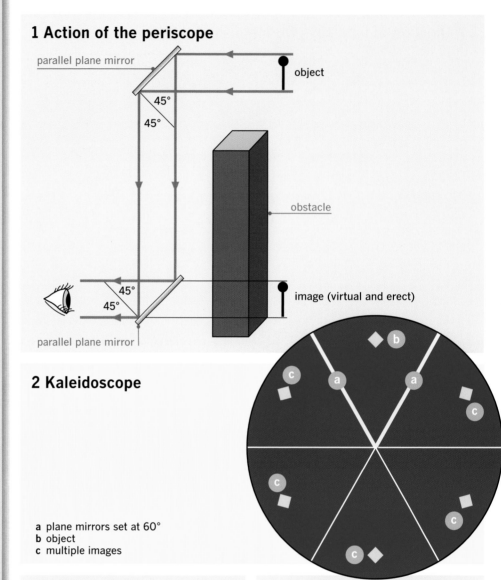

parallel plane mirror

45°
45°

object

obstacle

45°
45°

image (virtual and erect)

parallel plane mirror

2 Kaleidoscope

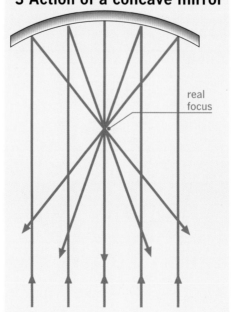

a plane mirrors set at 60°
b object
c multiple images

3 Action of a concave mirror

real focus

4 Action of a convex mirror

virtual focus

virtual rays

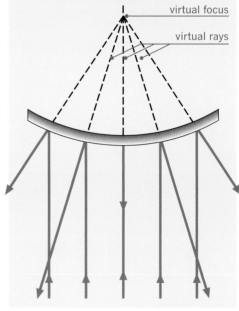

Reflection 3

1 Definitions associated with a concave mirror

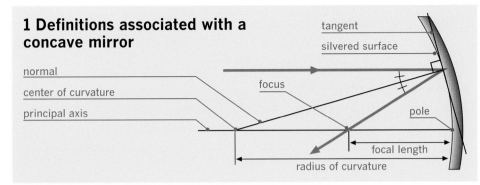

2 Definitions associated with a convex mirror

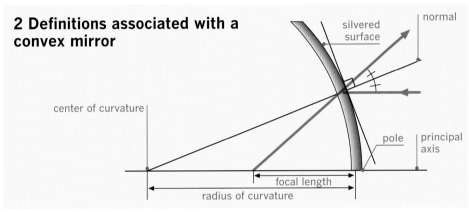

3 Caustic curve formation in a spherical mirror

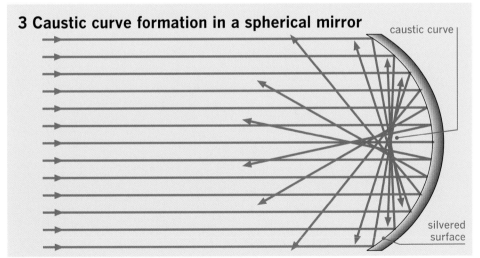

4 Elimination of caustic curve using parabolic reflector

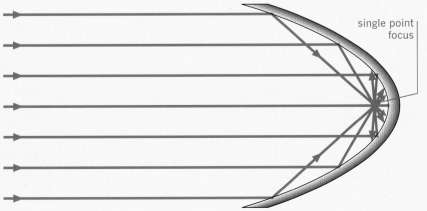

1 Definitions associated with a concave mirror

● A spherical *concave* mirror can be regarded as part of a sphere whose center is called the center of curvature. The distance from there to the mirror is the radius of curvature.

● A ray of light striking the mirror is reflected through the *focus* (half way between the mirror and the center of curvature). The *laws of reflection* are satisfied. The *angle of incidence* and the angle of reflection are found by drawing the *tangent* to the mirror at the point where light rays strike it and then the *normal* to this tangent.

2 Definitions associated with a convex mirror

● A spherical *convex* mirror is also regarded as part of a sphere. The focus and center of curvature are behind the mirror. The focus is half way between the mirror and the center of curvature, thus the radius of curvature is twice the focal length.

3 Caustic curve formation in a spherical mirror

● Light rays parallel to the principal axis incident on a spherical mirror are focused not through a single point but through a series of points lying on the radius of curvature. This effect is *spherical aberration*. It results from the mirror's focal length for marginal rays being less than for paraxial rays.

4 Elimination of caustic curve using parabolic reflector

● In a *parabolic reflector* all rays parallel to the principal axis are reflected through a single focus.

● Searchlight and car headlights use parabolic reflectors. All the light is reflected as a parallel beam.

Key words

center of curvature	principle axis
concave	virtual image
convex	
focus	

The three rays used to find the images formed by reflection at a curved mirror

- In order to locate the image of an object formed by a *convex* or *concave* mirror three rays may be drawn from the top of the object. Any two of these rays is sufficient to fix the location.
- For a convex mirror the rays must be drawn as if they are coming from the focus or the *center of curvature*.
- The intersecting rays locate the top of the image. The image is then drawn from the point of intersection to the *principal axis*.
- Once the image has been located it is possible to comment on its position relative to the center of curvature and the *focus*, and describe it as:
    upright or inverted
    magnified, diminished or same size
    real or *virtual*.

1 Ray parallel to principal axis

- A ray parallel to the principal axis which is reflected back through the focus or appears to diverge from it.

2 A ray arriving through the focus

- A ray through the focus which is reflected parallel to the principal axis.

3 A ray returning along the same path

- A ray passing through the center of curvature which strikes the mirror at a right angle to the path of the ray and is reflected back along the same path.

Reflection 4

1 Ray parallel to principal axis

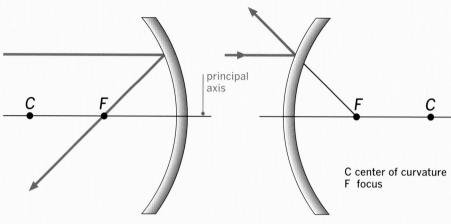

C center of curvature
F focus

Concave: reflected through focus, *F*   Convex: reflected as though it came from *F*

2 A ray arriving through the focus

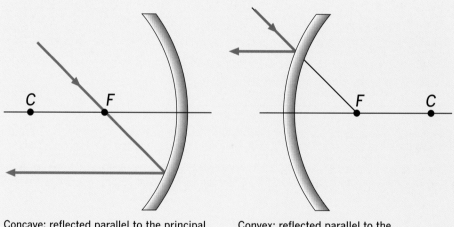

Concave: reflected parallel to the principal axis   Convex: reflected parallel to the principal axis

3 A ray returning along the same path

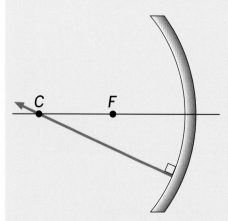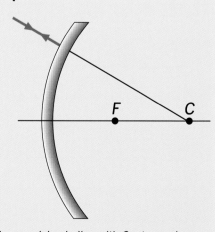

A ray arriving through the center of curvature, *C*, returns along the same path   A ray arriving in line with *C* returns along the same path

Reflection 5

Key words

center of curvature	infinity
concave	plane
convex	virtual image
focus	

1 Images formed by a concave mirror

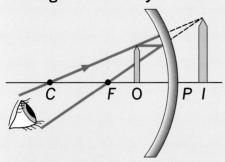

Object O between focus, F, and pole, P: image is virtual – used as a magnifier

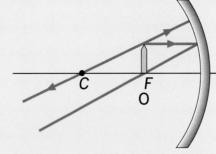

Object O at F: image at infinity – used as a reflector in a spotlight

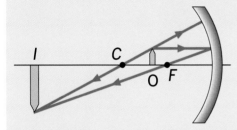

Object between F and center of curvature, C: image is real

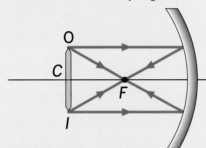

Object beyond C: image is real – used as a reflector behind a projector lamp

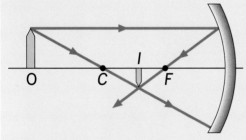

Object beyond C: image is real

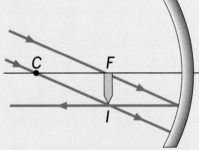

Object at infinity: image is real – used in a reflecting telescope

2 Images formed by a convex mirror

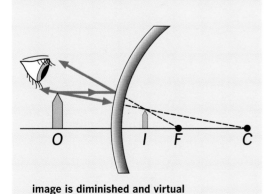

image is diminished and virtual

3 Convex mirror giving a wide field of view

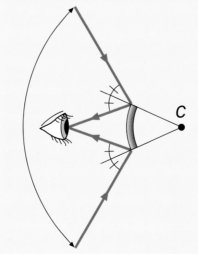

1 Images formed by a concave mirror

- The nature of the image formed by a *concave* mirror depends on the position of the object.
- When the object is between the *focus* and the mirror the image is upright, magnified and *virtual* since it is behind the mirror.
- When the object is at the focus it is not possible to locate the image since the rays normally used to locate an image are parallel. The image is said to be at *infinity*.
- When the object is between the *center of curvature* and the focus a real, inverted and magnified image is formed.
- When the object is at the center of curvature a real, inverted image the same size as the object is formed at the same point.
- When the object is beyond the center of curvature an inverted, diminished real image is formed between the focus and the center of curvature.
- An object at infinity forms an inverted real image at the focus.

2 Images formed by a convex mirror

- A *convex* mirror always forms a diminished, upright, virtual image no matter what the position of the object.

3 Convex mirror giving a wide field of view

- A convex mirror gives a much wider field of view than a *plane* mirror of similar size.
- Convex mirrors are used as rear view mirrors in cars and security mirrors in shops.

Refraction 1

Key words

angle of incidence	vacuum
reflection	
refraction	
refractive index	

Refraction
- The speed of light is constant for any medium. The change of speed on passing from one medium to another causes *refraction* as light rays bend.

1 Refraction and reflection
- When a light ray passes into a medium with a different optical density, part of the ray is *reflected* and part refracted.
- When a light ray passes from a less to a more dense medium, the *angle of incidence* is greater than the angle of refraction. When it passes the other way, the converse is true.
- The ratio sine of angle of incidence : sine of angle of refraction is the *refractive index* for light passing from one medium into another. For media 1 and 2, refractive index is $_1\mu_2$. If 1 is a *vacuum* (or air) the ratio is the absolute refractive index, μ_2.

2 Real and apparent depth
- When a submerged object is viewed from above the surface of water it appears closer to the surface than it is. This is due to light rays from the object being bent away from the normal as they pass out of the water (the more dense medium) into air (the less dense medium).
- The ratio of the real depth of the object to its apparent depth equals the refractive index of water.

3 Apparent depth used to measure refractive index
- Real depth of the mark is S_3–S_1. (Difference in readings when the microscope is focused on the surface of the liquid and on the mark in the empty beaker.)
- Apparent depth of the mark is S_3–S_2. (Difference in readings when the microscope is focused on the surface of the liquid and on the mark in the beaker full of water.)

1 Refraction and reflection

In this example medium y is more dense than medium x.
If x is a vacuum, then
$$\frac{\sin d}{\sin e} = \mu \quad \text{refractive index}$$

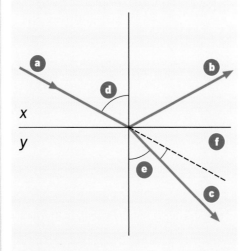

x

y

a incident ray
b reflected ray
c refracted ray
d angle of incidence
e angle of refraction
f angle of deviation

2 Real and apparent depth

$$\mu = \frac{\text{real depth}}{\text{apparent depth}}$$

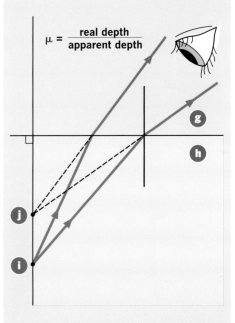

g air
h water
i object
j image position

3 Apparent depth used to measure refractive index

Focus microscope on mark. Record reading S_1

Pour in water and focus on mark. Record reading S_2

Focus on lycopodium powder and record reading S_3

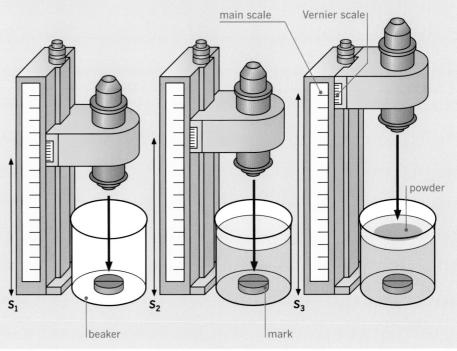

main scale   Vernier scale

powder

S_1 S_2 S_3

beaker   mark

Refraction 2

1 Critical angle

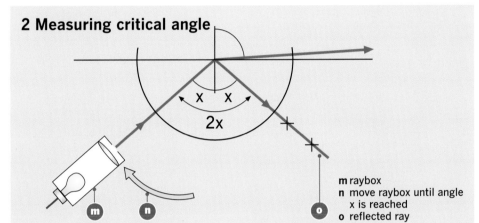

f source
g air
h water
i partial transmission
j partial reflection
k grazing emergence
l total reflection

2 Measuring critical angle

x x
2x

m raybox
n move raybox until angle x is reached
o reflected ray

3 Deviation through prism

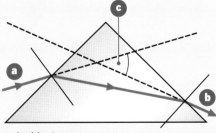

a incident ray
b emergent ray
c angle of deviation

4 Total internal reflection

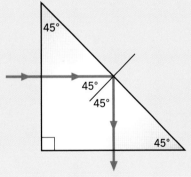

45°
45°
45°
45°

5 Prism turning ray 180°

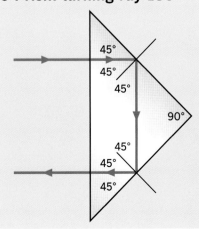

45°
45°
45°
90°
45°
45°
45°

6 Image formation with prism

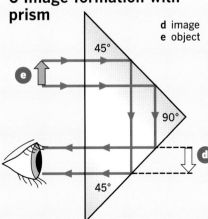

d image
e object

45°
90°
45°

---

1 Critical angle

- When a ray of light strikes the interface between two media, some is *refracted*, some *reflected*.
- When a ray of light passes from a more to a less optically dense medium (from water to air) at some *angle of incidence*, the angle of refraction is 90° and the ray is refracted along the interface between the two media. This is called the *critical angle*, c. When the angle of incidence is greater than the critical angle no light is refracted and total internal reflection takes place.

2 Measuring critical angle

- The *refractive index* equals the reciprocal of the sine of the critical angle i.e. $\mu = 1/\text{sine } c$.

3 Deviation through prism

- A light ray passing from air into a glass *prism* at other than a right angle is refracted towards the *normal*. On passing from prism back into air it is refracted away from the normal. The angle of deviation gives the overall change in direction of the light ray.

4 Total internal reflection

- No refraction takes place when a light ray passes from air into a glass prism at a right angle to the surface.
- Total internal reflection occurs if the light ray strikes another surface inside the prism at greater than the critical angle. Ray shown is turned 90°.

5 Prism turning ray 180°

- A 45° prism can also reflect light through 180°. Thus a prism can reflect light in the same manner as a mirror.

6 Image formation with prism

- An image viewed using a prism is *virtual*, inverted and the same size as the object.

Key words

absorption
endoscope
fiber optics
refractive index

1 Optical fiber

● Each time a light ray strikes the inside of the fiber, total internal reflection takes place. The ray passes from side to side down an optical fiber with very little loss due to *absorption* in the glass, and emerges almost normally.

2 Light pipe

● Several optical fibers are taped together to form a light pipe. The many uses of light pipes include medicine, engineering, and providing illumination in difficult conditions.

● To reduce leakage of light at points of contact between fibers, each fiber is coated with cladding to promote total internal reflection. The cladding is a layer of glass of lower *refractive index* than the glass from which the fiber is made.

● Light pipes transport beams of light. Changes in the orientation of the fibers along the length of the pipe present no problems.

3 Medical use

● If an image is to be used it is essential that each fiber retains the same position relative to the others in the bundle throughout its length.

● Such arrangements are more difficult to manufacture than light pipes, but are essential components of instruments such as the *endoscope* which a surgeon uses to view internal parts of a patient's body.

4 Transmission of signals

● Optical fibers are increasingly used to carry television, telephone and computer signals. Such signals are generated as pulses of light from lasers. Optical fibers are preferred to traditional copper wires because of their high information-carrying capacity, freedom from noise caused by electrical interference, lower mass and signal loss, and greater security.

Refraction 3

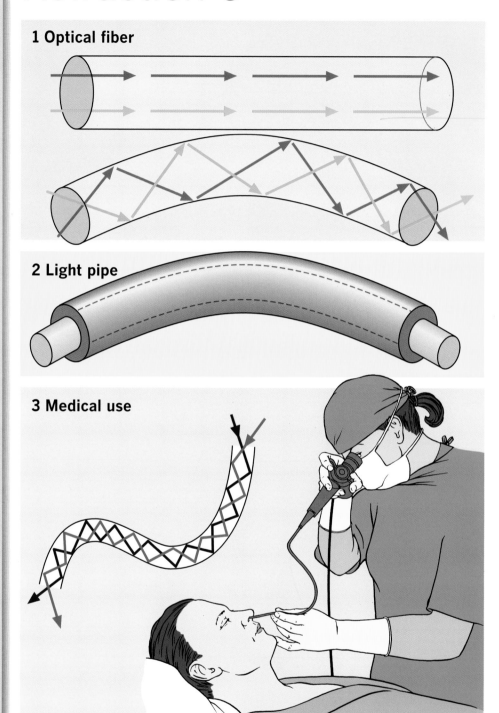

1 Optical fiber

2 Light pipe

3 Medical use

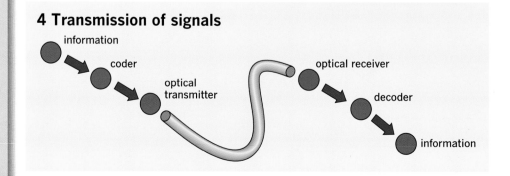

4 Transmission of signals

information

coder

optical transmitter

optical receiver

decoder

information

The human eye

1 The eye

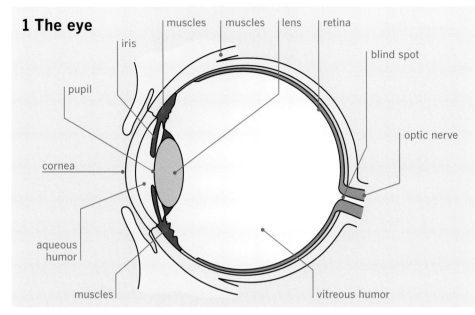

iris
muscles   muscles   lens   retina

blind spot

pupil

optic nerve

cornea

aqueous humor

muscles

vitreous humor

2 Focusing

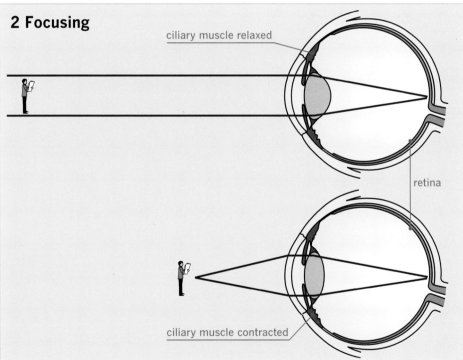

ciliary muscle relaxed

retina

ciliary muscle contracted

3 Control of light entering eye

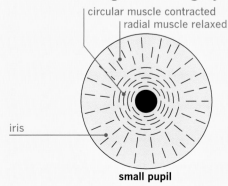

circular muscle contracted
radial muscle relaxed

iris

small pupil

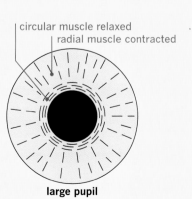

circular muscle relaxed
radial muscle contracted

large pupil

Key words

accommodation	retina
cornea	
focal length	
focus	
lens	

1 The eye

- Light is *focused* on the *retina*, a layer of light sensitive cells, by the *cornea* and the *lens*. When the retina detects light, an impulse is sent along the optic nerve to the brain. The point where the optic nerve leaves the eye is called the blind spot and is not itself sensitive to light. Within the wall of the eye the choroid layer contains heavy pigmentation which prevents light from being reflected.

2 Focusing

- The eye can focus on objects over a range of distances. This is called *accommodation* and occurs by altering the *focal length* of the lens. The lens is held by suspensory ligaments attached to a ciliary body which is a ring of muscle.
- To view distant objects, the ciliary muscle relaxes. This pulls on the suspensory ligaments which, in turn, pull on the lens. The lens is stretched thinner at the center and its focal length increases.
- To view near objects, the ciliary muscle contracts. This reduces the tension on the suspensory ligaments allowing the lens to thicken at the center, decreasing its focal length.

3 Control of light entering eye

- The amount of light entering the eye through the pupil is controlled by the iris which is composed of both circular and radial muscles.
- In bright light the circular muscles contract and the radial muscles relax. This reduces the size of the pupil, limiting the amount of light that can enter the eye.
- In dim light the circular muscles relax and the radial muscles contract, increasing the size of the pupil, allowing as much light as possible into the eye.

Key words

concave	retina
convex	
cornea	
focus	
lens	

1 Short sight correction

- A short sighted person can see close objects, but light rays from distant objects converge in front of the retina. Correction is made using a *concave lens* which makes light rays diverge slightly before being *focused* by the *cornea* and lens onto the *retina*.

2 Long sight correction

- A long sighted person can see distant objects, but light rays from close objects converge behind the retina. It is corrected using a *convex* lens. This makes light rays converge slightly before being focused by the cornea and lens onto the retina.

3 Rods and cones

- The retina consists of rod and cone cells.
- Rods allow the eye to see in low light and are responsible for night vision. They do not register objects as clearly as cones and do not respond to different colors.
- Cones work best in good illumination and are responsible for daylight vision. They register a clear image and respond to different colors.

4 Color vision

- There are three types of cones, each sensitive to one of the three primary colors. It is thought that a color is perceived by one, two or three cone types being stimulated to some extent.
- Some people have red and green absorption curves so close together that they cannot distinguish between these two colors and are red-green color blind.
- Another type of color blindness results from the complete absence of one type of cone. A person with this defect can only see colors formed by mixing the two primary colors corresponding to the cone types present.

Defects of vision

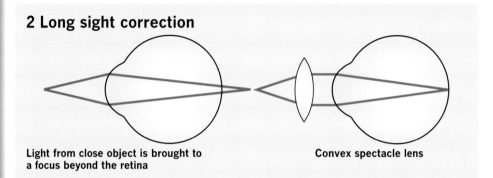

1 Short sight correction

Light from distant object is brought to a focus in front of the retina

Concave spectacle lens

2 Long sight correction

Light from close object is brought to a focus beyond the retina

Convex spectacle lens

3 Rods and cones

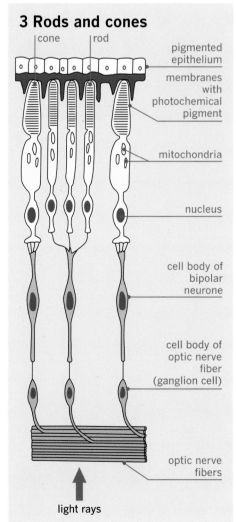

cone   rod

pigmented epithelium

membranes with photochemical pigment

mitochondria

nucleus

cell body of bipolar neurone

cell body of optic nerve fiber (ganglion cell)

optic nerve fibers

light rays

4 Color vision

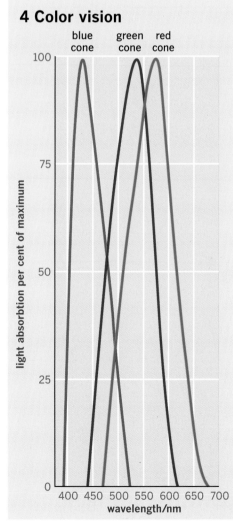

blue cone   green cone   red cone

light absorbtion per cent of maximum

wavelength/nm

Lenses 1

Key words

diopter
concave
convex
focal length
focus

lens
prism
virtual image

1 Two types of image

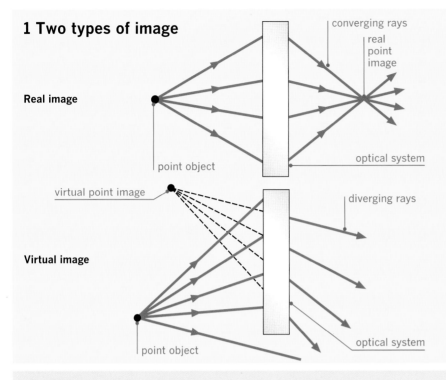

2 Three prisms forming an image

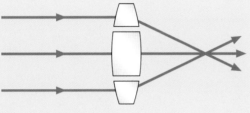

3 Continuously curved surface forming an image

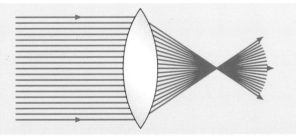

4 Lens shapes

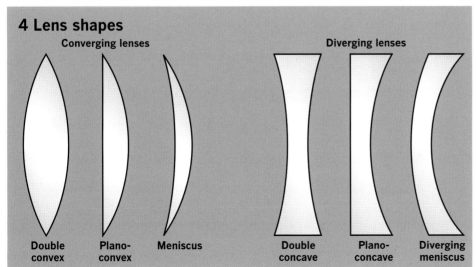

Converging lenses

Double convex Plano-convex Meniscus

Diverging lenses

Double concave Plano-concave Diverging meniscus

1 Two types of image
- A real image is formed when rays of light actually pass through it.
- An image is described as *virtual* if rays of light of light seem to come from it but do not actually do so.
- A *convex* lens is a converging lens and has real foci. A *concave* lens is a diverging lens and has virtual foci.

2 Three prisms forming an image
- A *lens* can be thought of as a series of *prisms*. A ray of light is refracted by each prism through a common *focus*.

3 Continuously curved surface forming an image
- Lenses have a continuous curved surface. A light ray striking the lens at any point on one surface is refracted through a common focus.

4 Lens shapes
- Lenses have a variety of types and are named according to their shape. For example, a plano-convex lens has one flat and one convex side. Similarly a bi-concave or double-concave lens has two concave sides.
- A meniscus lens has one concave and one convex side.
- The power of a lens is related to its *focal length*. The shorter the focal length the more the lens converges or diverges light. The power, F, of a lens is the reciprocal of its focal length, f, measured in meters; $F = 1/f$.
- The unit of power is the radian per meter, rad m^{-1}. The focal length equals distance, in meters, divided by angle of deviation, measured in radians. This has replaced the *diopter*, which was 1 radian per meter.
- The sign convention for power is the same as that used for focal length i.e. positive for converging lenses and negative for diverging lenses.

Lenses 2

Key words

concave	principal axis
convex	refraction
focal length	
focus	
lens	

1 Focal points of lenses

- All *lenses* have two foci since light passes through them in either direction. For symmetrical bi-*convex* and bi-*concave* lenses the foci are equal distances on either side of the lens and the *focal length* each side of the lens is also equal.

2 Ray diagrams locating image formed by lenses

- The position of the image of a small object perpendicular to the axis of a lens can be located by drawing two of three possible rays from the top of the object. The point of intersection of the rays indicates the top of the image.
- A ray parallel to the principal axis which, after being *refracted* by the lens, passes through the principal *focus* (convex lens) or appears to diverge from it (concave lens).
- A ray which passes through the (optical) center of the lens. This ray is drawn straight with no deviation.
- For convex lens—ray which, after passing through the principal focus, is refracted by the lens and leaves it parallel to the *principal axis*.
- For concave lens—ray which appears to pass through the principal focus but is refracted by the lens and leaves it parallel to the principal axis.
- No matter at what distance an object is placed from a concave lens, a virtual, upright and diminished image is always formed. Concave lenses are used in spectacles to correct short sight.
- The magnification, m, of a lens is the ratio of the height of the image to the height of the object. Magnification has no unit or sign. If a magnified image is formed magnification is greater than 1, and if a diminished image is formed magnification is less than 1.

1 Focal points of lenses

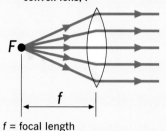

Primary focal point of a convex lens, F

f = focal length

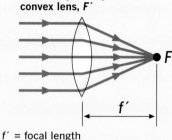

Secondary focal point of a convex lens, F´

$f´$ = focal length

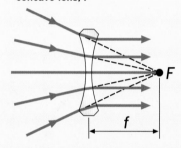

Primary focal point of a concave lens, F

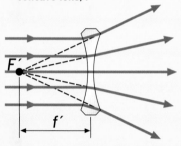

Secondary focal point of a concave lens, F´

2 Ray diagrams locating image formed by lenses

Convex lens

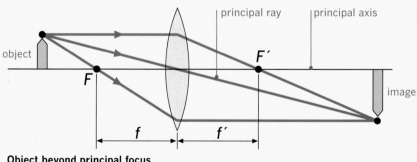

principal ray   principal axis

object

image

Object beyond principal focus

Concave lens

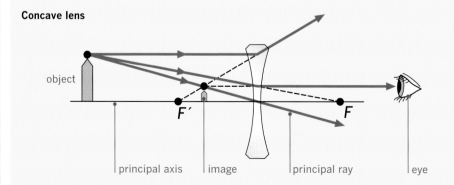

object

principal axis   image   principal ray   eye

Lenses 3

1 Position and nature of image formed by convex lens

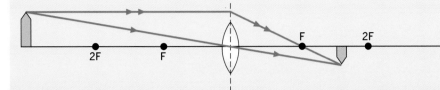

object distance more than twice focal length

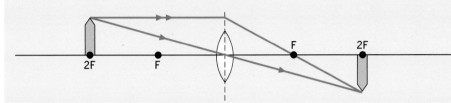

object distance exactly twice focal length

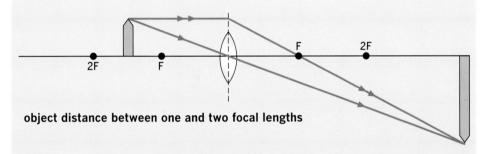

object distance between one and two focal lengths

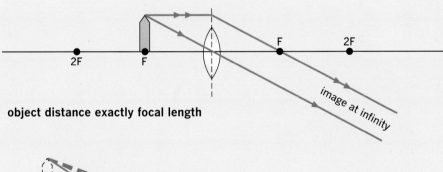

object distance exactly focal length

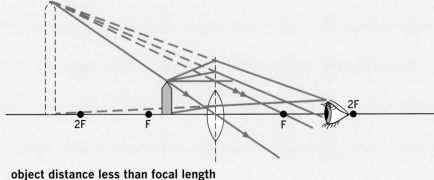

object distance less than focal length

Key words

convex
diverging lens
focal length
lens
virtual image

Images formed by convex lenses

- The image formed by a *convex lens* depends on its distance from the lens.
- The position of an image formed by a object can be found by calculation using the formula:
$1/u + 1/v = 1/f$
u—distance between the object and the center of the lens, v—distance from the image to the center of the lens, f—*focal length* of the lens.
- The focal length of a convex lens is taken as positive, that of a *diverging lens* as negative. A positive value for u or v indicates that it is real, a negative value indicates it is *virtual*.

1 Position and nature of image formed by convex lens

- When an object is at a distance of more than twice the focal length of the lens a real, inverted and diminished image is formed.
- When an object is at a distance of exactly twice the focal length of the lens a real, inverted image which is exactly the same size as the object is formed at the same distance on the opposite side of the lens.
- When an object is at a distance between one and two focal lengths from the lens a real, magnified inverted image is formed.
- When an object is at a distance exactly equal to the focal length of the lens the rays drawn to locate the image are parallel. An image is said to form at infinity.
- When an object is at a distance of less than the focal length a virtual, upright and magnified image is formed.

Color

Key words

diffraction	refraction
dispersion	spectrum
electromagnetic spectrum	wavelength
prism	

1 Producing a pure spectrum

- Visible light is a small part of the *electromagnetic spectrum*. Each color corresponds to light of a different *wavelength*.
- White light is a mixture of light of all colors. When white light passes through a *prism* different wavelengths are *diffracted* by different amounts. This effect is called *dispersion* and the resulting visible *spectrum* of colors can be shown on a screen.
- In the visible spectrum there is a gradual color change from one color to the next. The spectrum, however, is shown as consisting of seven colors; red, orange, yellow, green, blue, indigo and violet.
- The colors of the visible spectrum correspond to the colors of the rainbow. A rainbow is formed when sunlight (which is white light) is *refracted* by droplets of water in the atmosphere and dispersion takes place.
- The red light has the longest wavelength and is refracted the least while the violet light has the shortest wavelength and is refracted the most.

2 Recombining white light

- If a pair of prisms, one upright and one inverted, are placed next to each other the first prism disperses white light into its component colors while the second recombines the colors forming white light.

3 Newton's disc

- Newton's disc consists of a series of seven segments corresponding to the colors of the visible spectrum. When the disc is rotated rapidly about its center, the colors appear to merge forming white light.

1 Producing a pure spectrum

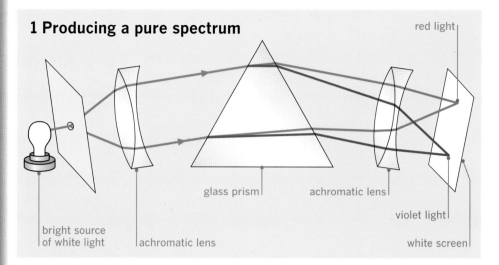

red light

glass prism

achromatic lens

violet light

bright source of white light

achromatic lens

white screen

2 Recombining while light

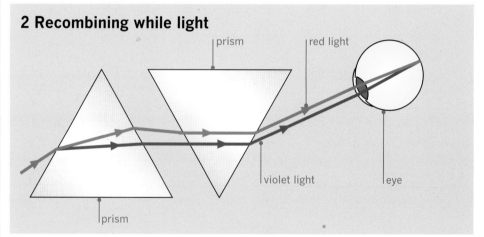

prism

red light

violet light

eye

prism

3 Newton's disc

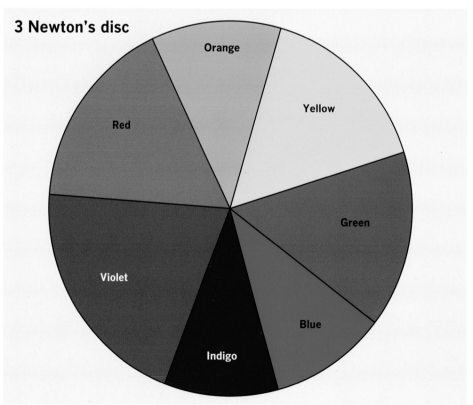

Orange

Yellow

Red

Green

Violet

Blue

Indigo

Color mixing

1 Primary colors

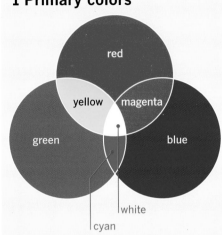

red
yellow | magenta
green | blue
white
cyan

2 Mixing of light

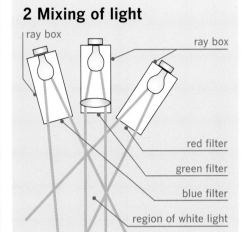

ray box
ray box
red filter
green filter
blue filter
region of white light

3 Colored light – absorption and reflection

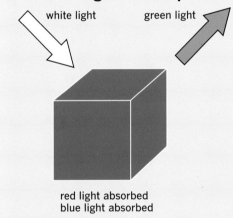

white light | green light | red light

red light absorbed
blue light absorbed

red light absorbed

4 Primary pigments

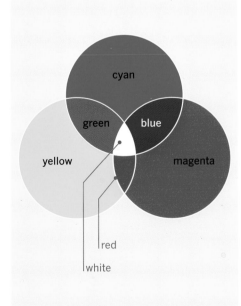

cyan
green | blue
yellow | magenta
red
white

5 Mixing of pigments

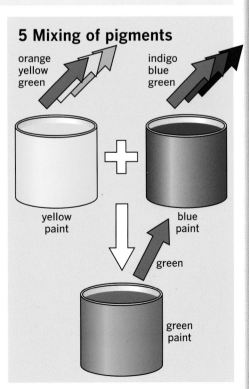

orange
yellow
green

indigo
blue
green

yellow paint

blue paint

green

green paint

Key words

absorption
primary colors
reflection
secondary colors

1 Primary colors

- Red, blue and green are the three *primary colors* of light. All other colors are made by combinations of primary colors.
- The *secondary colors*, yellow, magenta and cyan, are formed by mixing two primary colors.

2 Mixing of light

- Mixing of light occurs by addition.
- White light forms when light of the three primary colors is mixed.
- When a secondary color is mixed with its complementary color white light is formed.

3 Colored light—absorption and reflection

- An object's color is determined by the light it absorbs and reflects.
- A green box appears green when viewed in white light. It *absorbs* red and blue light and *reflects* green light.
- The same box when viewed in red light appears black since it absorbs the red light and reflects no light.

4 Primary pigments

- Primary pigments are colors which cannot be made by mixing other colored pigments. These pigments are used to make paints.

5 Mixing of pigments

- Mixing of pigments occurs by subtraction.
- Paints are seldom pure colors but mixtures of colors in which one color may predominate.
- Blue paint appears blue because it absorbs all the colors in white light except green, blue and indigo. Yellow paint absorbs all the colors except orange, yellow and green. When the two paints are mixed, all the colors of white light are absorbed except green, which is reflected. Mixing blue paint and yellow paint makes green paint.

Key words

convex	objective lens
focal length	virtual image
focus	
lens	
magnification	

1 Magnifying glass

- A magnifying glass consists of a single *convex lens*. When in use the object is placed so that the distance to the lens is less than the *focal length* of the lens and the eye is placed close to the other side of the lens.
- A magnifying glass produces an upright, magnified *virtual image*. Magnification, m, equals the height of the image/ height of the object.
- The *magnification* is also **equal to v/u.** v—distance from the image to the center of the lens. u—distance from the object to the center of the lens.
- **m = v/u; using the lens equation 1/u + 1/v = 1/f it follows that m = v/f − 1**
- A lens with a short focal length thus has a large magnifying power.

2 Microscope

- A magnifying glass is also a simple microscope, but it has limitations. The focal length of a lens can be decreased by making its surfaces more curved, but this results in serious distortion of the image.
- A compound microscope uses two convex lenses of short focal lengths. The *objective lens* forms a real, magnified and inverted image of an object placed just outside its principal *focus*. The image is just inside the principal focus of the second lens or eyepiece, which acts as a magnifying glass and produces a magnified virtual image of the first image.
- Microscopes commonly have a choice of objective lenses ranging from low power x10 to high power x40. They may also have a choice of eyepieces such as x5 and x10. The total magnification of a compound microscope is the product of the powers of the objective lens and the eyepiece.

Optical instruments 1

1 Magnifying glass

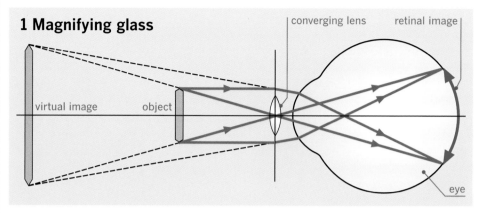

2 Microscope

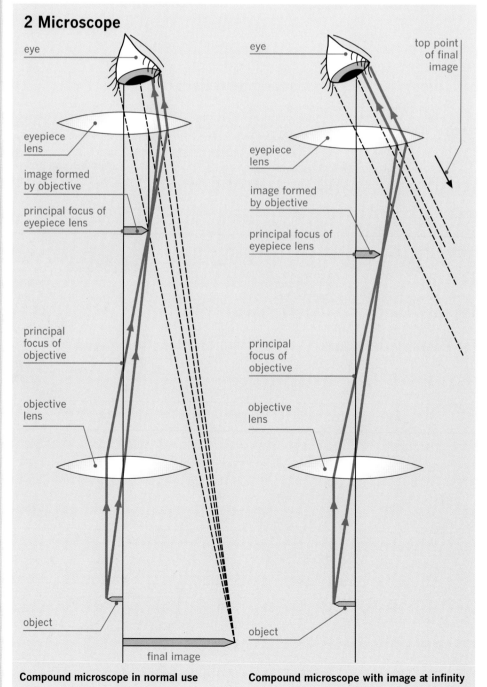

Compound microscope in normal use   Compound microscope with image at infinity

Optical instruments 2

1 Simple telescope

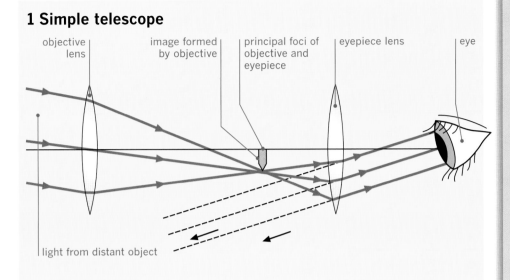

2 Terrestrial telescope

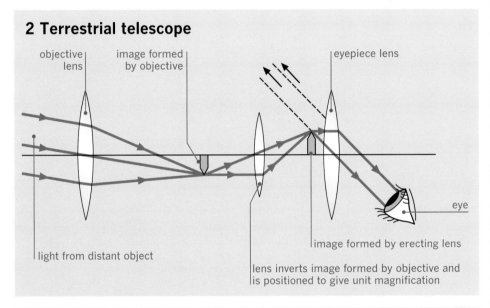

3 Galilean telescope

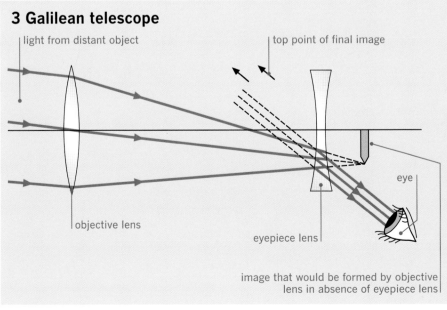

Key words

concave	*reflecting*
convex	*telescope*
focal length	*refracting*
focus	*telescope*
infinity	*virtual image*
objective lens	

Refracting telescopes

● *Refracting telescopes* use lenses, but large lenses are heavy, difficult to support and have two ground surfaces. *Reflecting telescopes* use mirrors which can be made much larger, are more easily supported and have a single ground surface.

1 Simple telescope

● A simple telescope has two *convex* lenses. The objective has a long *focal length* while the eyepiece has a short focal length. The lenses are arranged so that their principal foci coincide.

● The *objective lens* forms a real, diminished, inverted image of a distant object at its principal *focus*. The eyepiece acts as a magnifying glass forming a magnified *virtual image* of the first image. In normal adjustment, this image is at *infinity*.

2 Terrestrial telescope

● A simple telescope produces an inverted image. This is a problem for viewing objects on Earth.

● A terrestrial telescope has an erecting lens between objective and eyepiece. The image of the objective forms at twice the focal length of the erecting lens. A second real, upright image of the same size forms at the same distance on the opposite side of the inverting lens. The eyepiece forms a magnified third image at infinity.

3 Galilean telescope

● A Galilean telescope uses a convex objective lens of large focal length and a *concave* eyepiece of small focal length to produce an erect image.

● The image of the objective lens forms at the principal focus on the opposite side of the eyepiece. The converging light rays falling on the eyepiece behave like a virtual object and an upright virtual image forms at linfinity.

Lasers

1 Spontaneous emission

- When *atoms* are excited, *electrons* are promoted to high *energy levels*. They normally return to lower energy levels spontaneously. *Radiation* is emitted in all directions and is incoherent.

2 Stimulated emission

- If a *photon* of exactly the correct energy approaches an excited atom, an electron may fall to a lower energy level and emit another photon with the same *phase*, frequency and direction of travel as the first, which is unaffected. This is called stimulated emission and is the basis of a *laser*.

3 Optical pumping

- In a laser there must be more electrons in upper energy levels than lower (an inverted population).
- An inverted population can be produced by illuminating laser material with light (optical pumping).
- In a two energy level system, when the electron population in the higher level increases, the pumping radiation induces stimulated emission so no build up of electrons occurs.
- In a three energy level system, the pumping radiation promotes electrons from E1 to E3 which fall to E2 by spontaneous emission. An inverted population arises between E2 and E1.
- Spontaneous emission of a photon due to an electron transition between E2 and E1 may trigger stimulated emission of more photons, giving the laser effect.

4 Ruby laser

- A ruby rod laser, a three-level laser, consists of a synthetic crystal of aluminum oxide containing small amounts of chromium.
- Optical pumping radiation is provided by intense flashes of yellow-green light from a flash tube. Electrons emit red light on falling to level 1.

1 Spontaneous emission

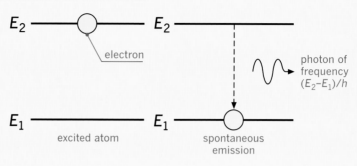

excited atom — spontaneous emission — photon of frequency $(E_2 - E_1)/h$

2 Stimulated emission

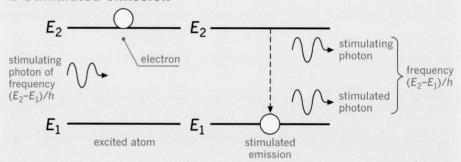

stimulating photon of frequency $(E_2 - E_1)/h$ — excited atom — electron — stimulating photon / stimulated photon — frequency $(E_2 - E_1)/h$ — stimulated emission

3 Optical pumping

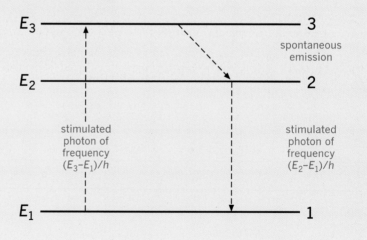

spontaneous emission — stimulated photon of frequency $(E_3 - E_1)/h$ — stimulated photon of frequency $(E_2 - E_1)/h$

4 Ruby laser

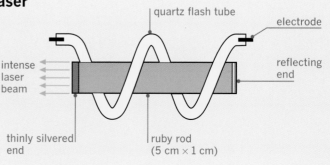

quartz flash tube — electrode — reflecting end — intense laser beam — thinly silvered end — ruby rod (5 cm × 1 cm)

Electric charge

Key words

atom	nucleus
charge	proton
electron	
ion	
neutron	

1 Positive and negative

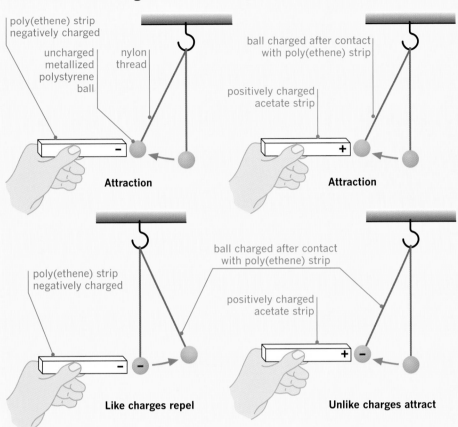

Attraction

Attraction

Like charges repel

Unlike charges attract

- poly(ethene) strip negatively charged
- uncharged metallized polystyrene ball
- nylon thread
- ball charged after contact with poly(ethene) strip
- positively charged acetate strip
- poly(ethene) strip negatively charged
- ball charged after contact with poly(ethene) strip
- positively charged acetate strip

1 Positive and negative

- When a negatively *charged* strip is placed close to a neutral polystyrene ball the ball becomes polarized. *Electrons* on the ball are repelled by the negatively charged strip, resulting in the side of the ball facing the strip becoming positively charged and the side facing away from the strip negatively charged. The ball is therefore attracted to the strip.
- A similar effect is observed when a positively charged strip is placed close to the same ball. In this case, the side of the ball facing the strip becomes negatively charged and the side facing away becomes positively charged. The result is the same and the ball is attracted to the strip.
- A negatively charged strip repels a negatively charged ball but attracts a positively charged ball. Like charge repel while unlike charge attract.

2 Atomic model

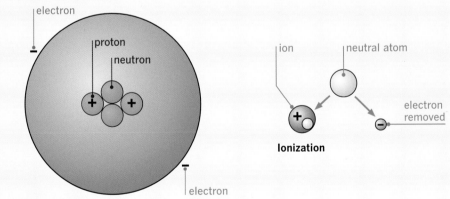

- electron
- proton
- neutron
- electron
- ion
- neutral atom
- electron removed

Ionization

2 Atomic model

- An *atom* consists of a *nucleus* containing *protons* and *neutrons*, surrounded by electrons. Electric charge is the result of loss (to give a positive charge) or gain (to give a negative charge) of electrons. The particles in the nucleus of an atom remain unchanged.
- An atom can become an *ion* either by the loss or gain of one or more electrons.

3 Charging by friction

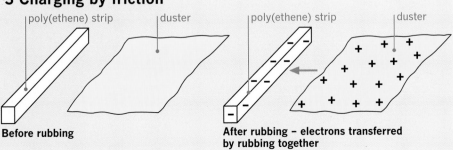

- poly(ethene) strip
- duster
- poly(ethene) strip
- duster

Before rubbing

After rubbing – electrons transferred by rubbing together

3 Charging by friction

- Before charging by friction there is no imbalance of electrons on either the poly(ethene) rod or the duster.
- When the rod is rubbed with the duster electrons are transferred from the duster to the rod. The result is that the duster becomes positively charged while the rod becomes negatively charged. As a result the poly(ethene) rod and duster will be attracted to each other.

Key words

charge
conductor
electron
electroscope
insulator

1 Gold-leaf electroscope

● A gold leaf *electroscope* is used to detect electric *charge*. When the metal cap becomes charged this is transferred to the metal plate and gold leaf. Since the metal plate and the gold leaf carry the same charge they repel each other and the gold leaf rises.

2 Charge-sharing

● A poly(ethene) strip becomes negatively charged because *electrons* are transferred to it when it is rubbed. If a charged strip is placed in contact with an uncharged strip no charge is transferred because poly(ethene) is an electrical *insulator* and electrons are unable to flow through it.

● If a negatively charged strip is placed on the metal cap of an electroscope charge is transferred because metals are electrical *conductors* and electrons are able to flow through them. The gold leaf is repelled by the metal plate indicating they carry the same negative charge.

3 Testing the sign of a charge

● If a negatively charged poly(ethene) strip is placed on the metal cap of a negatively charged electroscope electrons flow from the strip into the metal part of the electroscope. The gold leaf moves even further away from the metal plate indicating that the amount of negative charge on the electroscope has increased.

● If a positively charged acetate strip is placed on the metal cap of a negatively charged electroscope electrons flow from the metal part of the electroscope to the strip. The gold leaf falls nearer to the metal plate indicating that the amount of negative charge on the electroscope has decreased.

The electroscope

1 Gold-leaf electroscope

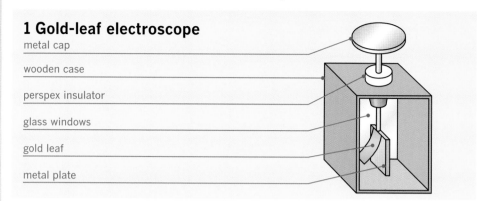

metal cap

wooden case

perspex insulator

glass windows

gold leaf

metal plate

2 Charge-sharing

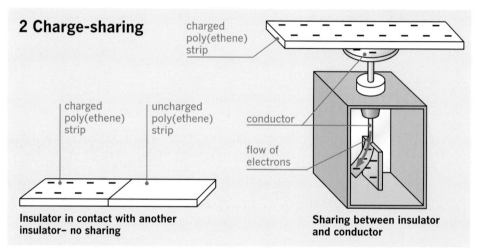

charged poly(ethene) strip

charged poly(ethene) strip

uncharged poly(ethene) strip

conductor

flow of electrons

Insulator in contact with another insulator– no sharing

Sharing between insulator and conductor

3 Testing the sign of a charge

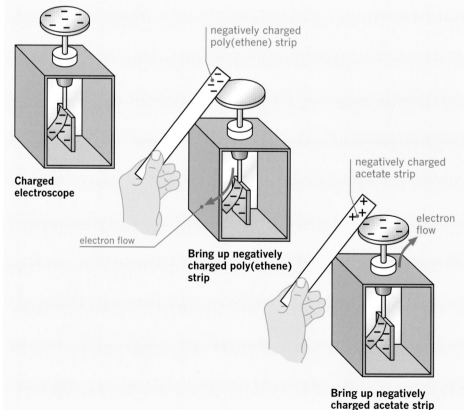

Charged electroscope

negatively charged poly(ethene) strip

electron flow

Bring up negatively charged poly(ethene) strip

negatively charged acetate strip

electron flow

Bring up negatively charged acetate strip

Charging by induction

Key words

conductor
electron
electroscope
induction
insulator

1 Charging by induction

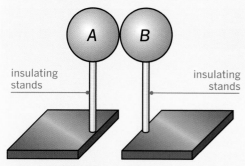

Two uncharged metal spheres (*A* and *B* in contact)

insulating stands   insulating stands

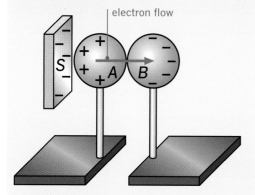

electron flow

Bring up negatively charged strip (*S*)

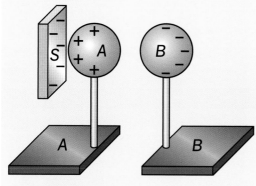

Move spheres apart

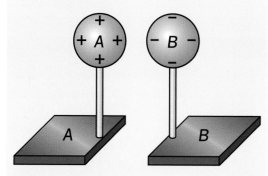

**Remove *S*
A is now positively charged
B is now negatively charged**

2 Charging an electroscope by induction

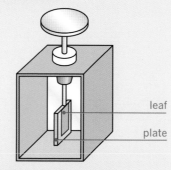

leaf

plate

Uncharged electroscope

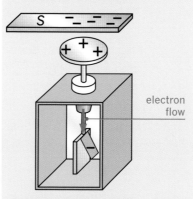

electron flow

Bring up charged strip S

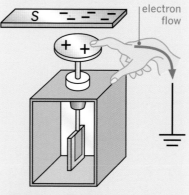

electron flow

Earth top with finger

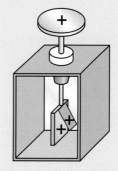

**Remove finger then remove *S*
Electroscope is left positively charged**

1 Charging by induction

- *Electrons* flow through electrical *conductors*.
- When a negatively charged strip is placed close to but not touching an *insulated* metal ball, electrons are repelled from the side next to the strip and accumulate on the other side. One side of the ball becomes positively charged and the other becomes negatively charged.
- When the metal ball is in contact with a second metal ball electrons flow; negative charge accumulates on the second ball, leaving the first ball short of electrons—positively charged. The balls retain their opposite charge when they are separated and the charged strip removed.
- No charge was transferred from the strip to the balls. The strip simply *induced* electrons to move from one ball to the other.

2 Charging an electroscope by induction

- When an *electroscope* is uncharged there is no repulsion between the gold leaf and the metal plate.
- When a negatively charged strip is placed close to but not touching the metal cap, it repels electrons from the cap leaving it positively charged. Electrons flow to the metal plate and gold leaf which become negatively charged and repel each other.
- With the charged strip in place, the metal cap retains induced positive charge. Electrons flow to earth if the cap is touched; both metal plate and gold leaf lose negative charge and no longer repel. Electroscope is overall positively charged.
- When the charged strip is removed, positive charge flows through the electroscope; the metal plate and gold leaf again repel as they are now positively charged.

Key words

charge
corona
electron
electrostatic
  precipitator
van de Graaff

1 van de Graaff generator

- A negative *charge* is produced on the poly(ethene) roller by friction between the roller and the rubber belt, inducing a positive charge on an earthed metal comb which is sprayed off the points onto the outside of the belt and carried upwards towards another metal comb. When the positively charged belt reaches the comb the negative charge induced on it is sprayed off the points leaving the dome positively charged.

2 Electric wind

- Charge accumulates at the most highly curved parts of an object.
- Charge accumulates at each of the four points of the mill and is discharged to the surrounding air by point or *corona* discharge. The "wind" streams away from each point causing the mill to spin around.

3 Lightning conductor

- Lightning results from a build up of negative charge in the atmosphere which induces a positive charge on structures below. *Electrons* flow to earth, or discharge, from the atmosphere in a flash of light.
- A tall structure may be damaged by lightning discharging through it. A lightning conductor, a thick strip of good conducting material such as brass or copper, provides lightning with a low-resistance path to earth.

4 Electrostatic precipitator

- An *electrostatic precipitator* prevents ash particles in wastes gases from coal-fired power stations from being released into the atmosphere.
- The particles become positively charged on passing through a positively charged wire grid. They are attracted to earthed metal plates where they are deposited. Periodic mechanical shaking removes the ash.

Applications of electrostatics 1

1 van de Graaff generator

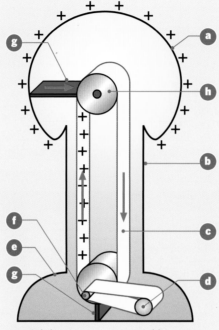

a metal dome
b insulating column
c rotating rubber belt
d electronic motor
e metal base
f poly(ethene) roller
g metal combs

2 Electric wind

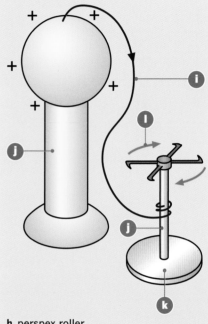

h perspex roller
i wire
j insulating supports
k Hamilton's mill
l direction of rotation

3 Lightning conductor

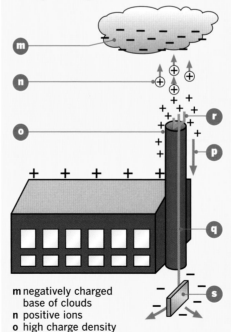

m negatively charged base of clouds
n positive ions
o high charge density
p electric flow
q thick copper conductor
r pointed end of conductor
s large metal plate buried in the ground

4 Electrostatic precipitator

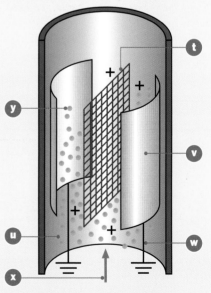

t positively charged fine wire grid
u chimney
v metal plates
w earth connection to metal plates
x smoke and dust particles rising
y positively charged particles deposited on plates

Applications of electrostatics 2

Key words

charge
earth
potential
  difference

1 Electrostatic powder coating

a compressed air
b powder hopper
c fluidized powder
d particle charging region
e earthed object

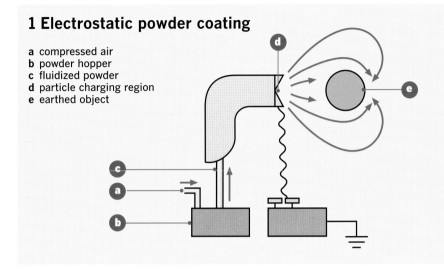

2 Ink jet printer

f ink reservoir
g pump
h ultrasonic oscillator
i gun
j charging cylinder
k output from
  computer
l deflection plates
m paper
n gutter

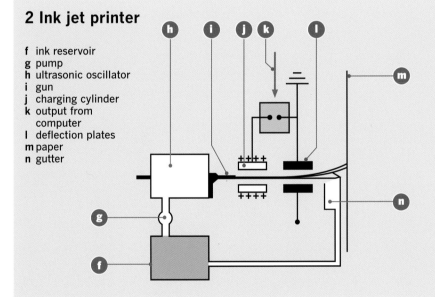

3 Electrostatic finger printing

o high voltage charger
p metal plate
q fine powder gains a
  positive charge
r specimen
s powder becomes
  negatively charged

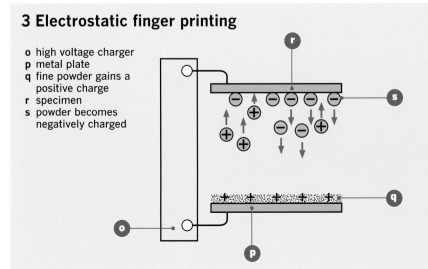

1 Electrostatic powder coating

● The powder coating is fluidized in a stream of compressed air. As the stream passes out of the gun the particles become positively *charged*. The object to be coated is *earthed* and therefore negatively charged relative to the powder particles. The powder particles are attracted to the object and will adhere to it.

2 Ink jet printer

● The jet of ink becomes positively charged as it passes through the charging cylinder. The *potential difference* across the deflecting plates is varied in such a way as to direct the jet of ink onto the paper in a pattern corresponding to what is to be printed.
● Since the jet of ink is positively charged any droplets of ink that form will also be positively charged and will be repelled. These droplets collect in the gutter and are recycled to the ink reservoir.

3 Electrostatic finger printing

● The positive terminal of the charger is attached to the metal plate while the negative terminal is attached to the specimen.
● A dark background of fine particles is sprinkled on the metal plate where they become positively charged.
● The larger particles on the specimen become negatively charged and are attracted to the positively charged metal plate. Since the plate is covered in a dark background of fine particles the pattern of the larger particles from the specimen are easily seen.

Key words

charge
corona
electron
photoconductive
  cell

1 The complete process for a rotating drum copier

- *Xerography*—from the Greek words for "dry" and "writing" is another word for the photocopying process, referring to the fact that the process does not use liquid ink.
- When a document is placed on the platen of a photocopier, the cover is closed to exclude light and the button is pressed to start the copying procedure.
- The charging corotron, containing a fine *corona* wire, is charged to several thousand volts. The photoconductive surface of the receptor plate (in the form of a rotating drum) passes the charging corotron and the surface of the receptor plate gains a positive *charge* of several hundred volts.
- At the same time, traces of bright light are seen escaping around the edges of the cover. This light captures an image of the document; the image is reflected by angled mirrors and focused onto the surface of the receptor plate.
- The light areas of the image cause the receptor plate to lose *electrons*, while positive charge remains in the dark areas. An image of the document is thus formed as a pattern of electric charge on the receptor plate.
- The receptor plate rotates past the developing unit. Toner particles are mixed with beads which transfer them to a roller. The roller brings toner into contact with the receptor plate, where it adheres to the charged areas of the drum (representing the dark parts of the document).
- A sheet of paper passing into the machine is charged by a corotron. This charge causes transfer of the toner from the receptor plate.
- The surface of the paper is heated to fuse the toner to the paper, and it passes out of the machine.

Applications of electrostatics 3

The complete process for a rotating drum copier

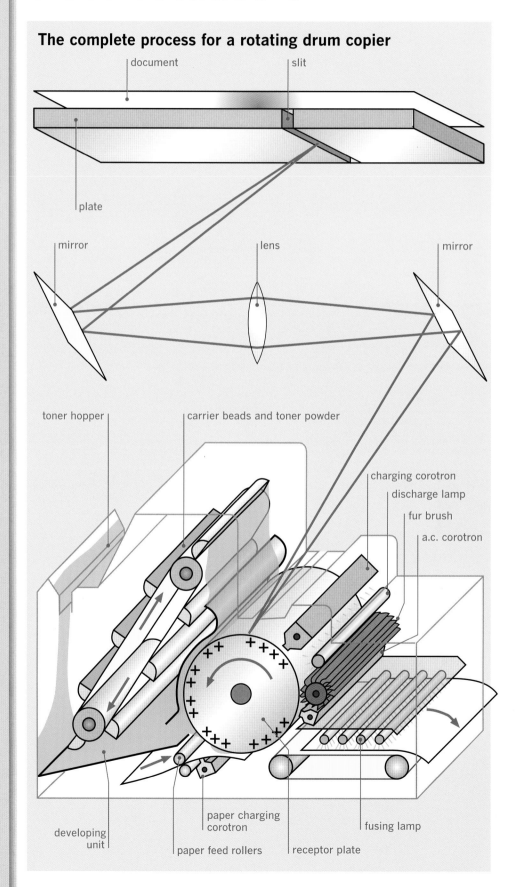

document   slit

plate

mirror   lens   mirror

toner hopper   carrier beads and toner powder

charging corotron

discharge lamp

fur brush

a.c. corotron

developing unit

paper charging corotron

paper feed rollers   receptor plate

fusing lamp

Applications of electrostatics 4

1 Receptor plate

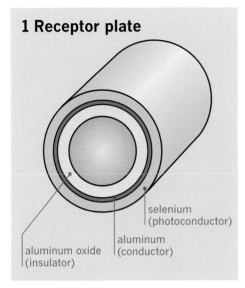

selenium (photoconductor)

aluminum (conductor)

aluminum oxide (insulator)

2 Charging receptor plate

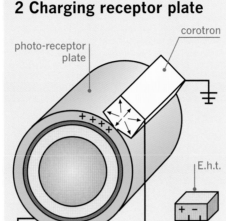

photo-receptor plate

corotron

E.h.t.

3 Exposure

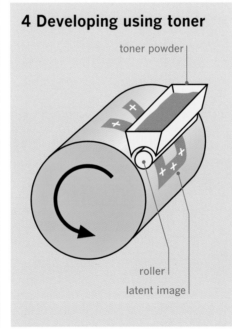

lens

back of mirror

photo-receptor plate

latent image on receptor plate

4 Developing using toner

toner powder

roller

latent image

5 Transfer onto paper

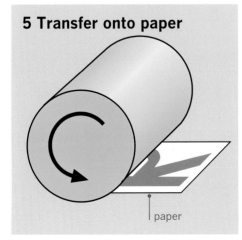

paper

6 Forming permanent copy

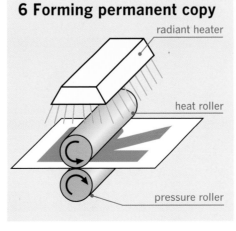

radiant heater

heat roller

pressure roller

© Diagram Visual Information Ltd.

Key words

charge
neutral
photoconductive
  cell
reflection

1 Receptor plate
- The receptor plate is coated with a photoconductor such as selenium (or the less toxic poly(vinyl) carbazole) . Electrons are released when light shines on a photoconductor.

2 Charging receptor plate
- The receptor plate becomes positively charged by rotating it in contact with a corotron.

3 Exposure
- The document to be copied is illuminated. Light *reflected* by the document is focused and reflected by a mirror onto the receptor plate.
- Light reflected from white areas of the document falls on the receptor plate. Areas of the coating receiving light release electrons, *neutralizing* the positive *charge* carried. Dark areas of the document (text or illustration) do not reflect light. No light from these areas is received by the receptor plate so those parts of the receptor plate remain positively charged.
- An image of the document composed of positive charge is formed.

4 Developing using toner
- Toner consists of very fine particles of carbon black which are given negative charge. When they come into contact with the receptor plate they adhere to the positively charged areas as the receptor plate rotates.
- This results in a black image of the original sheet of paper composed of toner particles on the receptor plate.

5 Transfer onto paper
- The image formed on the receptor plate is transferred to a sheet of paper.

6 Forming permanent copy
- The paper passes between rollers which heat and compress it, fixing the toner powder in place.

Key words

alpha particle	electrostatics
charge	ionizing radiation
earth	isotope
electricity	radioactivity
electron	

1 Friction and static charge

- Static *electricity* is generated whenever two materials touch and then separate. *Electrons* are transferred between the materials leaving one positively *charged* the other negatively charged.
- A build-up of static electricity occurs when the rate of charge generation is greater than the rate of charge dissipation. The rapid build up of a very high potential leads to electrostatic discharge (ESD) sparks and shocks.

2 Earthing static charge

- Static electricity may result from the movement of fluidized solids, liquids or gases through or over a material. Precautions must be taken to prevent ESD where the generation of sparks could result in fires and/or explosions.
- In manufacturing processes involving transferring fluidized solids, such as flour, chocolate powder etc. pipes must be *earthed*.
- The hoses used to transfer gas and diesel into vehicles in petrol stations are made of a special form of conducting rubber.
- The charge which builds up on the surface of aircraft during flight is discharged to earth on landing.

3 Neutralizing static charge

- During the manufacture of poly(ethene) and other plastic film, charge builds up on the film. If it is not neutralized the film cannot be wound onto a roller safely as each layer repels the previous layer, since they carry the same charge.
- The charge is neutralized using a charge bar. This contains a strip of the *radioactive isotope* polonium-210 which emits radiation in the form of *alpha particles*, *ionizing* the air around them. These ions neutralize the charge of the poly(ethene).

Problems created by electrostatic charge

1 Friction and static charge

Hair brushes gain static from friction of combing.

Balloons rubbed on garments contain static electricity and can stick to walls.

2 Earthing static charge

Hoses used to transfer gasoline are made from conducting rubber.

3 Neutralizing static charge

Newly made plastic film creates positive static charges on the outside and negative charges on the inside.

Installing a neutralizing bar removes positive outside charges.

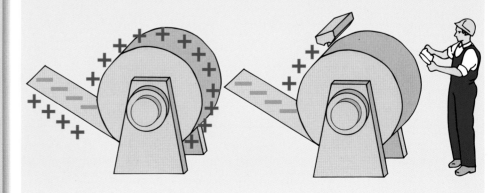

Capacitance

1 Capacitance varies with dielectric used

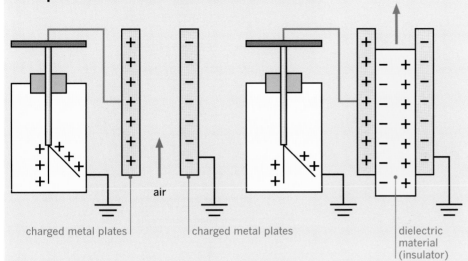

charged metal plates

air

charged metal plates

dielectric material (insulator)

2 Capacitance varies with area of plates

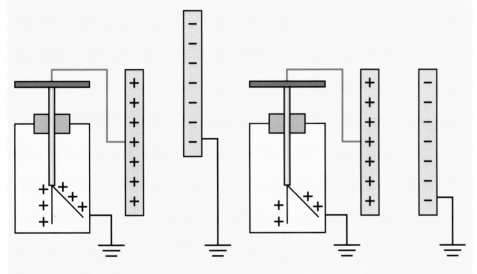

3 Capacitance varies with separation of the plates

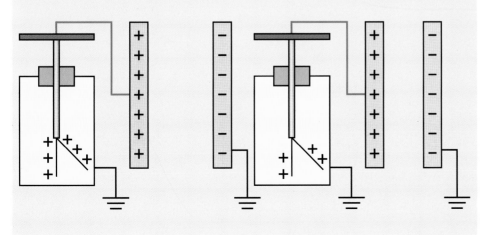

1 Capacitance varies with dielectric used

- A metal plate is shown to be charged by connecting it to an *electroscope*. The gold leaf rises indicating that it and the metal plate carry similar *charge* and thus repel each other.
- There is an *electric field* between positively and negatively charged plates which are placed next to, but not touching, each other.
- Positively charged *nuclei* of *dielectric* material molecules are attracted towards the negatively charged plate, electrons move the other way.
- Dielectric molecules become distorted with excess positive charge at one end and excess negative charge at the other, forming electric *dipoles*.
- Within the dielectric, positive and negative ends of adjacent dipoles balance out, but the surfaces are charged with opposite sign to the plate they touch. *Potential difference* between the plates is reduced.
- The force between oppositely charged plates is always reduced when an insulating material replaces a vacuum. The material is said to have *permittivity*. A material with a high permittivity significantly reduces the force between the plates compared to a vacuum (or air).
- *Capacitance* increases if the plates are separated by a dielectric with a high permittivity.

2 Capacitance varies with area of plates

- Capacitance increases as the area of overlap between the positively and negatively charged plates increases.

3 Capacitance varies with separation of the plates

- Capacitance increases as the separation distance between the positively and negatively charged plates decreases.

Practical capacitors

1 Non-electrolytic capacitors

- *Capacitors* have many uses in electrical circuits.
- Choice of capacitor depends on its value, stability and the frequency of any *alternating current* that will flow.
- *Dielectric* material breaks down at a particular potential gradient. The nature and thickness of the dielectric determines the working potential difference of a capacitor.
- Waxed paper capacitors are only used where frequencies are less than 1 MHz. Their stability is also poor. Mica, plastic and ceramic capacitors are more stable and can be used at much higher frequencies.

2 Electrolytic capacitors

- *Electrolytic capacitors* have much higher *capacitance*.
- Their dielectric is a thin (as little as 10^{-4} mm) film of aluminum oxide, formed by passing a current through a strip of paper soaked in aluminum borate sandwiched between two strips of aluminum foil. A layer of oxide forms on one aluminum strip (the *anode*). The remaining borate solution is connected to the second aluminum strip which becomes the *cathode*.
- A *current* of around 1 mA must pass through the capacitor in the correct direction to maintain the dielectric. The anode is marked with a + and must be connected at a higher potential difference than the cathode.

3 Variable capacitors

- A variable capacitor, used to tune radio receivers, consists of two sets of interleaving plates. The capacitance is determined by the degree of overlap.
- Air is the dielectric in such capacitors and losses are low at all frequencies. Breakdown occurs at relatively low potential differences so the dielectric should be relatively thick.

1 Non-electrolytic capacitors

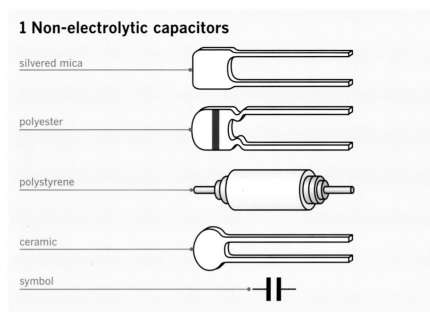

silvered mica

polyester

polystyrene

ceramic

symbol

2 Electrolytic capacitors

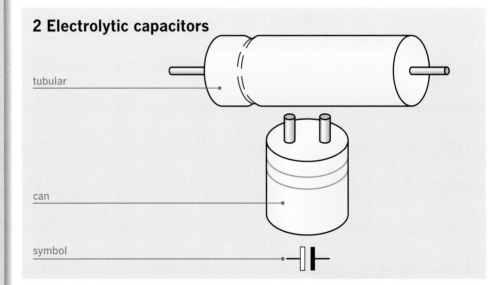

tubular

can

symbol

3 Variable capacitors

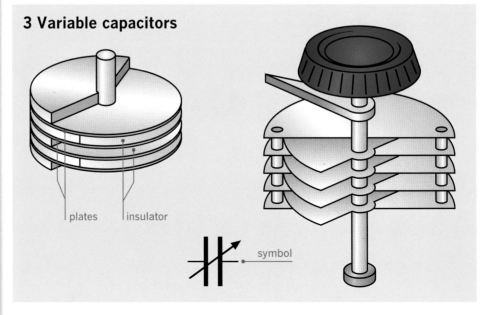

plates   insulator

symbol

Color coding and size

Key words

capacitance
capacitor
electrolytic
  capacitor

1 Non-electrolytic capacitors

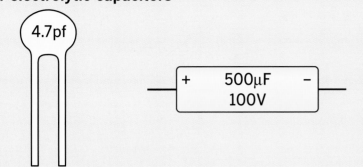

2 Identifying size capacitor

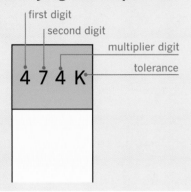

letter	tolerance
F	± 1%
G	± 2%
J	± 5%
K	± 10%
M	± 20%

3 Color coding

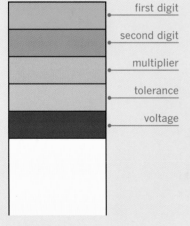

0	black
1	brown
2	red
3	orange
4	yellow
5	green
6	blue
7	violet
8	gray
9	white

color	tolerance
black	± 5%
brown	± 10%
red	± 20%

color	voltage
brown	100
red	250
yellow	400

4 Capacitors in a circuit

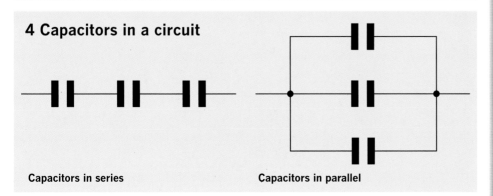

Capacitors in series   **Capacitors in parallel**

1 Non-electrolytic capacitors

- The unit of *capacitance*, the farad, **F**, is a large unit so microfarads, μF (10^{-6} F) or nanofarads, nF (10^{-9}F), or picofarads, pF (10^{-12}F) are used.
- The capacitance of non-electrolytic *capacitors* is generally limited to a few microfarads, and in the case of mica capacitors, the limit is around 0.01 μF. *Electrolytic capacitors* can have values up to 100,000 μF.

2 Identifying capacitor size

- Large capacitors generally have their value printed on them. For smaller capacitors different conventions exist.
- There are a variety of different marking conventions used to indicate the size of a capacitor.
- Small disk type capacitors may carry three numbers followed by a letter. The first two numbers indicate the first and second digits of the capacitance and the third number is the multiplier (as a power of 10). From these values the capacitance is given in **pF**. The letter indicates the tolerance.

3 Color coding

- Ceramic capacitors may be coded by a series of colored bands. The first two numbers indicate the first and second digits of the capacitance and the third number is the multiplier. The fourth and fifth bands correspond to tolerance and operating voltage.

4 Capacitors in a circuit

- When capacitors are connected in series in a circuit their combined capacitance, **C**, is given by:
$$\frac{1}{C} = \frac{1}{C_1} + \frac{1}{C_2} + \frac{1}{C_3}$$
- When capacitors are connected in parallel in a circuit their combined capacitance, **C**, is given by:
$$C = C_1 + C_2 + C_3$$

© Diagram Visual Information Ltd.

Key words

charge
conduction
electric field
electron

1 Attractive and repulsive forces

- A body may be positively charged (having a shortage of *electrons*) or negatively charged (having an excess of electrons).
- Bodies having the same *charge* repel each other, those with opposite charge attract each other.

2 Electric field patterns

- Charge on an isolated *conducting* sphere is uniformly spread over its surface due to the repulsion of like charges, resulting in a radial field pattern. The field outside the sphere is the same as it would be if the charge acted in the center of the sphere.
- *Electric fields* are represented by electric field lines. The direction of these lines is the direction in which a positive charge would accelerate. Since a positive charge would be repelled by another positive charge, it would accelerate away from it, thus electric field lines point away from a positive charge. Conversely, a positive charge would be attracted towards a negative charge thus electric field lines point towards a negative charge. The number of lines per unit cross-section area is proportional to the field strength.

3 Electric force field

- When two positive point charges are brought close together electric field lines are directed away from both showing that a repulsive force exists between them. There is a similar pattern of field lines for two negative point charges except that the field lines are directed towards the charges.
- When a positive and a negative point charge are brought close together, electric field lines are directed away from the positive charge towards the negative charge, showing that a force of attraction exists between them.

Electric fields

1 Attractive and repulsive forces

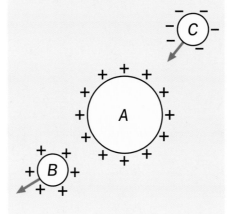

3 Electric force field

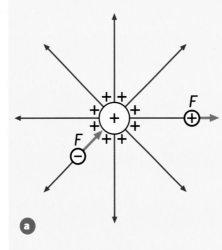

2 Electric field patterns

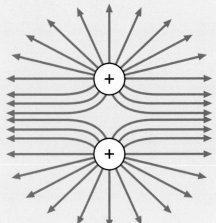

Two positive point charges

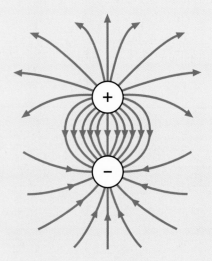

Two opposite point charges

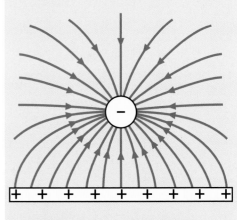

Point charge next to a charged sheet

Electric fields and Gauss's theorem

1 Electric field line

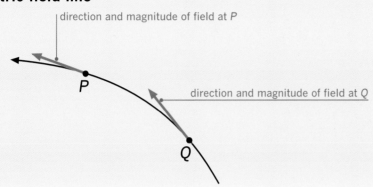

direction and magnitude of field at *P*

P

direction and magnitude of field at *Q*

Q

2 Electric field due to a dipole

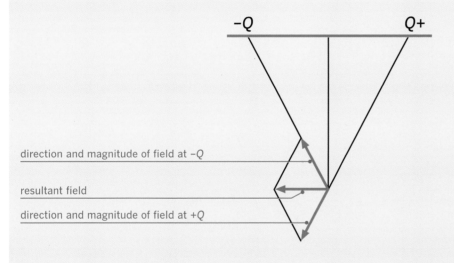

−*Q*   *Q*+

direction and magnitude of field at −*Q*

resultant field

direction and magnitude of field at +*Q*

3 Simple Gaussian surface

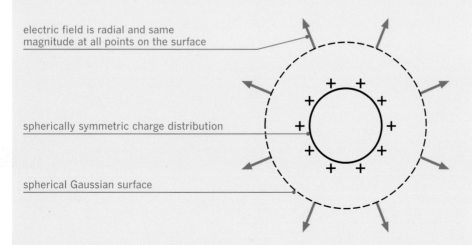

electric field is radial and same magnitude at all points on the surface

spherically symmetric charge distribution

spherical Gaussian surface

1 Electric field line
- The direction of the field at any point on an *electric field* line is the *tangent* to the field line at that point.

2 Electric field of a dipole
- The direction of an electric field line is given by the direction in which a positive *charge* would accelerate along it. Since like charges repel and unlike charges attract, field lines are directed away from a positive charge and towards a negative charge.
- The resultant field is parallel to the axis of the *dipole*.

3 Simple Gaussian surface
- A Gaussian surface can be any shape that completely encloses a volume of space and is often referred to as a closed surface.
- When a sphere is charged the electric field is spread symmetrically over its surface.
- A small positive point charge Q placed at any point in an electric field experiences a force, F. Field strength, E, at that point is: $E = \dfrac{F}{Q}$
- Calculate field strength, E (in a vacuum) of point charge $+Q$ at position P (distance between P and Q = r by considering small charge $+Q_0$ at P. Using Coulomb's law, force F on Q_0 is: $F = \dfrac{QQ_0}{4\pi r^2 \epsilon_0}$
  E is force per unit charge ($E = \dfrac{F}{Q_0}$
  so $F = \dfrac{E}{Q_0}$
  Therefore $E = \dfrac{Q}{4\pi r^2 \epsilon_0}$
  (ϵ_0 is the *permittivity* of a vacuum).
- Charge density, σ, is charge per unit area. Since a sphere's surface area is s $4\pi r^2$: $\sigma = Q / (4\pi r^2)$. $E = \sigma/\epsilon_0$

© Diagram Visual Information Ltd.

Key words

charge	neutral
conduction	polarization
earth	van de Graaff
electron	
induction	

1 Showing an electric current is a flow of electric charge

- When the *van de Graaff* is running, positive *charge* accumulates on the dome. If a metal plate is connected to the dome by a *conducting* wire, positive charge will also accumulate on the metal plate.
- The metallized ball becomes *polarized* due to *induction*. The side facing the positively charged plate will become negatively charged and therefore attracted to the plate.
- Once the ball touches the positive plate it acquires a positive charge and is then repelled by the positive plate and attracted by the second metal plate which is *earthed* to the base of the van de Graaff generator.
- When the ball touches the second plate it acquires *electrons* and becomes *neutral*. The process of being attracted to the positively charged plate is then repeated.
- Electrons move around the circuit carrying charge. The current produced causes a deflection on the ammeter.

2 Metallized ball transfers charge

- The direction in which a current moves around a circuit is a cause of some confusion. Prior to the properties of electrons being known, in the nineteenth century, scientists decided to adopt a convention whereby a current flowed from positive to negative.
- Subsequent to this, it was discovered that electrons carried a negative charge and therefore actually flowed from negative to positive in a circuit.
- As a result we talk about conventional current as flowing from positive to negative, and actual current flowing from negative to positive.

Electric current 1

1 Showing electric current is a flow of electric charge

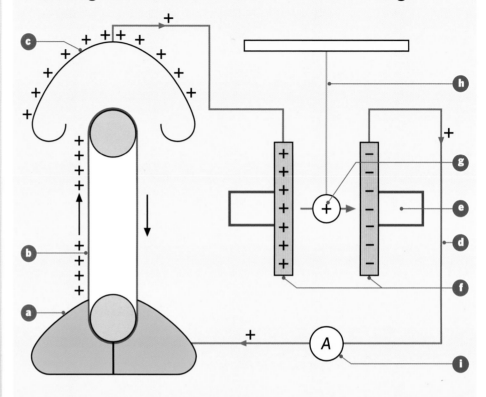

a van de Graaff generator
b rubber belt
c metal dome
d copper wire
e insulating handles
f metal plates
g metalized ping-pong ball
h nylon thread
i sensitve ammeter

2 Metallized ball transfers charge

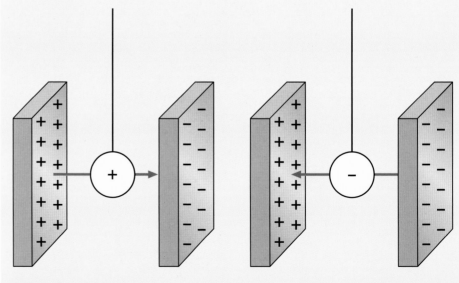

A flow of positive charge =
a conventional current

A flow of negative charge =
a flow of electrons

Electric current 2

V-I characteristics

1 Ohmic conductor

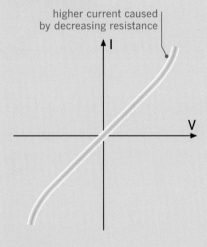

2 Filament lamp

lower current caused by decreasing resistance

3 Thermistor

higher current caused by decreasing resistance

4 Thermionic valve

saturation current

zero reverse current

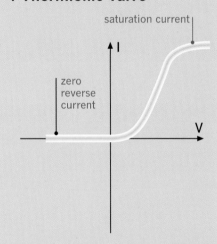

5 Gas

small saturation current

spark discharge

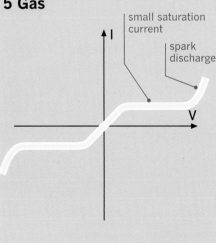

6 Semiconductor diode

mA

very small reverse current

avalanche breakdown

μA

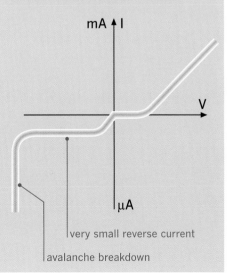

Key words

diode
direct proportion
Ohm's law
resistance

semiconductor
thermionic valve
thermistor

1 Ohmic conductor

- When the current flowing through a conductor, such as a metal wire, is *directly proportional* to the potential difference allied across it the current is said to be ohmic and obeys *Ohm's law*. Its *resistance* does not alter with the potential difference applied across it provided its temperature remains constant.

2 Filament lamp

- A filament lamp is ohmic over a narrow range of current. However, as the current increases, the temperature of the tungsten wire increases until it becomes white hot, increasing the resistance of the wire causing the curve to become less steep.

3 Thermistor

- A *thermistor* is made of *semiconductor* material. As its temperature increases its resistance decreases causing the graph to bend upwards.

4 Thermionic valve

- A *thermionic valve* passes current in one direction only. Current increases with potential difference up to the saturation current where the resistance of the valve begins to increase.

5 Gas

- The saturation current of a gas is relatively small. A spark discharge results in a rapid decrease in resistance.

6 Semiconductor diode

- Current passes when the potential difference is applied in one direction but is almost zero when the polarity is reversed. A *diode* has a small resistance when the current flows in one direction and a large resistance when it flows in the other. If a large potential is applied in the reverse direction, the diode breaks down.

© Diagram Visual Information Ltd.

Key words

battery
charge
current
electron

1 Electric current direction

- By convention, all *current* is assumed to be due to the movement of positive *charges* therefore when current direction is marked on a circuit it is from positive to negative.
- In metals an electric current is the movement of negative charge in the form of *electrons*. Electrons move from negative to positive i.e. in the opposite direction to the conventional current. To differentiate from the conventional current, this is called the real current.

2 Flow of electric charge

- In a circuit charge is provided by a *battery* or other source. It flows along a conductor when there is a potential difference, V, between points.
- The unit of charge is the coulomb (**C**). One coulomb is the quantity of electrical charge carried past a given point in a circuit when a current of 1 ampere flows for 1 second.

3 Current in a conductor

- A conductor of length, **L**, and cross-section area, **A**, has **n** "free" electrons per unit volume. Each electron carries a charge **e**.
  Volume of conductor = **AL**
  Number of free electrons = **nAL**
  Total charge, **Q**, of free electrons = **nALe**
- The charge, **Q**, travels length, **L**, in time, **t**, with an average drift velocity of **v**. The resulting steady current, **I**, is given by:

$$I = \frac{Q}{t} = \frac{nALe}{t}$$

but $v = \dfrac{L}{t}$ and therefore $t = \dfrac{L}{v}$

so the drift velocity is given by:

$$v = \frac{I}{nAe}$$

For a current of 1 ampere passing through an SWG gauge copper wire the drift velocity is 0.6 mm s^{-1}.

Electric current 3

1 Electric current direction

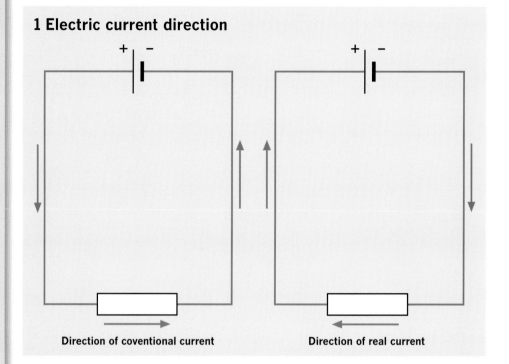

Direction of coventional current   Direction of real current

2 Flow of electric charge

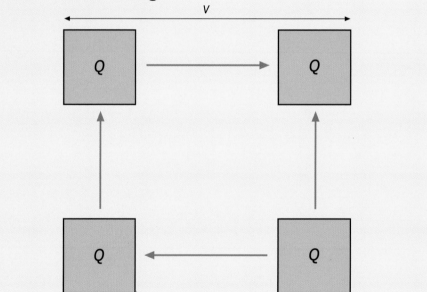

3 Current in a conductor

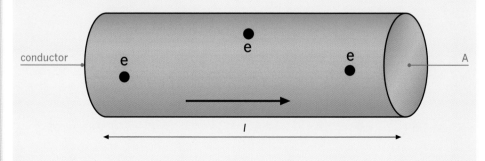

Electric current 4

Key words

charge
conservation of
  energy, law of
current

electromotive
  force (e.m.f).
potential
  difference

1 Kirchhoff's first law

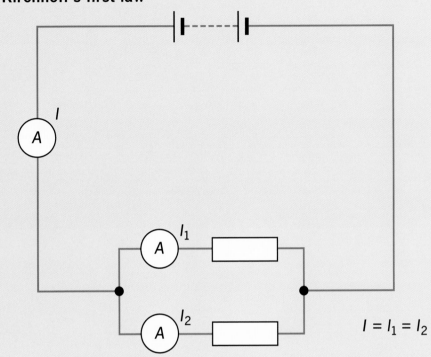

$$I = I_1 = I_2$$

2 Kirchhoff's second law

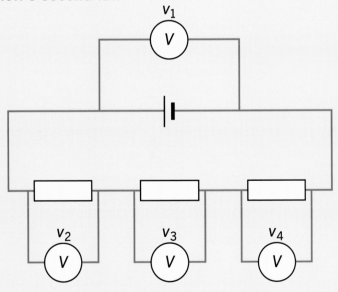

3 Conversion of electrical energy into power

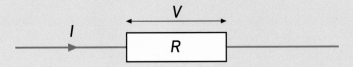

1 Kirchhoff's first law

- In a circuit, the *current* arriving equals the current leaving.
- Since current is the transfer of *charge*, charge is conserved and flows in a circuit without being destroyed or accumulating at any particular point.
- This can be verified by measuring the current at different points in a circuit.

2 Kirchhoff's second law

- Around any closed circuit or loop, the algebraic sum of the *e.m.f.* equals the algebraic sum of the products of the current, I, and resistance, R. This can be expressed as $\Sigma E = \Sigma IR$.
- This can be verified by measuring the *potential difference* (P.D.) at different points in a circuit.
- This law is another way of stating the law of *conservation of energy* using electrical quantities.

3 Conversion of electrical energy into power

- When a current flows electrical energy is converted into other forms of energy. The power of a device is the rate at which this conversion occurs.
- If the P.D. across a device is V, the current through it is I. The electrical energy, W, converted in time t is given by $W = ItV$.
- Power, P, is the rate at which energy is converted: $P = \dfrac{ItV}{t} = IV$
- Device converting electrical energy into heat energy is called a passive resistor. The rate of production of heat is also IV. Since $R = \dfrac{V}{I}$

  this can expressed as:
  $$P = IV = \frac{V^2}{R} = I^2R$$
- Heat energy losses increase as the square of the current so if the current is doubled the heat losses will be quadrupled.

© Diagram Visual Information Ltd.

Key words

electromotive force (e.m.f.)	Ohm's law
galvanometer	resistance
potential difference	Wheatstone bridge

Electric current 5

1 Wheatstone bridge circuit

- A *Wheatstone bridge* circuit allows *resistance* to be measured far more accurately than is possible using an ammeter and voltmeter. It is based on the principle that when the ratio of **P/Q** is equal to that of **R/S** then no current flows through the *galvanometer* and therefore the *potential difference* across the galvanometer must be zero.
- Using *Ohm's law*
  $(V = IR)$ $I_1P = I_2R$ and $I_1Q = I_2S$.
  $I_1P = I_2R$ thus $\dfrac{P}{Q} = \dfrac{R}{S}$
  $\dfrac{I_1P}{I_1Q} = \dfrac{I_2R}{I_2S}$

2 Comparing e.m.f.s

- When the reading on the galvanometer is zero the ratio of the *e.m.f.s* of the cells, E_1/E_2 must be equal to the ratio of the resistance in the circuit containing E_1 ($L_1 + L_2$) and the resistance of the circuit containing E_2 (L_1) i.e. ($L_1 + L_2$) / L_1. This values of L_1 and L_2 are found by moving the contact from the galvanometer, often called the jockey, along the wire.

3 Comparing resistances

- A potential divider can be used to compare two resistances. When the reading on the galvanometer is zero the ratio of the resistances either side of the jockey on the potential divider, L_1/L_2 is equal to the ratio of the two resistors **P/Q**.
  $$\frac{L_1}{L_2} = \frac{P}{Q}$$

4 Comparing p.d.s

- When the galvanometer reads zero there is no current flowing through it therefore the potential difference across it must equal zero. This will occur when the potential difference across L_1 is equal to the potential difference across the resistor **Q**.

1 Wheatstone bridge circuit

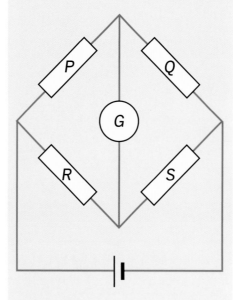

2 Comparing e.m.f.s

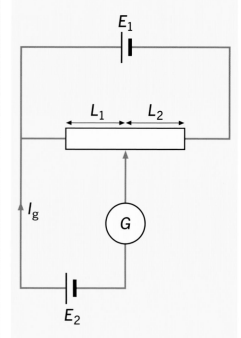

3 Comparing resistances

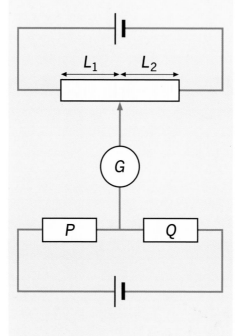

4 Comparing p.d.s

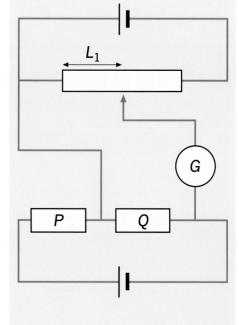

Ohm's law

1 Testing current, voltage, and resistance in a circuit

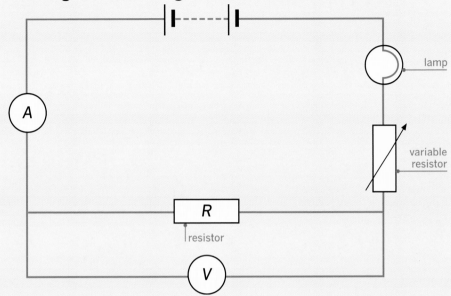

lamp

variable resistor

R

resistor

A

V

2 Relating current and voltage

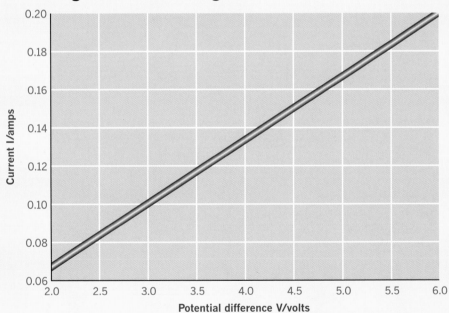

Current I/amps (y-axis): 0.06, 0.08, 0.10, 0.12, 0.14, 0.16, 0.18, 0.20

Potential difference V/volts (x-axis): 2.0, 2.5, 3.0, 3.5, 4.0, 4.5, 5.0, 5.5, 6.0

3 Ohm's law

$$V = I \times R \qquad \text{Voltage} = \text{Current} \times \text{Resistance}$$

$$R = \frac{V}{I} \qquad \text{Resistance} = \frac{\text{Voltage}}{\text{Current}}$$

$$I = \frac{V}{R} \qquad \text{Current} = \frac{\text{Voltage}}{\text{Resistance}}$$

Where voltage is given in volts (V), current in amps (A), ans resistance in ohms (Ω).

Key words

battery	potential
conductor	difference
Ohm's law	
parallel	

1 Testing current, voltage, and resistance in a circuit

- A resistor, **R**, is connected in series with a *battery*, lamp and variable resistor. An ammeter is connected in series with the resistor and a voltmeter is connected in *parallel*.
- When the value of the variable resistor is changed this alters the *potential difference* across resistor and therefore its current. The current and the potential difference are recorded for several different values.
- The lamp provides a visual indication of how the total resistance of the circuit is changing. When the value of the variable resistor is high the current falls and the lamp becomes dimmer.

2 Relating current and voltage

- The graph of current against voltage is a straight line indicating the current in the resistor is proportional to the potential difference across it. This assumes that the temperature of the resistor has remained constant.
- This relationship is known as *Ohm's law*. *Conductors* which obey this law are called ohmic conductors.
- The gradient of the graph, I/V = 0.0333.

3 Ohm's law

- Potential difference or voltage, current and resistance are connected by a simple mathematical equation.
- The gradient of the graph is equal to I/V. The resistance of a resistor is given by **V**/I therefore the resistance of **R** is given by the reciprocal of the gradient of the graph. R = 1 / 0.0333 = 30 Ω.

Key words

*alternating
  current (AC)*
current
magnetic field
solenoid

1 Moving coil meter

- Most direct current meters are the moving coil type. This consists of a coil of copper wire, wound around a soft iron cylinder, which rotates inside a strong *magnetic field* provided by a permanent magnet.
- The magnetic field produced in the narrow air gap between the coil and the permanent magnet is radial. The field lines in the gap appear to radiate from the central axis of the cylinder and are always parallel to the plane of the coil as it rotates.
- The coil is pivoted on jewelled bearings and its rotation is resisted by hair springs above and below it. The springs are also the means by which current enters and leaves the coil.
- When a *current* passes through the coil it generates a magnetic field. This interacts with the magnetic field of the permanent magnet causing the coil to rotate.

2 Moving iron meter

- The deflection of an *alternating current* meter cannot depend upon the direction of the current since this is continually changing.
- In a moving iron meter two soft iron rods are mounted inside a *solenoid* parallel to its axis. One rod is fixed while the other is attached to a pointer.
- When current passes either way through the solenoid the soft iron rods are magnetized in the same direction and repel each other. The rod which is not fixed moves away until it is stopped by the restoring couple of the hair springs.
- This type of coil can be used for measuring direct current or alternating current. The scale is non-linear, being closer for smaller currents.

Electric meters 1

1 Moving coil meter

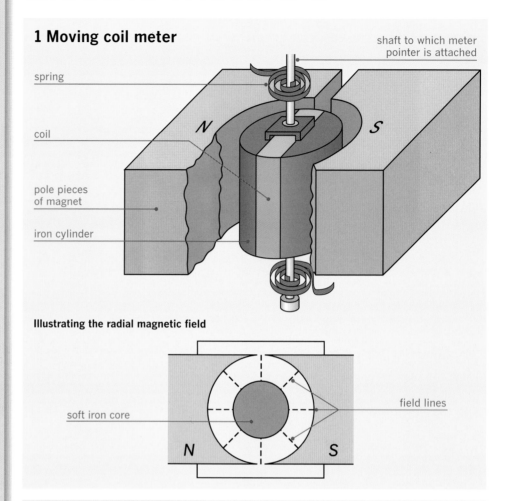

shaft to which meter pointer is attached

spring

coil

N   S

pole pieces of magnet

iron cylinder

Illustrating the radial magnetic field

soft iron core

field lines

N   S

2 Moving iron meter

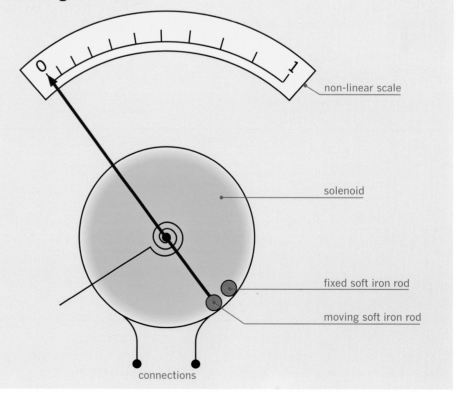

non-linear scale

solenoid

fixed soft iron rod

moving soft iron rod

connections

Electric meters 2

Key words

current   resistance
Ohm's law
parallel
potential
  difference

1 Moving coil meter as ammeter

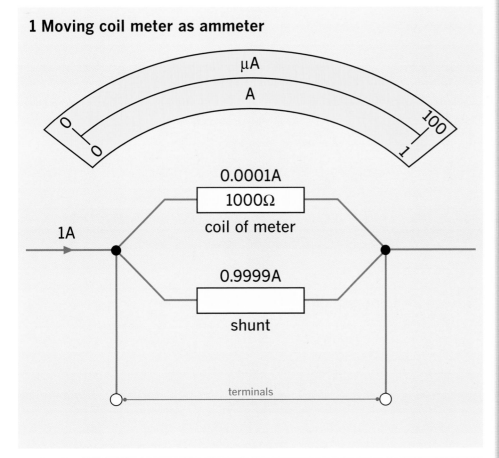

2 Moving coil meter as voltmeter

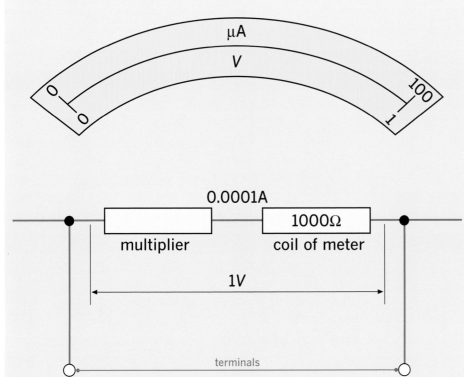

Moving coil meter

- A moving coil meter has a *resistance* of 1,000 Ω, due mainly to the coil, and gives a full scale deflection when a *current* of 100 μA passes through it.

1 Moving coil meter as ammeter

- A resistor of very low value (called a shunt) is connected in *parallel* with the meter to convert it to an ammeter reading 0–1 A.
- The meter and the shunt are in parallel therefore the *potential difference* across the meter equals the potential difference across the shunt. Applying *Ohm's law* (V = IR):
  0.0001 A x 1000 Ω = 0.9999 x resistance of shunt =
  $$\frac{0.0001 \times 1000}{0.9999} = 0.1 \ \Omega$$

2 Moving coil meter as voltmeter

- A resistor of very high value (called a multiplier) is connected in series with the meter to convert it to a voltmeter reading 0–1 V.
- Applying Ohm's law (V = IR) the potential difference across the multiplier and meter in series =
  0.0001 x (1000 Ω + resistance of multiplier)
  The meter must give a full scale deflection when a potential difference of 1 V is applied across it therefore:
  0.000 1 x (1000 Ω + resistance of multiplier) = 1 Ω
  Resistance of multiplier = 9000 Ω
- Voltmeters are graded according to their resistance per volt at full scale deflection. Here, applying 1 V would give a full scale deflection corresponding to a current of 100 μA therefore the resistance per volt (R = V/I) is 10000 Ω. The higher the resistance per volt the more accurate the voltmeter as the smaller the current it draws.

1 Resistors in series

- When resistors are connected in series the *potential difference* across the network is divided between the resistors $V = V_1 + V_2 + V_3$. The same *current*, I, is in each resistor.
- From *Ohm's law* $V = IR$ therefore $R = V/I$. An expression can be written for each resistor:
  $R_1 = V_1/I$; $R_2 = V_2/I$; $R_3 = V_3 I$.
- It follows that $IR = IR_1 + IR_2 + IR_3$: dividing throughout the equation by I gives $R_T = R_1 + R_2 + R_3$ where R_T is the total effective resistance.
- When resistors are connected in series the total effective resistance of the network is equal to the sum of the individual resistors.

2 Resistors in parallel

- When resistors are connected in *parallel* the current in each resistor is dependent on the size of the resistance $I = I_1 + I_2 + I_3$. The same potential difference is across each resistor.
- From Ohm's law $V = IR$ therefore $I = V/R$. An expression can be written for each resistor:
  $I_1 = V/R_1$; $I_2 = V/R_2$; $I_3 = V/R_3$.
- It follows that $V/R = V/R_1 + V/R_2 + V/R_3$: dividing throughout the equation by V gives: $1/R_T = R_1 + R_2 + R_3$ where R_T is the total effective resistance.
- When resistors are connected in parallel the reciprocal of the total effective resistance of the network is equal to the sum of the reciprocals of the individual resistors.

3 Resistors in series and parallel

- When resistors are arranged in a mixture of series and parallel circuits within a network the effective resistance of each part of the network is found separately before the total effective resistance is calculated.

Resistors 1

1 Resistors in series

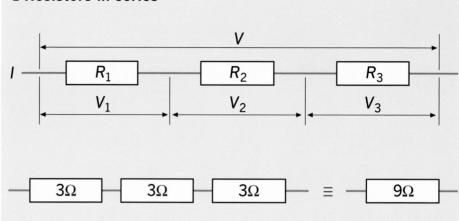

2 Resistors in parallel

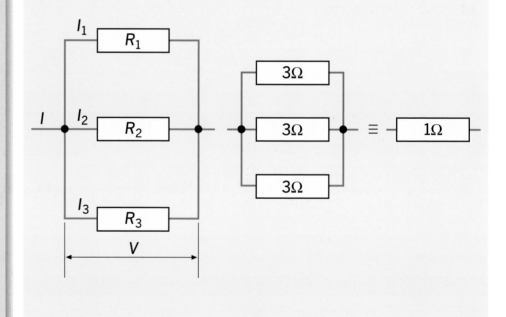

3 Resistors in series and parallel

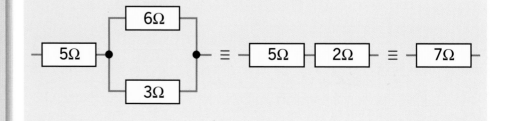

Resistors 2

Key words

conductor
resistance

1 Carbon resistor

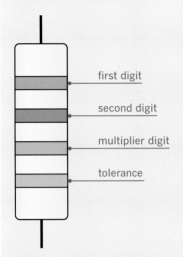

	first digit
	second digit
	multiplier digit
	tolerance

0	black
1	brown
2	red
3	orange
4	yellow
5	green
6	blue
7	violet
8	gray
9	white

color	tolerance
gold	± 5%
silver	± 10%
red	± 20%

- Resistors come in a variety of types which are used in different ways in circuits.
- Carbon resistors are composed of carbon black, clay and a resin binder. The mixture is molded into rods by heating. Carbon is the *conducting* material in the mixture. The value of the resistance is determined by the proportion of carbon present.
- The stability of carbon resistors is poor and their tolerance is usually ± 10% at best. However, they are cheap to produce and are good enough for many applications.
- The value of a carbon resistor may be given in numbers or as a sequence of colored bands.

2 Carbon film resistor

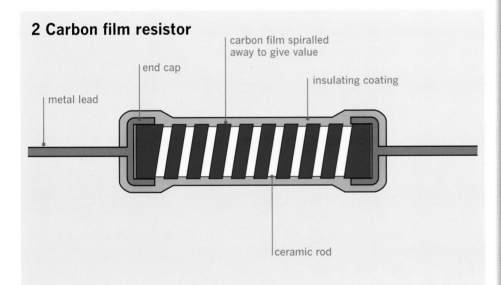

carbon film spiralled away to give value

end cap

insulating coating

metal lead

ceramic rod

- Carbon film resistors consist of a ceramic rod upon which is deposited a film of carbon. The value of the resistor depends on the thickness of this film, and can be increased by cutting a spiral groove in the coating. The carbon film is protected by a coating of epoxy resin.
- This type of resistor is more stable than a carbon resistor and its tolerance is commonly ±2%.

3 Wire-wound resistor

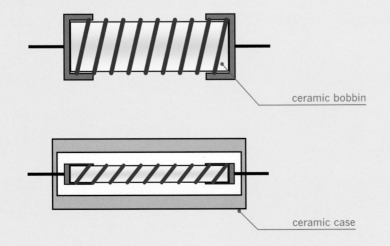

ceramic bobbin

ceramic case

- Wire-wound resistors are very stable and have a very low tolerance. They also have the advantage over carbon resistors that they can be manufactured to have a large power rating.
- This type of resistor is based on the fact that the *resistance* of a wire increases with its length. For high precision resistors manganin (an alloy of copper, manganese and nickel) is used while for general commercial resistors nickel-chromium wire provides resistors which are sufficiently accurate.

Key words

battery	electromotive
cell	force (e.m.f.)
charge	galvanometer
electrolyte	generator
	insulator

1 Galvanometer e.m.f.

- The *e.m.f.* of a *battery* or *generator* is the energy, in whatever form, converted into electrical energy when unit *charge* passes through it. Its unit is the volt. The e.m.f. of a source is 1 V when 1 joule of one form of energy is changed into electrical energy when 1 coulomb passes through it.
- A *galvanometer* can measure the e.m.f. produced when wires of different metals are connected.

2 E.m.f. of simple cell

- A simple *cell* is formed by placing two different metals either side of a piece of blotting paper which has been soaked in a solution of an *electrolyte* such as sodium chloride.

3 Daniel cell

- Early cells, such as the Daniel cell, were described as wet cells as they consisted of rods of different metals suspended in liquid electrolytes such as dilute sulfuric acid. The e.m.f. of the Daniel cell is 1.1 V.

4 Dry cell

- In dry cells the electrolyte is a paste. In a carbon-zinc cell the electrolyte is a paste of ammonium chloride. The e.m.f. of this cell is 1.5 V.

5 Car battery

- Cells which are discarded after use are described as primary cells while those that can be recharged are secondary cells or accumulators.
- A car battery, or lead accumulator, consists of plates of lead and lead oxide in sulfuric acid, separated by layers of *insulator*. When the battery is discharging a chemical reaction takes place; this is reversed when the battery is being recharged.
- The e.m.f. of a car battery is normally 12 V.

Electromotive force

1 Galvanometer measuring e.m.f

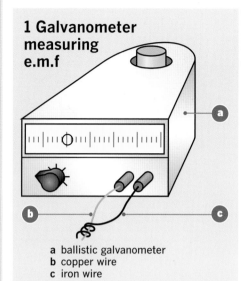

a ballistic galvanometer
b copper wire
c iron wire

2 E.m.f. of simple cell

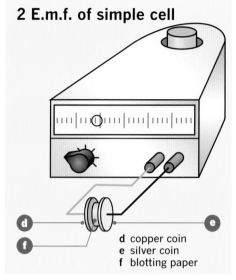

d copper coin
e silver coin
f blotting paper

3 Daniel cell

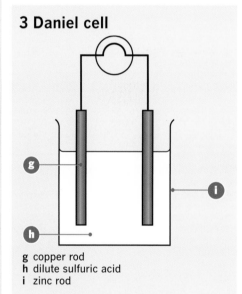

g copper rod
h dilute sulfuric acid
i zinc rod

4 Dry cell

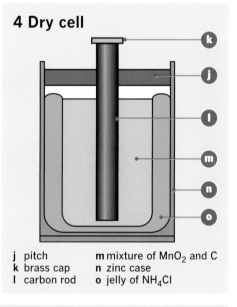

j pitch
k brass cap
l carbon rod
m mixture of MnO_2 and C
n zinc case
o jelly of NH_4Cl

5 Car battery

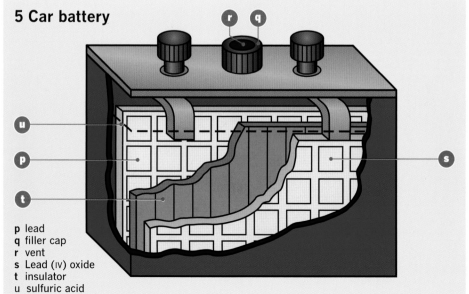

p lead
q filler cap
r vent
s Lead (IV) oxide
t insulator
u sulfuric acid

Applications of the Wheatstone network 1

Key words

corrosometer
explosimeter
resistance
Wheatstone
  bridge

1 The explosimeter

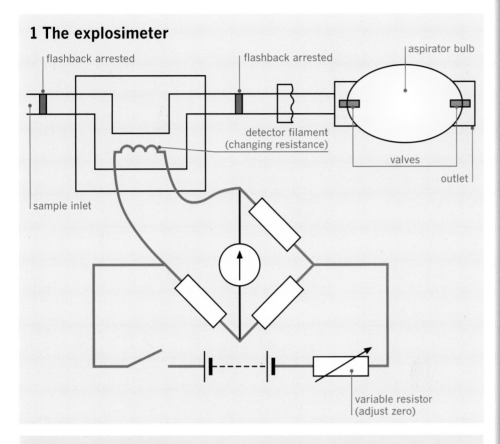

flashback arrested

flashback arrested

aspirator bulb

detector filament
(changing resistance)

valves

outlet

sample inlet

variable resistor
(adjust zero)

2 The corrosometer

reference element

measuring element

The circuit

variable resistor (with corrosion dial)

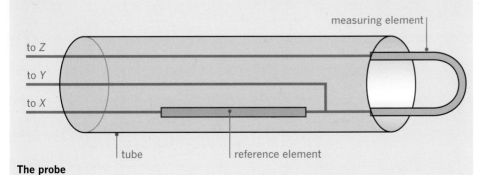

measuring element

to Z

to Y

to X

tube

reference element

The probe

1 The explosimeter

- The *resistance* of a material varies with its temperature. This can be expressed by its temperature coefficient of resistance which is the fractional increase in resistance at 0°C per unit rise of temperature.
- Metals have positive coefficients i.e. their resistance increases with temperature rise. The value of the coefficient is of the order of 1/275 per°C.
- An *explosimeter* is used to measure the concentration of combustible gases present in a sample, in a location such as a mine. The greater the concentration the greater the heat produced when the sample is burnt.
- Initially the *Wheatstone bridge* is balanced. The sample is then introduced to the hot wire. Combustible gases are ignited and burn in the presence of the wire. The more heat is produced, the hotter the wire becomes and therefore the more its resistance increases. This disturbs the Wheatstone bridge which gives a reading.
- Flashback arrestors are installed in the device as a safety feature to prevent the explosimeter igniting a sample external to it.

2 The corrosometer

- A *corrosometer* is used to measure the metal loss due to corrosion.
- When the measuring element comes into contact with the metal its resistance is altered. This causes an imbalance in the Wheatstone bridge circuit which is rectified by the variable resistor. The amount of rectification is an indication of the amount of metal loss.

Key words

resistance
strain
Wheatstone
  bridge

1 Electric strain gauge

- An electric *strain* gauge converts mechanical strain into a change in *resistance* in itself. This is possible because the resistance of a wire depends on its length and cross-sectional area.
- One form of strain gauge consists of a very fine wire (of a nickel-iron-chromium alloy) bonded to a slip of thin paper. It is attached to the component to be tested using a strong adhesive so that whatever strain is experienced by the component will also be experienced by the wire.
- As the component is stretched so is the gauge wire. This increases its length and decreases its cross-section, both of which increase its resistance. This change in resistance can be detected by a *Wheatstone bridge* suitably calibrated to indicate the magnitude of the strain.

2 Strain gauge pressure transducer

- Initially the strain gauge windings above and below the flexible cross member are under the same strain and therefore Wheatstone bridge circuit is balanced.
- When a force is applied to the diaphragm the force rod is pushed down, causing the flexible cross member down at its center. The insulating pillars below the cross member splay out from each other resulting in an increase in the strain experienced by the windings around them.
- This causes the windings to stretch, thereby becoming longer and thinner, which increases their resistance. The result is an imbalance in the Wheatstone bridge circuit which is detected and converted into a measure of the strain.

Applications of the Wheatstone network 2

1 Electric strain gauge

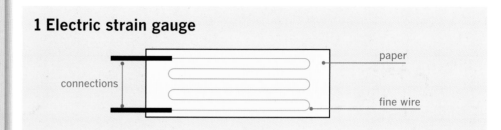

2 Strain gauge pressure transducer

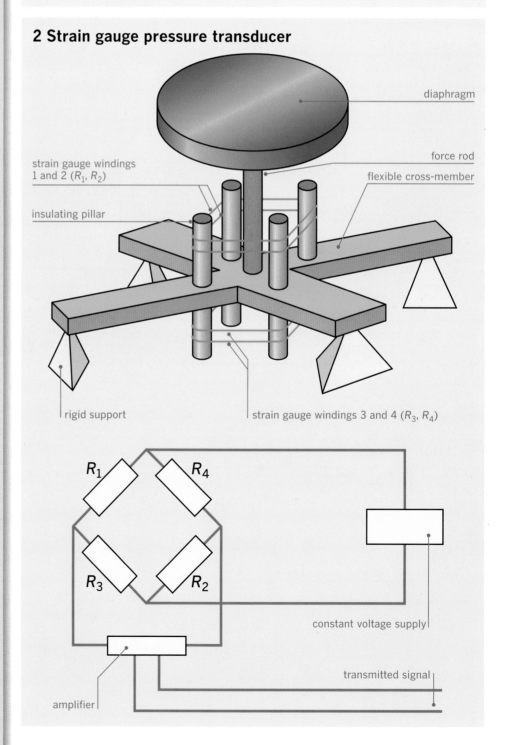

Electric power

Key words

current   power
electrical energy
fuse
potential
  difference

1 The watt and the kilowatt

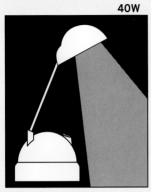

40W

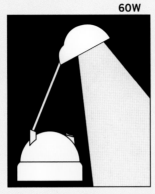

60W

100W

2 Power rating of appliances

Lamp 60W

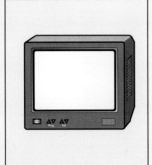

Television 650W

Drill 900W

Fan heater 1,000W

Iron 1200W

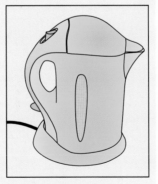

Kettle 1500W

3 Operating current and calculation of fuse required

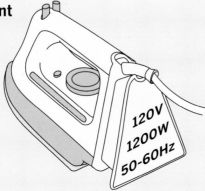

120V
1200W
50-60Hz

1 The watt and the kilowatt

- The *power* of an electrical device is the rate at which it converts *electrical energy* into other forms of energy. The higher the power the more electrical energy is consumed per unit time.
- The unit of power is the watt (**W**). One watt is the transfer of **1** J of electrical energy into other forms of energy each second.
- Electrical energy is often measured in kilowatt hours kWh. One kilowatt hour is the amount of electrical energy which is converted to other forms of energy when an electrical device which has a power rating of 1 kilowatt is used for 1 hour.
  1 kWh = 1 x 1,000 x 60 x 60 = 3,600,000 J = 3.6 MJ

2 Power rating of appliances

- All electrical devices have a power rating. Devices which are designed to heat in some way, such as irons, kettles and fan heaters have the highest ratings.

3 Operating current and calculation of fuse required

- Electrical power can be calculated using the equation:
  Power = Current x Potential difference
- The information given on an electrical device can be used to calculate the operating current and therefore the size of *fuse* that should be fitted to it.
- The operating *current* of an iron which has a power rating of 1200 W when connected to a 120V supply is:
  Current = $\frac{1200 \text{ W}}{120 \text{ V}}$ = 10 A

© Diagram Visual Information Ltd.

Key words

electrode	infrared
energy levels	ultraviolet light
evaporation	
filament	
flourescence	

1 Filament lamp

- A *filament* lamp consists of a thin wire filament enclosed in a glass bulb. Such lamps operate at very high temperatures in order to emit light and therefore the filament is made of tungsten which has a very high melting point (3400 °C).
- The glass bulb is filled with an inert gas such as nitrogen or argon. The gas reduces the *evaporation* of tungsten and prevents it being deposited on the inside of the bulb where it would cause blackening. The bulb cannot be filled with air as at high temperatures the tungsten would undergo a chemical reaction with oxygen.
- In addition to producing light energy, filament lamps also produce *ultraviolet* radiation and *infrared* radiation (heat). The efficiency of filament lamps as producers of light is very low, of the order of 10 percent.

2 Fluorescent lamp

- A *fluorescent* lamp consists of a glass tube with an *electrode* at each end. The tube contains mercury vapor and the inside surface is coated with a phosphor material.
- When a high voltage is applied across the electrodes electrons migrate between them, colliding with atoms of mercury. Energy is transferred to the mercury atoms causing electrons to be promoted to higher *energy levels*. When the electrons fall back to their ground state, energy is released as ultraviolet radiation.
- The phosphor coating on the inside of the tube is a fluorescent material. It absorbs the ultraviolet radiation from the mercury vapor and emits visible light.
- Fluorescent lamps do not emit unwanted ultraviolet radiation and produce relatively little heat, therefore they are typically 4 to 6 times more efficient than filament lamps.

Electric lighting

1 Filament lamp

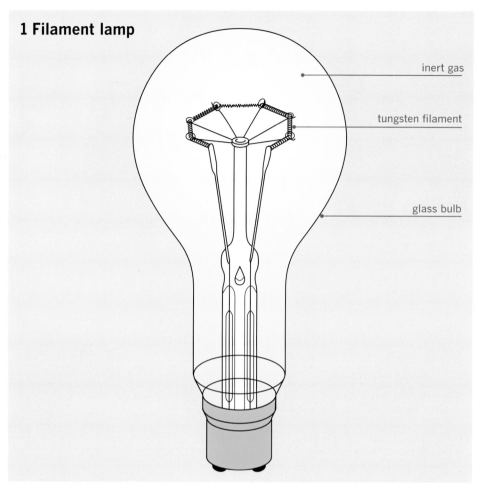

inert gas

tungsten filament

glass bulb

2 Fluorescent lamp

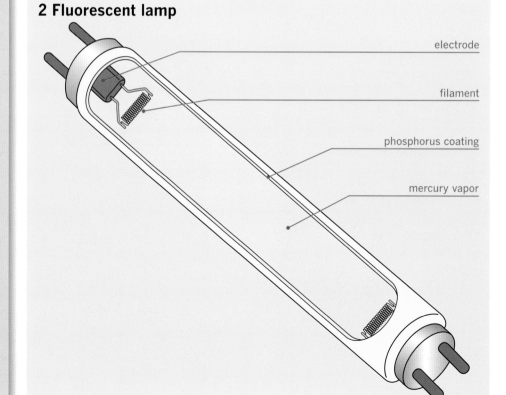

electrode

filament

phosphorus coating

mercury vapor

Electrolysis

1 Copper voltameter

Circuit for a voltameter

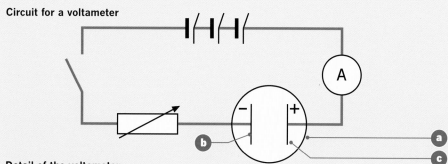

Detail of the voltameter

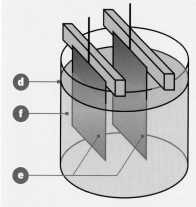

Flow of current in the voltameter

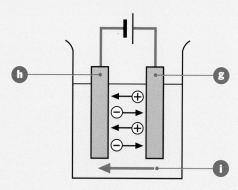

a voltameter
b cathode
c anode
d beaker

e copper plates
f saturated copper sulfate solution with addition of small amount of dilute sulfuric acid

g anode
h cathode
i direction of conventional current

2 Electrolysis of copper

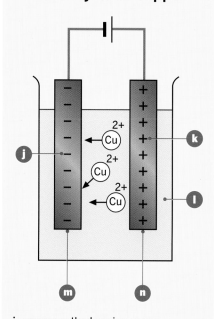

j copper cathode gains mass
k copper anode loses mass
l copper sulfate solution
m copper deposited
n copper dissolved

3 Electrolysis of water

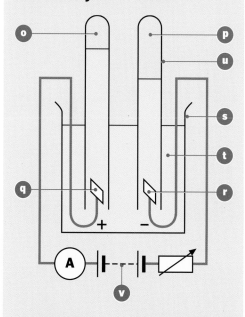

o oxygen gas
p hydrogen gas
q platinum anode
r platinum cathode
s tall beaker

t slightly acidified water
u inverted burette
v 12 V DC supply

Key words

anion	electrolysis
anode	electrolyte
cathode	ion
cation	voltameter
charge	

1 Copper voltameter

- *Electrolysis* causes chemical change when an electric current passes through an *electrolyte* (either a melted or an aqueous solution of an ionic substance). *Ions* transfer current through the electrolyte.
- Negative ions (*anions*) are attracted to the *anode* (positive electrode) while positive ions (*cations*) are attracted to the *cathode* (negative electrode).
- A *voltameter* measures the size of an electric *charge* by detecting changes to anode and cathode.

2 Electrolysis of copper

- The following reactions occur.
  At the anode: $Cu \rightarrow Cu^{2+} + 2e^-$
  At the cathode: $Cu^{2+} + 2e^- \rightarrow Cu$
- Copper goes into solution at the anode which becomes smaller. Conversely, copper is deposited from the solution on the cathode which becomes larger.
- The anode's loss in mass equals the cathode's gain in mass. The concentration of Cu^{2+} ions in solution remains constant so its color neither fades nor deepens.
- If a block of impure copper forms the anode, pure copper is deposited at the cathode. Solid impurities fall and accumulate below the anode.

3 Electrolysis of water

- Pure water ionizes to a very small extent as follows: $H_2O \rightleftharpoons H^+ + OH^-$. Due to the low concentration of ions it is a very poor conductor of electricity, but this increases if a small amount of an ionic substance such as dilute sulfuric acid is added.
- The following reactions occur at the electrodes.
  anode $4OH^- \rightarrow O_2 + 2H_2O + 4e^-$
  cathode $4H^+ + 4e^- \rightarrow 2H_2$
  Twice as much hydrogen as oxygen is produced.

Key words

magnet
magnetic field

Magnetic field

- The direction of a *magnetic* field at a point is the direction of the force that acts on a north magnetic pole there.
- The pattern of field lines indicates the shape and direction of the field. The number of field lines per unit cross section area indicates field strength.

1 Single magnet

- In a bar *magnet* the magnetic field is concentrated at the ends of the bar. Field lines are directed away from the N pole and towards the S pole.

2 Combined fields of magnet and Earth

- The magnetic field around a bar magnet alters when it is placed in an applied field.

3 Two north poles (end on)

- Like magnetic poles, either N—N or S—S, repel each other. This is shown by the pattern of field lines when like poles are placed close together.

4 North and south poles (end on)

- Unlike magnetic poles, N—S, attract each other. The magnetic field lines are directed out of the N pole and into the S pole.

5 Magnets broadside on

- When two bar magnets are placed broadside to each other repulsion occurs at both poles if they are in the same orientation, and attraction if they are in the opposite orientation.

6 Effects on soft iron

- When a bar magnet is placed close to a piece of soft iron it induces magnetism in the soft iron. The part of the soft iron closest to the N pole acts as if it was the S pole of a magnet, while the part closest to the S pole acts as if it was an N pole.

Magnetic fields of magnets

1 Single magnet

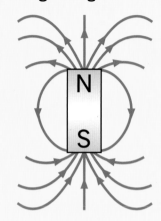

2 Combined fields of magnet and Earth

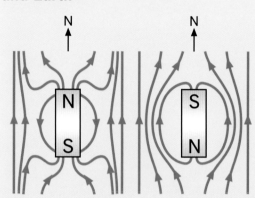

3 Two North poles (end on)

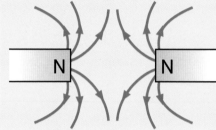

4 North and South poles (end on)

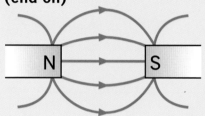

5 Magnets broadside on

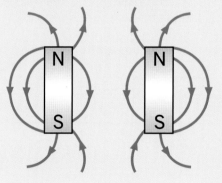

6 Effect on soft iron

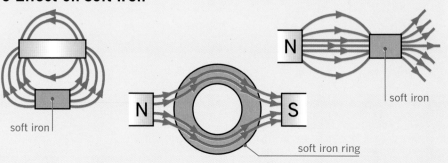

Magnetic fields due to an electric current 1

Key words

current
magnetic field

1 A current produces a magnetic field

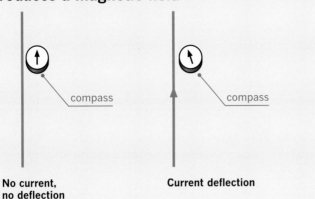

**No current,
no deflection**

Current deflection

compass

compass

1 A current produces a magnetic field
- When a *current* is passed through a wire it creates a *magnetic field* around the wire which is demonstrated by the deflection of a plotting compass. While the current is flowing the compass needle deflects but as soon as the current is switched off the compass needle returns to pointing north.

2 Field patterns produced by currents

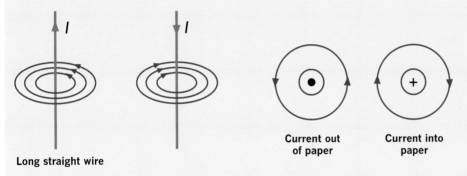

Long straight wire

Current out of paper

Current into paper

2 Field patterns produced by currents
- The magnetic field around a wire carrying a current consists of a series of concentric circles. The direction of the field is determined by the direction of the current.
- Conventionally, if a wire is represented is section, a current coming out of the page is represented by a dot (●) while a current passing into the paper is represented by a cross (+). The dot and cross represent the tip and tail of an arrow respectively.

3 Determining a field pattern

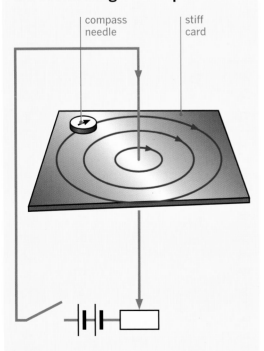

compass
needle

stiff
card

3 Determining a field pattern
- The shape and direction of the magnetic field around a wire carrying a current can be found by placing plotting compasses at different locations around the wire. The needle of a plotting compass lines up with the magnetic field line and indicates its direction.

4 Right hand screw rule

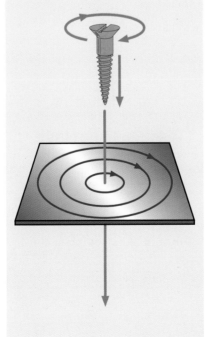

4 Right hand screw rule
- The direction of the magnetic field around a wire carrying a current can be predicted using the "right hand screw rule." If a right-handed screw moves forward in the direction of the conventional current then the direction of rotation of the screw gives the direction of the magnetic field lines.

Magnetic fields due to an electric current 2

1 Field pattern produced by wire loop

- When an electric *current* is passed through a loop of wire each part of the loop can be regarded as a single wire. The current passes in the opposite direct in each part of the loop therefore the *magnetic field* lines will have the opposite orientation.

2 Field pattern produced by solenoid

- A *solenoid* is a long cylindrical coil composed of many loops. The field pattern for a solenoid can be thought of as the summation of the field pattern for each loop. It is similar to that of a bar *magnet*.

3 Right hand grip rule

- The polarity of a solenoid can be predicted using the "right hand grip rule." If the right hand is placed over a solenoid with fingers pointing in the same direction as the conventional current passing through each coil, the direction of the N pole of the solenoid is given by the thumb.
- If the direction of the current is reversed its polarity is also reversed.
- *Electromagnetism* may be described as temporary magnetism since it only exists when a current passes through a *conductor*.
- In general, the field produced by a permanent magnet can be reproduced by passing a current through a suitably shaped conductor. This supports the idea that all magnetic effects are due to electric currents which, in the case of permanent magnets, are the result of the movement of *electrons* within the *atoms*.
- Static charge gives rise to electric fields. Moving charge i.e. current, gives rise to both electric and magnetic fields.

1 Field pattern produced by wire loop

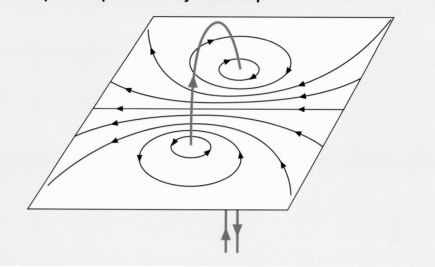

2 Field pattern produced by solenoid

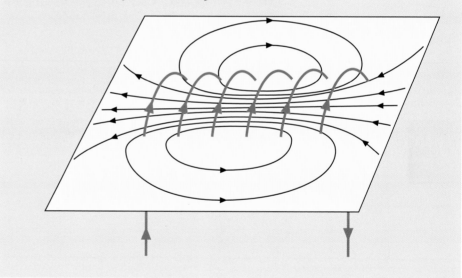

3 Right hand grip rule

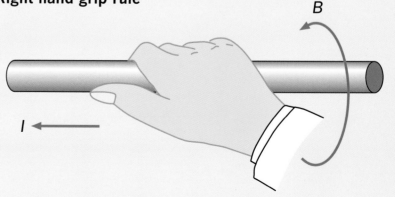

Magnetic field of Earth 1

Key words

magnet
magnetic field

1 Earth's magnetic field

mndpn points vertically downward

axis of rotation

North pole

mnpdn points vertically upwards

South pole

Magnetic north pole dip needle (mnpdn)

2 Earth's magnetic field in terms of electric currents

magnetic axis of the Earth magnet

S

N

electric currents in the Earth's core

3 Migration of north magnetic pole

84°N
90°N
82°N
80°N
78°N
76°N
74°N
72°N

2000
1999

1995
1990
1985
1980
1955

1920
1915
1910
1900

1 Earth's magnetic field

- Earth is surrounded by a *magnetic field*. It is as if Earth contains a huge imaginary bar *magnet* but the source of the magnetic field is much more complicated than this.
- It is thought that the field is the result of the movement of molten iron in the outer core of the Earth some 3,000 km or more below the surface.

2 Earth's magnetic field in terms of electric currents

- Magnetic North is the place to which compass needles point. However since the end of a compass needle marked N points north it follows that Earth's magnetic north pole is actually a south magnetic pole.
- Earth's magnetic N pole is not fixed either in terms of polarity or of location.
- Evidence obtained from rocks containing minerals of iron indicate that the polarity of Earth's magnetic field has reversed many times in its history. These iron minerals aligned with Earth's magnetic field while the rock was still molten and forming. Their orientation provides a record of Earth's field when the rock was formed.
- It has been suggested that a reversal of polarity occurs when the circulation of molten iron in Earth's outer core is disrupted and then reestablishes itself in the opposite direction.

3 Migration of north magnetic pole

- The position of the north magnetic pole can move erratically from day to day but more usually it migrates typically 10 – 40 kilometers each year.
- The north magnetic field drifted steadily north and west over the last century and appears to be heading towards Siberia in this one.

© Diagram Visual Information Ltd.

Key words

magnetic field
satellite

Magnetic field of Earth 2

1 Resolving Earth's magnetic field strength

- Earth's *magnetic field* strength, B_R can be resolved into horizontal, B_H, and vertical, B_V, components: $B_H = B_R \cos \alpha$ and $B_V = B_R \sin \alpha$, where α is the angle of dip, the angle between the horizontal and the magnetic pole.
- A compass needle is only affected by B_H since is only moves in the horizontal plane.

2 The dip circle

- A dip needle is essentially a magnetized needle, such as is found in a compass, but suspended vertically so that it moves freely about its center.
- At the north magnetic pole the vertical component of Earth's magnetic field strength is at its maximum and the horizontal component is zero. A dip needle points vertically downward at this point on Earth.
- At the magnetic equator the vertical component of Earth's magnetic field strength is zero and the horizontal component is at its maximum. Anywhere on the magnetic equator a dip needle lies horizontal.
- The dip angle indicates the position of a location in terms of latitude relative to Earth's magnetic poles. In the southern hemisphere it is the opposite end of the dip needle which indicates the dip angle.

3 Angle of declination

- The angle of declination is the angle between the geographical North Pole and the magnetic north pole. Since the location of the magnetic north pole is not constant, it is necessary for people relying on a compass that navigation to make periodic amendments to their instruments and charts. The increasing use of *satellites* for navigation has made this less of a problem in recent years.

1 Resolving Earth's magnetic field strength

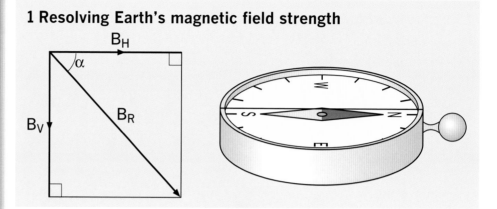

2 The dip circle

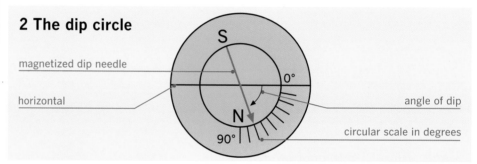

magnetized dip needle

horizontal

angle of dip

circular scale in degrees

3 Angle of declination

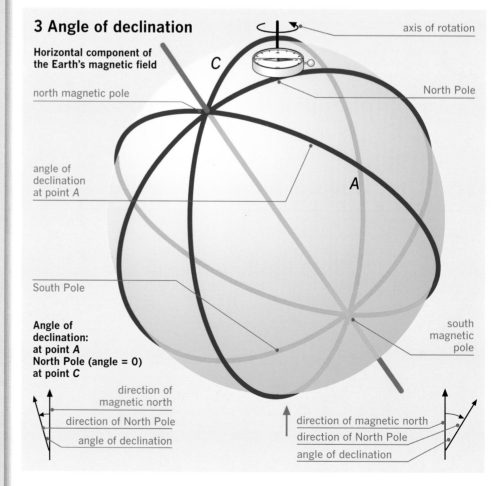

Horizontal component of the Earth's magnetic field

north magnetic pole

angle of declination at point A

South Pole

Angle of declination: at point A North Pole (angle = 0) at point C

axis of rotation

North Pole

south magnetic pole

direction of magnetic north

direction of North Pole

angle of declination

direction of magnetic north

direction of North Pole

angle of declination

Forces in magnetic fields 1

1 Current-carrying wire in a magnetic field

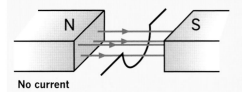

No current

current flowing

I

2 Current balance

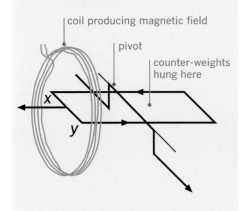

coil producing magnetic field

pivot

counter-weights hung here

x

y

3 Fleming's Left-Hand rule

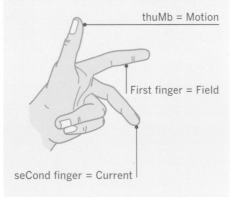

thuMb = Motion

First finger = Field

seCond finger = Current

4 Motion of a charge moving in a magnetic field

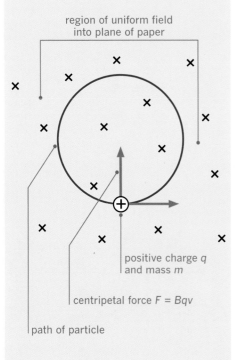

region of uniform field into plane of paper

positive charge *q* and mass *m*

centripetal force $F = Bqv$

path of particle

5 Helical motion of particle in uniform field

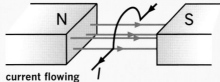

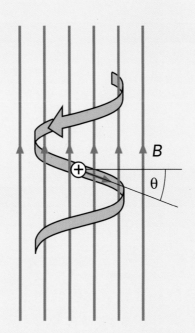

B

θ

Key words

conductor
current
flux
helical motion
magnetic field

1 Current-carrying wire in a magnetic field

- A circular *magnetic field* is generated around a *current*-carrying wire. The direction of the field reinforces the applied magnetic field below it and opposes that above it, resulting in the wire being thrust upwards.

2 Current balance

- A horizontal wire loop, balanced at its center, has one end within a magnetic field produced by a coil. This part of the loop moves down when current passes through it. The size of the force is measured by adding counter weights to the opposite end of the loop.

3 Fleming's Left-Hand Rule

- This relates motion, magnetic field and current in motors.

4 Motion of a charge moving in a magnetic field

- The force exerted on a current-carrying *conductor* in a magnetic field is the resultant of the forces acting on the charges.
- For a particle carrying a charge, q, moving at velocity, v, in a conductor at an angle θ to a uniform magnetic field of *flux* density, B, the force exerted on the particle, $F = Bqv\sin\theta$.
- If the charged particle enters the uniform magnetic field at a right angle then θ = 90°, sin θ = 1 and $F = Bqv$.
- The direction of the force is at right angles to the field and the direction of motion, resulting in the particle being deflected in a circular path.

5 Helical motion of particle in uniform field

- If a charged particle enters the uniform magnetic field other than at a right angle then sin θ ≠ 1 the particle is deflected in a *helical* path.

Key words

conductor
current
Hall effect
Magnadur
magnetic field

potential
difference

1 Force between current carrying wires

- When *current* passes in the same direction through parallel wires, the circular *magnetic field* around both wires has the same direction—either clockwise or counterclockwise. Overlapping parts of the fields between the wires are opposite in direction so the wires are forced together.
- When current passes in opposite directions through parallel wires the direction of the circular magnetic field around the wires is different. Overlapping parts of the fields between the wires are in the same direction so the wires are forced apart.

2 The Hall effect

- When a current carrying *conductor* is placed in a magnetic field it has a small potential difference across its sides at right angles to the field.
- This effect is caused by forces acting on the charge carriers in the conductor. These forces act at right angles to the magnetic field and the current and cause the charge carriers to be pushed sideways. Their concentration increases on one side of the conductor thus leading to a *potential difference* across it.

3 Measuring Hall voltage

- A current of around 50 mA is passed through the Hall slice (such as a piece of doped germanium). If the connections to the Hall slice are not exactly opposite each other there will be a potential difference between them irrespective of whether a magnetic field is applied to the slice. In this case the balance control is used to zero the meter.
- If a *Magnadur* magnet is placed face down on the Hall slice the voltmeter indicates that a potential difference now exists across it.

Forces in magnetic fields 2

1 Force between current carrying wires

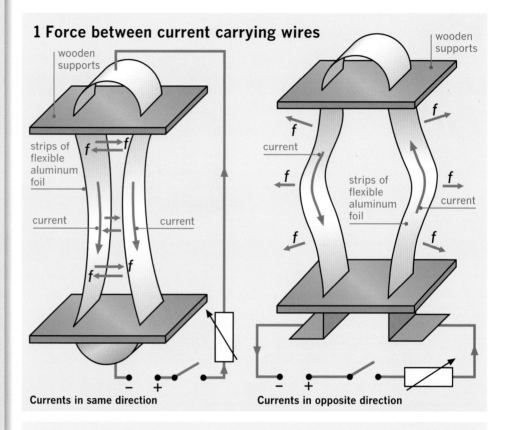

Currents in same direction

Currents in opposite direction

2 The Hall effect

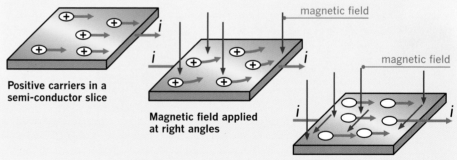

Positive carriers in a semi-conductor slice

Magnetic field applied at right angles

Electric field established across the slice

3 Measuring Hall voltage

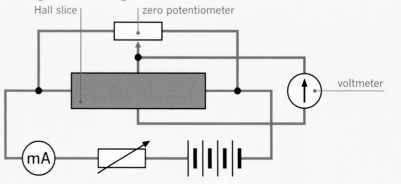

Electromagnets 1

1 Experimental electromagnet

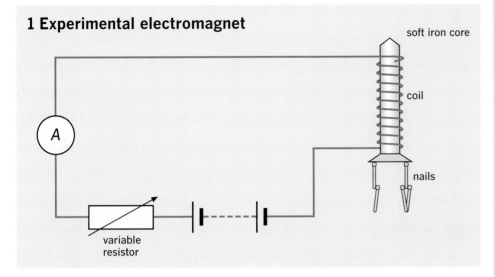

soft iron core

coil

nails

A

variable
resistor

2 Horseshoe electromagnet

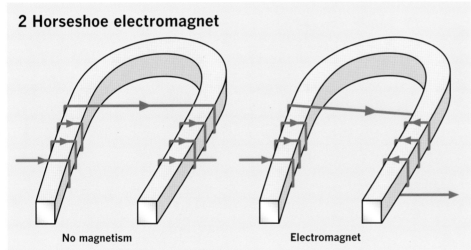

No magnetism

Electromagnet

3 Practical electromagnet

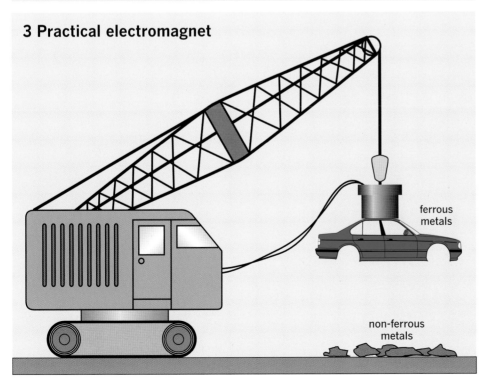

ferrous
metals

non-ferrous
metals

Key words

current   magnetism
electromagnet
electromagnetism
magnet
magnetic field

Electromagnetism

● *Electromagnetism* is called temporary *magnetism* since it only exists while a *current* is passing. An *electromagnet* can be switched on and off unlike a permanent *magnet*.

1 Experimental electromagnet

● When a current passes through a wire a *magnetic field* is generated around it however, to make a practical electromagnet, the wire is wound into a coil.

● An electromagnet's strength can be found by measuring the weight of iron which it can support. A simple comparison of the strengths of electromagnets can be made using small articles e.g. nails or paper clips.

● The strength of an electromagnet increases when the number of turns of wire in the coil increases.

● The strength of an electromagnet increases when the current passing through the coils increases.

● The strength of an electromagnet increases when the coil is wound around a core of soft iron.

2 Horseshoe electromagnet

● A horseshoe electromagnet can be made by winding a coil around each limb of a soft iron core.

● If the coils are wound around the limbs in the same direction the magnetic fields cancel each other out and the core is not magnetized.

● If the coils are wound around the limbs in opposite directions the limbs are magnetized with opposite polarity.

3 Practical electromagnet

● Electromagnets are used in scrap yards as a convenient way of moving ferrous metals (iron and steel) and separating them from non-ferrous metals such as aluminum, copper and brass.

Key words

current
electromagnet
magnetic field
sound waves

1 Electric door bell

- When the switch is closed the circuit is complete and *current* flows through the coil. The soft iron core becomes magnetic and attracts the armature. As the armature moves it strikes the gong while at the same time breaking the circuit. The soft iron core ceases to be magnetic and the steel spring returns the armature to its original position, completing the circuit once again. The cycle is repeated for as long as the switch remains closed causing the bell to ring.

2 Door bell with chimes

- When the switch is closed the coil of insulated copper wire becomes an *electromagnet* and the soft iron collar is pulled down into it causing the poly(ethene) bobbin to strike the lower metal plate. The spring is compressed and forces the poly(ethene) bobbin and soft iron collar back up again to strike the upper metal plate. The bobbin will continue to oscillate up and down in this way while the switch is closed.

3 Telephone ear piece

- A variable current passes through the coil in the ear piece. This produces changes in the strength of the *magnetic field* below the diaphragm which causes it to move up and down making *sound waves*.

4 Magnetic relay

- When the switch is closed current flows through the coil and the soft iron core becomes magnetic. As one end of the armature is attracted downward towards the core the other end moves upwards closing the contacts.

Electromagnets 2

1 Electric door bell

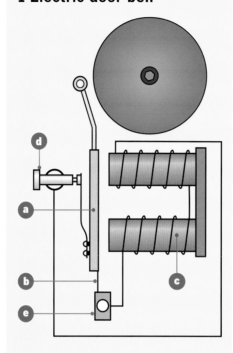

a armature
b steel spring
c soft iron core
d screw to adjust tension
e push button to close switch

2 Door bell with chimes

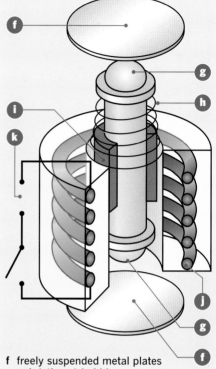

f freely suspended metal plates
g poly(ethene) bobbin
h loosely coiled spring
i soft-iron collar
j coil of insulated copper wire
k supply

3 Telephone ear piece

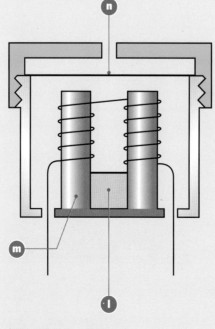

l permanent magnet
m soft iron
n magnetic diaphragm

4 Magnetic relay

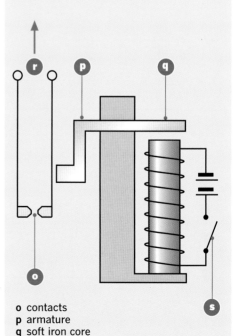

o contacts
p armature
q soft iron core
r to circuit to be switched
s switch

Electromagnetic induction 1

Key words
conductor
current
galvanometer
generator
magnetic field

1 Moving a conductor in a magnetic field

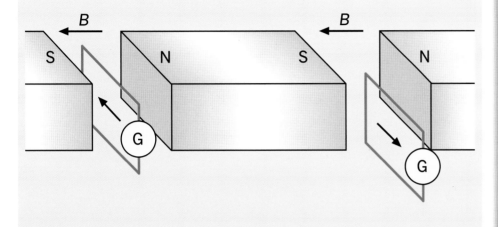

2 Right-hand rule

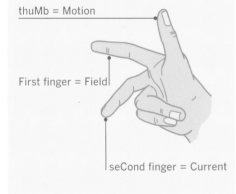

thuMb = Motion

First finger = Field

seCond finger = Current

3 Moving a magnetic field around a conductor

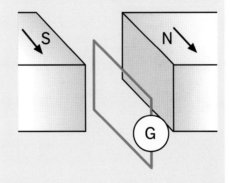

4 Moving both magnetic field and conductor

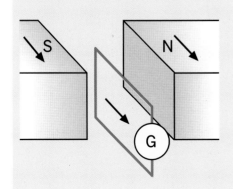

5 Conductor moving within magnetic field

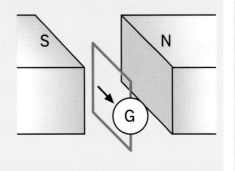

1 Moving a conductor in a magnetic field

● When a *conductor* is moved in a *magnetic field* in such a way that it cuts the magnetic field lines a current is induced in it. This occurs when the conductor is moved horizontally or vertically through a magnetic field but not when it is moved from one magnetic pole to the other along the field lines.

● Moving one end of a loop either into or out of a magnetic field causes a deflection on the *galvanometer* while the loop is moving.

2 Right-hand rule

● Fleming's Right-hand rule, used for electric *generators*, relates motion, magnetic field, and *current*.

3 Moving a magnetic field around a conductor

● A current is also induced if the conductor remains stationary and the magnetic field is moved. What is important is that the conductor is moving relative to the magnetic field and that it cuts the magnetic field lines.

4 Moving both magnetic field and conductor

● There is no induced current when the conductor and magnetic field move together in the same direction or when the conductor remains stationary inside the magnetic field. This is because magnetic field lines are not cut by the conductor.

5 Conductor moving within magnetic field

● When a closed loop is moved entirely within a magnetic field, a current is induced, moving in the same direction at both ends of the loop. The result is that they cancel each other out giving zero current.

© Diagram Visual Information Ltd.

Key words

conductor	galvanometer
electromagnetic induction	generator induction
electromotive force (e.m.f.)	magnetic field potential
flux	difference

Faraday's law of electromagnetic induction

- Faraday suggested an explanation of *electromagnetic induction* based on *magnetic field* lines. He proposed that an *e.m.f.* is induced in a *conductor* either when it cuts field lines or when there is a change in the number of lines linking it i.e. passing through it. These often amount to the same thing.
- The number of field lines per unit cross-sectional area represents the magnitude, B, of the *flux* density. Where the flux density acts at right angles to and over an area, A, the magnetic flux, $F = BA$.
- If F is the flux through the cross-sectional area A of a coil of N turns the total flux through it, or flux linkage, is NF since the same flux, F, links each of the N turns.
- Faraday's law of *induction* states that the induced e.m.f. is directly proportional to the rate of change of flux linkage or rate of flux cutting.

1 Flux changes and e.m.f.

- When part of the loop passes between the magnetic poles there is a change in the flux. A deflection on the galvanometer indicates that an e.m.f has been induced.
- When the whole of the loop passes through the flux there is no net change in the flux and no e.m.f. is induced.

2 Rotating conductor in a magnetic field

- When a coil of wire is rotated in a magnetic field each turn of wire cuts through the flux inducing an e.m.f. The result is a *potential difference* across the coil thus a current flows through it. This is the basis of an electric *generator*.

Electromagnetic induction 2

1 Flux changes and e.m.f

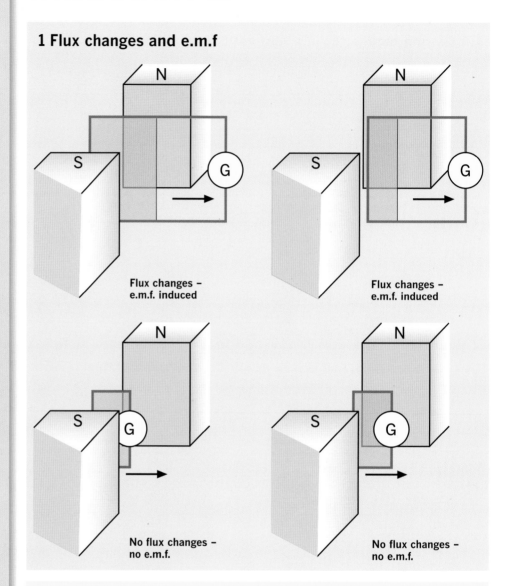

Flux changes –
e.m.f. induced

Flux changes –
e.m.f. induced

No flux changes –
no e.m.f.

No flux changes –
no e.m.f.

2 Rotating conductor in a magnetic field

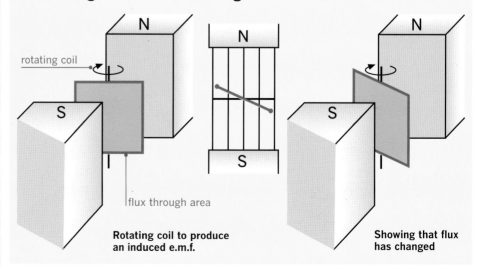

rotating coil

flux through area

Rotating coil to produce
an induced e.m.f.

Showing that flux
has changed

Generating electric power

Key words

alternating
  current (AC)
commutator
electromotive
  force (e.m.f.)

generator
magnet
magnetic field

1 AC generator

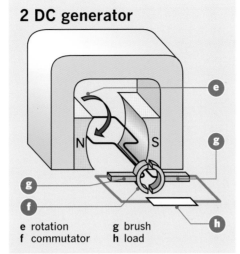

- **a** rotation
- **b** brushes
- **c** slip-rings
- **d** load

2 DC generator

- **e** rotation
- **f** commutator
- **g** brush
- **h** load

3 E.m.f. against time for AC generator

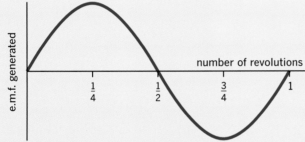

e.m.f. generated

number of revolutions

$\frac{1}{4}$ $\frac{1}{2}$ $\frac{3}{4}$ 1

Position of coil with respect to direction of magnetic field

zero e.m.f. –
coil vertical

maximum e.m.f. –
coil horizontal

zero e.m.f.

maximum
reversed e.m.f.

zero e.m.f.
T = time for one
complete circle

4 E.m.f. against time for DC generator

e.m.f. generated

number of revolutions

$\frac{1}{4}$ $\frac{1}{2}$ $\frac{3}{4}$ 1

Position of coil and commutator with respect to direction of magnetic field

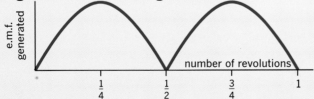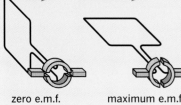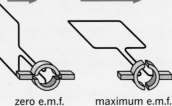

zero e.m.f.   maximum e.m.f.   zero e.m.f.   maximum e.m.f.   zero e.m.f.

1 AC generator

- A simple *alternating current generator* consists of a coil rotating inside a *magnetic field* produced by a permanent *magnet*. Current is taken off via slip rings.
- Brushes pressing against the slip rings transfer current to the load. Brushes are made of a soft conducting material, such as graphite.

2 DC generator

- A simple direct current generator is identical to an AC generator except that slip rings are replaced by a *commutator*.

3 E.m.f. against time for AC generator

- As the coil rotates the rate at which it cuts the magnetic field lines changes. When it moves through the vertical it passes along the field lines but does not cut them therefore no *e.m.f.* is produced. When it moves through the horizontal it passes through maximum flux density therefore maximum e.m.f. is induced.
- If Flemings Right-hand rule is used to predict the direction of the induced current in a single turn of a coil it is found that the direction of the current reverses each half turn.

4 E.m.f. against time for DC generator

- As the coil rotates the induced e.m.f. is zero when it moves through the vertical and maximum when moving through the horizontal.
- The commutator ensures that the output current of a DC generator does not reverse direction. As the induced current in the coil is reversed the output through the commutator is also reversed.

Key words

couple	magnetic field
current	
electromagnet	
generator	
magnet	

The DC electric motor

1 DC motor

- The structure of a simple DC motor is identical to that of a DC *generator*. The only difference in the devices is the direction of the energy transfer.
- In a generator: **kinetic energy → electrical energy**
  In a motor: **electrical energy → kinetic energy**
- A direct electric *current* (from a source such as a cell) passing through the coil creates a magnetic field around it. If the coil is positioned within a *magnetic field*, the field around the coil interacts with the applied field causing the coil to rotate.

2 Series wound motor

- In simple DC motors a permanent *magnet* often provides the field within which the coil rotates. In practical DC motors both the field and the coil are *electromagnets*.

3 Forces acting on the coil

- The direction of the force acting on each side of a coil can be predicted by applying Fleming's left-hand rule or the motor rule to each side.
- Opposite sides of the coil which are perpendicular to the applied magnetic field are acted on by vertical forces in opposite directions. A pair of forces acting in this way are called a *couple*.
- Opposite sides of the coil which are parallel to the applied magnetic field are acted on by forces directly perpendicular to that field.

4 Forces on coil at different parts of cycle

- Forces causing the coil to rotate are greatest when the coil is moving horizontally relative to the magnetic field lines, and least when the coil is moving through the vertical.

1 DC motor

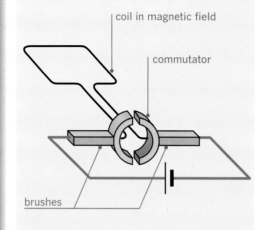

coil in magnetic field

commutator

brushes

2 Series wound motor

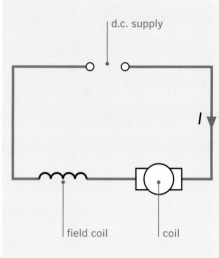

d.c. supply

I

field coil

coil

3 Forces acting on the coil

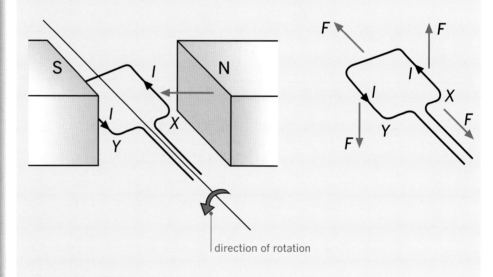

direction of rotation

4 Forces on coil at different parts of cycle

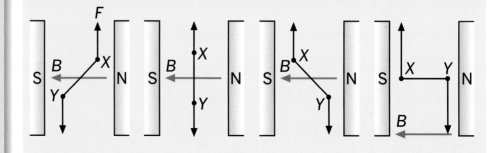

Transformer-induced e.m.f.s 1

Key words

current	magnetic field
electromotive	solenoid
force (e.m.f.)	transformer
flux	
magnet	

1 Inducing current two ways

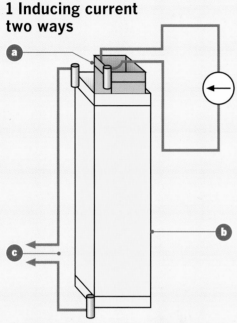

a, b   square cross-sectional solenoids
If **a** is moved out of **b** a current is
induced in **a**.
If the current in **b** is changed a current
is induced in **a**.
c   to smoothed DC supply and rheostat

- The outer *solenoid* forms part of a circuit whose *current* can be altered. A *magnetic field* forms around it when current flows.
- An *e.m.f.* is induced in the inner solenoid if it is moved in or out of the outer solenoid, cutting through magnetic field lines. This induced current changes direction as the inner solenoid is pushed in or pulled out.
- If the current passing through the outer solenoid is slowly reduced to zero the magnetic field around it slowly collapses. Magnetic field lines cut the inner solenoid and an e.m.f. is induced.

2 Continuously changing current

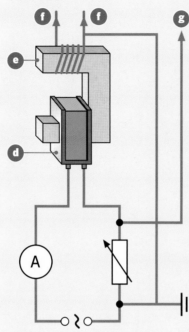

d   coil   f   to Y_2 input of CRO
e   iron yoke   g   to Y_1 input of CRO

- An AC reverses direction during each cycle. The polarity of the magnetic field generated when an AC passes through a conductor also reverses.
- The magnetic field generated around a coil connected to an AC supply grows and collapses twice each cycle owing to changes in polarity.
- When a coil is wrapped around a soft iron yoke, the yoke becomes a *magnet*. Field lines around the yoke grow and collapse, cutting turns of wire in a secondary coil, inducing an AC in it.
- This is the principle upon which *transformers* work.

3 Effect on e.m.f. of number of turns

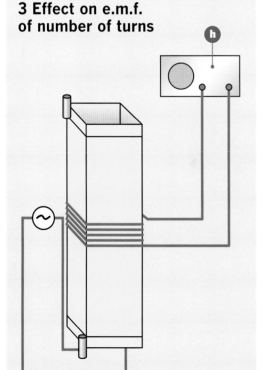

h   CRO

- If the number of turns of wire in a coil is increased the rate at which the *flux* is cut also increases therefore a greater e.m.f. is induced in the coil.

4 Effect on e.m.f. of solenoid area

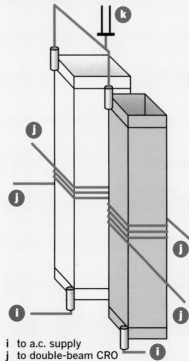

i   to a.c. supply
j   to double-beam CRO
k   probe (also to CRO)

- The ratio of the e.m.f.s induced in the coils equals the ratio of their areas.

© Diagram Visual Information Ltd.

Key words

eddy current	flux
electromotive	mutual
force (e.m.f.)	inductance
ferromagnetic	transformer

1 Effect on e.m.f. of rate of flux change

- The rate of change of *flux* can be increased or decreased by altering the frequency of the signal. As the rate of change of flux increases so does the induced *e.m.f.*

2 Power loss in a transformer

- A 6 V lamp provides the load on the secondary coil of the *transformer*.
- Electrical power can be calculated using the equation:
  Power = Current x Voltage.
  Input power at primary coil =
  $A_1 \times V_1$
  Output power at secondary coil =
  $A_2 \times V_2$
  Power loss in the transformer =
  $A_1 \times V_1 = A_2 \times V_2$

  Small energy losses (in the form of heat) do occur due to resistance in the windings, and *eddy currents* and flux leakage in the core.

3 Measuring mutual inductance

- A change in current in one coil or circuit can induce an e.m.f. in a neighboring coil or circuit. The phase difference between the coils or circuits is one quarter of a cycle.
- The *mutual inductance*, M, is defined by the equation:
  $$M = \frac{-\epsilon}{dI_p/dt}$$
  where ϵ is the e.m.f. induced in the secondary when the rate of change of current in the primary coil is dI_p/dt.
- The unit of mutual inductance is the henry (H). Two coils have a mutual inductance of 1 henry if an e.m.f. of 1 volt is induced in the secondary coil when the current in the primary coil changes at a rate of 1 ampere per second.
- The value of M is much higher when the coils have a *ferromagnetic* core.

Transformer-induced e.m.f.s 2

1 Effect on e.m.f. of rate of flux change

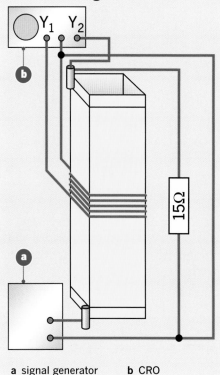

15Ω

a signal generator   b CRO

2 Power loss in a transformer

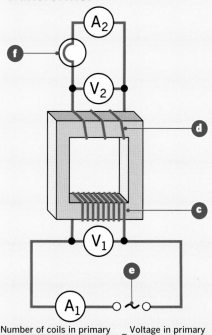

$$\frac{\text{Number of coils in primary}}{\text{Number of coils in secondary}} = \frac{\text{Voltage in primary}}{\text{Voltage in secondary}}$$

c primary turn coil   e a.c. mains
d secondary coil turn   f 6V lamp

3 Measuring mutual inductance

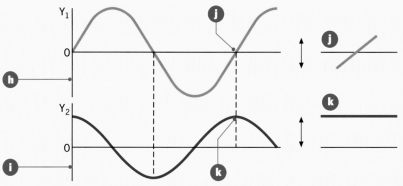

Circuit to measure mutual inductance

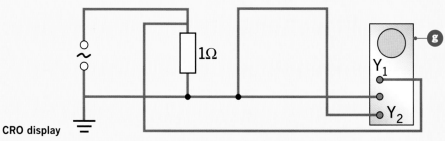

1Ω

CRO display

g CRO
h current in primary

i e.m.f. in secondary
j $\dfrac{dI}{dt}$

k E   M is computed from
$$E = \frac{MdI}{dt}$$

AC electric motors 1

1 Forces on induced currents

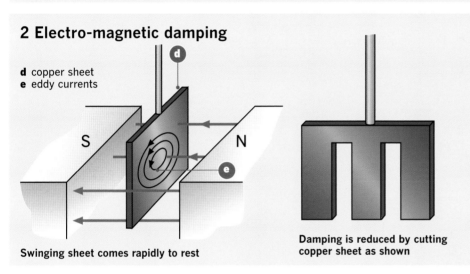

a aluminum ring
b iron ore
c coil

2 Electro-magnetic damping

d copper sheet
e eddy currents

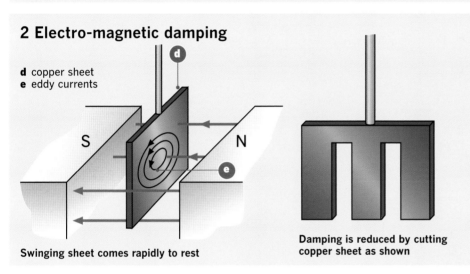

S   N

Swinging sheet comes rapidly to rest

Damping is reduced by cutting copper sheet as shown

3 3-phase electric motor

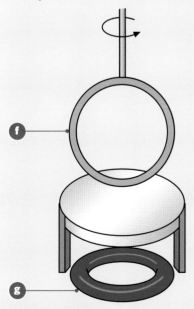

f conducting ring
g source of rotating magnetic field

4 Shaded-pole electric motor

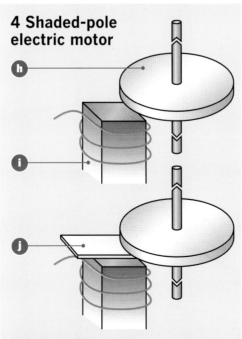

h aluminum sheet
i electromagnet
j aluminum plate, the insertion of which produces an unbalanced force on the eddy currents induced in **h**

1 Forces on induced currents

● When an *alternating current* is passed through the coil it induces an *eddy current* in the aluminum ring. The direction of the eddy current is such as to produce a *magnetic field* which opposes the one in the coil thus the aluminum ring is repelled up the iron core.

2 Electro-magnetic damping

● As the copper sheet swings it cuts the magnetic field lines and an eddy current is induced in it. The eddy current always tends to oppose the motion of the sheet so it rapidly comes to rest.

● If sections of the copper sheet arc removed then a much weaker eddy current is induced and the *damping* effect is much reduced.

3 3-phase electric motor

● In a 3-phase electric motor three pairs of stationary *electromagnets* are arranged at equal angles around a rotor. Each pair is connected to one phase of a three phase AC supply. The phases reach their maximum values one after another in a repeating cycle.

4 Shaded-pole electric motor

● A shaded-pole induction motor produces a rotating magnetic field by covering part of the pole of an electromagnet carrying alternating current with a conducting plate such a sheet of aluminum. The current induces eddy currents in the plate which create a second magnetic field adjacent to the first. The metal disc interprets the phase difference between the two fields as a moving field and responds by rotating.

Key words

electromagnet
magnetic field

1 3-phase electric power production

- Each of the coils is connected to one phase of a 3-phase AC supply. They provide the stationary *electromagnets* or stator in the electric motor. They are arranged at 120° to each other around a conductor or rotor.
- Each phase of the 3-phase AC rises to a maximum value in turn in a continuous cycle. During one rotation of the rotor each stator carries maximum current for part of the time, while the other windings carry smaller currents.

2 Producing rotating magnetic field

- Each phase of a 3-phase AC is fed into each coil in turn with the direction of the current reversing half way through the cycle. This produces a *magnetic field* which moves around the rotor.
- The rotor is often of a "squirrel cage" design. This consists of a number of copper rods contained in an iron cylinder. The rotor interprets the alterations of the magnetic field as a magnetic field sweeping around it, in other words a rotating field. The eddy currents induced in the copper rods cause it to rotate.

AC electric motors 2

1 3-phase electric power production

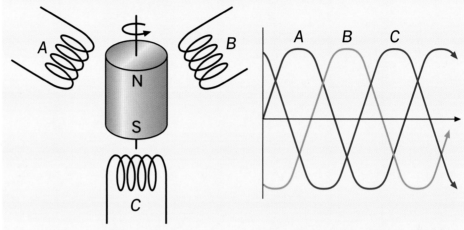

A, B, and C are coils at 120° to each other

An e.m.f. is induced by the rotating magnet in each coil

2 Producing rotating magnetic field

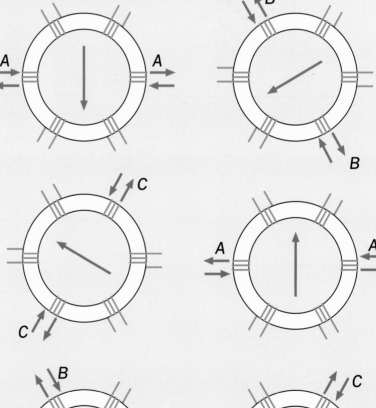

Electric power transmission 1

Key words

current
electrical energy
resistance
transformer

1 Transmission without transformer

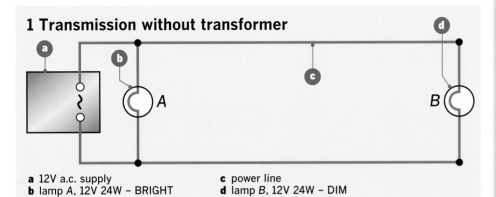

a 12V a.c. supply
b lamp A, 12V 24W – BRIGHT
c power line
d lamp B, 12V 24W – DIM

2 Transmission with transformer

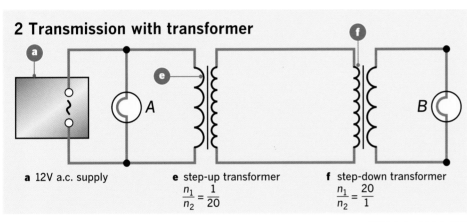

a 12V a.c. supply
e step-up transformer
$$\frac{n_1}{n_2} = \frac{1}{20}$$
f step-down transformer
$$\frac{n_1}{n_2} = \frac{20}{1}$$

3 Use of transformer

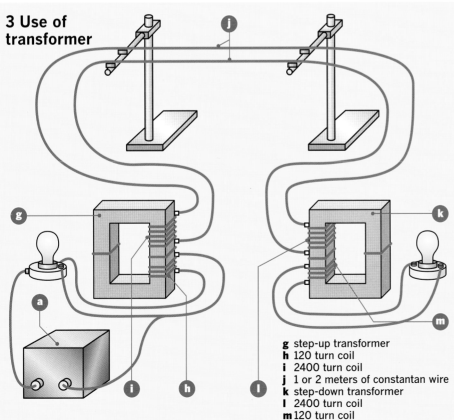

g step-up transformer
h 120 turn coil
i 2400 turn coil
j 1 or 2 meters of constantan wire
k step-down transformer
l 2400 turn coil
m 120 turn coil

1 Transmission without transformer

- The longer a wire the greater its *resistance* and the greater the loss of *electrical energy* from it as heat when a *current* flows through it.
- A drop in brightness of a lamp indicates a fall in power due to loss of electrical energy.
- Energy lost as heat from a wire, $E = I^2R$ (R—resistance of the wire; I—current). Loss of current results in a significantly larger energy reduction if electricity is transmitted long distances at large current values.
- Losses are significantly lower if electricity passes through wires with increased voltage and decreased current.

2 Transmission with transformer

- A step-up *transformer* increases voltage and decreases current.
- $V_{in}/V_{out} = n_1/n_2$ (n_1—number of turns in primary coil, n_2—number of turns in secondary coil).
- Input power = Output power (assuming 100% efficiency) and
  Power = Potential difference x Current
- If n_2 is twenty times n_1, e.m.f. induced in the secondary coil is twenty times that in the primary coil.
- Current decreases by a factor of 20 and energy losses decrease by a factor of 20^2 (400).
- In the step-down transformer n_1 is greater than n_2 thus e.m.f. is reduced and current increased.

3 Use of transformer

- step up: $n_1 = 120$, $n_2 = 2400$; voltage increases 20 fold.
- step down: $n_1 = 2400$, $n_2 = 120$; voltage decreases 20 fold.
- The similarity in brightness of the two lamps shows that little power has been lost through the wires.

© Diagram Visual Information Ltd.

Key words

current
electricity
potential
  difference
transformer

1 The grid system

- In a power station *electricity* is generated at a *potential difference* of 25,000 V. In order to reduce energy losses the potential difference is increased to 400,000 V using a step-up *transformer* for transmission through the super grid.
- Increasing the potential difference by a factor of 400,000 / 25,000 = 16 reduces the *current* by a factor of 16. Since the energy lost as heat from cables is proportional to the square of the current, this reduces the energy losses by a factor of $16^2 = 256$.
- A step-down transformer is used to reduce the potential difference to 132,000 V for transmission through the lower voltage grid.
- Electricity at a potential difference of 132,000 V is far too dangerous for domestic use so it is necessary to reduce the potential difference using step-down transformers.
- Heavy industry uses electricity at a potential difference of several thousand volts while electricity for home use is supplied at 120 V.

2 Pylon

- It is cheaper to suspend power lines from metal pylons that to bury them in the ground.
- The live cables are insulated from the pylon by large glass or porcelain insulators. A single neutral cable is run over the top of the pylon.

3 3-phase current

- If AC was transmitted in single phase the current would only reach its maximum positive and negative value once in each cycle. It is more economic to use 3-phase transmission where each phase is offset from its neighbor by 120°.

Electric power transmission 2

1 The grid system

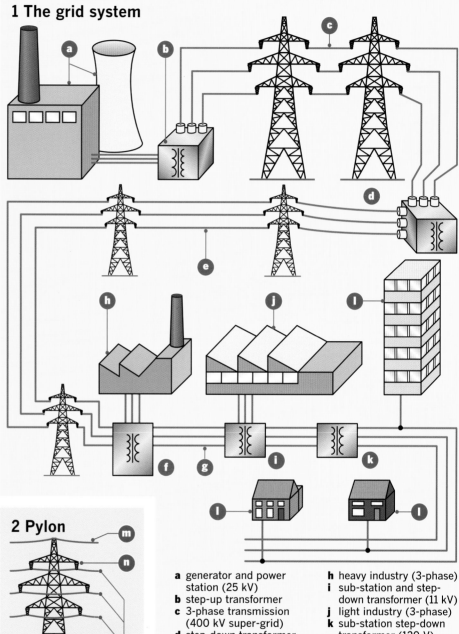

a generator and power station (25 kV)
b step-up transformer
c 3-phase transmission (400 kV super-grid)
d step-down transformer (grid switching point)
e 132 kV grid
f step-down transformer (distribution point)
g 33 kV grid

h heavy industry (3-phase)
i sub-station and step-down transformer (11 kV)
j light industry (3-phase)
k sub-station step-down transformer (120 V)
l domestic supply (single phase)
m single neutral cable
n insulators
o 3-phase transmission

2 Pylon

3 3-phase current

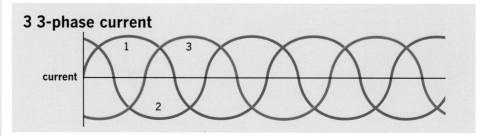

Transients: capacitor

1 Capacitor discharging through 1 MΩ resistor

Exponential decay
Time constant (T) = RC
                        = 1.0 s

The capacitor is charged by closing S_1 and discharged through R by closing S_2

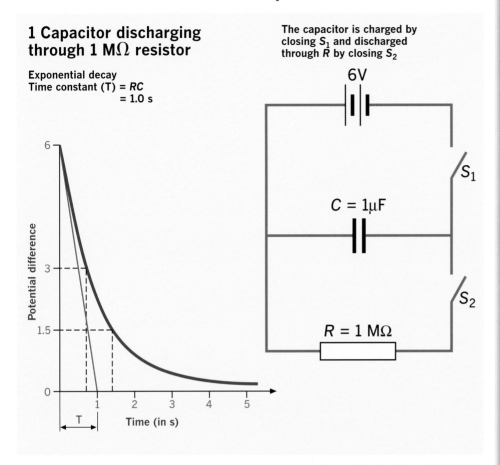

Key words

capacitor	half-life
current	potential
exponential	difference
exponential	
decay	

1 Capacitor discharging through 1 MΩ resistor

- When S_1 is closed *current* (I_c amps) flows and the *capacitor* (C farads) begins to charge. The current decreases progressively slowly to zero. *Potential difference*, V_c, initially rises rapidly and then progressively more slowly until reaching **6V**.
- The growth curves for I_c and V_c are both *exponential*. A graph of charge, Q, on the capacitor against time would have the same shape as V_c since $Q = V_cC$.
- S_1 is opened, S_2 closed, the capacitor discharges. The graph of voltage against time as the capacitor discharges is also exponential. In *exponential decay* curves a quantity decreases by the same fraction in equal time intervals. The time taken for half the original quantity to decay is the *half life* of the process.
- For capacitor value C, charged through resistor value R, and charging current constant at its starting value, the capacitor is considered fully charged after time **T** (the time constant). T = R x C seconds. (Although i decreases with time, **T** is a useful measure of a capacitor's charging and discharging time.)
- When a 1 μF capacitor discharges through a resistor of **1 MΩ**; time constant, T = R x C = 10^6 x 10^{-6} = 1s.
- Time taken for potential difference across the capacitor to fall to half its starting value (from 6 to 3 V) = $\log_e 2$ x T = 0.7 x 1 = 0.7 s.

2 Capacitor discharging through 2 MΩ resistor

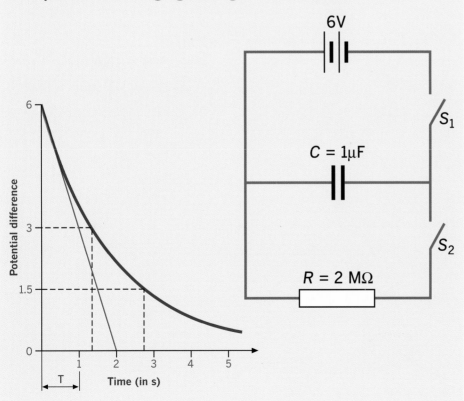

2 Capacitor discharging through 2 MΩ resistor

- If a **2 MΩ** resistor is used; T = 2 s
- The time taken for the potential difference of the capacitor to fall from 6 to 3V is 0.7 x 2 = 1.4 s.
- The larger the resistor, the longer the capacitor's discharge time.

Key words

current	exponential
electromagnetic	flux
induction	inductance
electromotive	resistance
force (e.m.f.)	self inductance

Inductor

- An inductor is a coil of wire which may either have a core of air or of some magnetic material. Inductors oppose current changes and are said to have *inductance*. Inductors use the symbol L and the unit of inductance is the henry (H).
- A *flux* is produced in the coil when the *current* passes. If the current changes the resulting flux change induces an *electromotive force* in the coil itself. This changing magnetic field type of *electromagnetic induction* is called *self induction*.
- The current in an inductor is greater if the inductance is low i.e. the coil has few turnings and does not surround a magnetic core. It is also greater if the frequency of the AC it carries is low, therefore the current changes value more slowly.

1 Investigating induction

- The induced electromagnetic force opposes the current change which causes it. When connected to a supply, the current passing through an inductor grows *exponentially* up to a maximum. The time taken for the current to rise from 0 to 0.5 A is the same as for 0.5–0.75 A and so on.
- The time constant for a circuit containing an inductor, L, and a resistor, R, is given by L/R thus it depends both on the inductance and *resistance*.

2 Effect of changing the time constant

- Increasing the size of the resistor, R, increases the time constant and decreases the maximum current that passes through the circuit.
- The time constant for a circuit containing a 1.0 henry inductor and a 2.0 ohm resistor is **2/1 = 2.0 s.**

Transients: inductor

1 Investigating induction

Exponential growth of current
Time constant
$$T = \frac{L}{R}$$
$$= 1.0 \text{ s } (T)$$
Time for current to grow from
0 to 0.5 A $= \text{Log}_e 2 \left(\frac{L}{R}\right)$
$$= 0.7 \left(\frac{L}{R}\right)$$
$$= 0.7 \text{ s}$$
Time for current to grow from
0.5A to 0.75A = 0.7 s

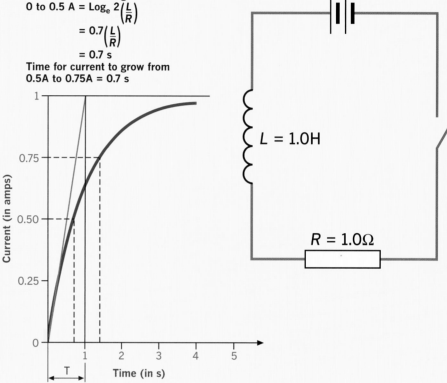

Transients in an inductor. When the switch is closed the growth of the current is recorded against time

2 Effect of changing the time constant

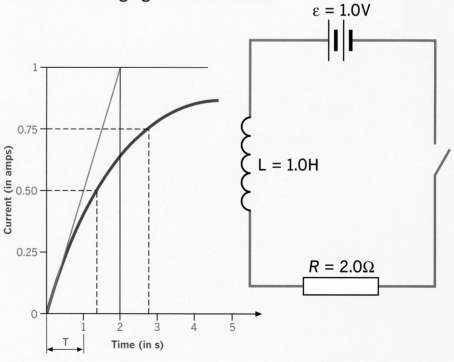

Radio

1 Transmission and reception

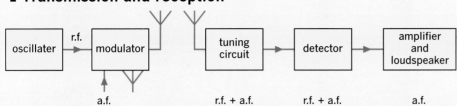

| oscillater | → r.f. → | modulator | | tuning circuit | → | detector | → | amplifier and loudspeaker |

a.f.   r.f. + a.f.   r.f. + a.f.   a.f.

2 AM and FM

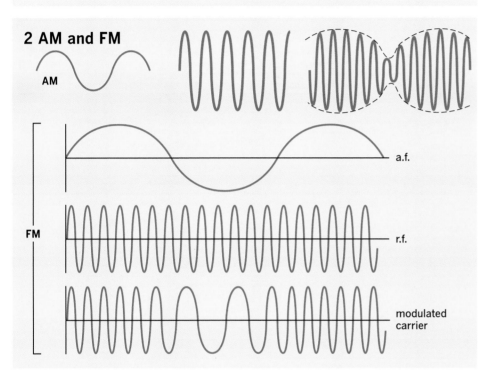

AM

FM

a.f.

r.f.

modulated carrier

3 Tuning circuit

aerial

coil L

variable capacitor C

earth

4 Demodulation

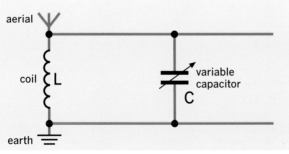

V

time

I

time

diode

amplitude modulated signal

capacitor

earphone

Key words

alternating current (AC)	electromagnetic spectrum
amplitude modulation	frequency
carrier wave	frequency modulation
demodulation	modulation
	oscillator

1 Transmission and reception

- Audio frequencies (a.f.) are *alternating currents* with *frequencies* below 20 kHv. Radio frequencies (r.f.) have frequencies above 20 kHz. In radio a.f. is combined with r.f. in order to send it over long distances.
- A transmitter is an *oscillator* that produces an r.f. current. If connected directly to an aerial it would send out an *electromagnetic* wave called a *carrier wave* Before transmission the r.f. signal is modified or *modulated* to carry the a.f.
- In a receiver the tuning circuit selects the wanted signal from the aerial The detector or *demodulator* separates the a.f. from the r.f. carrier signal.

2 AM and FM

- In *amplitude modulation* (AM) the speech or music from, for example, a microphone is used to vary the amplitude of the carrier wave so that it follows the wave shape of the a.f.
- In *frequency modulation* (FM) the frequency of the carrier wave varies with the information signal. It increases if the information signal is positive and decreases if it is negative.

3 Tuning circuit

- All radio waves of different frequencies induce a signal in the aerial of a radio receiver. If the aerial is connected to an L-C circuit only the signal whose frequency equals the natural frequency of the L-C circuit is selected. This is an example of electrical resonance. The radio is tuned to different radio stations by varying the value of C.

4 Demodulation

- In demodulation the a.f. which was added to the r.f. carrier wave is retrieved.

Key words

cathode ray
  oscilloscope
electron
fluorescence

1 Electron beam tracks screen

- A television is, in essence, a *cathode ray oscilloscope* with two time bases which cause a beam of electrons tracks across the screen in a sequence of horizontal lines. When *electrons* hit the screen they cause the *fluorescent* coating to glow. A picture is produced when an incoming signal alters the number of electrons which travel from the electron gun to the screen. On the screen of a black and white television this causes the brightness of spots to vary between white through different shades of gray to black.

- A complete new picture appears on the screen every 1/25th of a second. Each new picture is slightly different from the previous one but persistence of vision gives the effect of a continuous picture rather than a sequence of stills.

2 Color image formation

- In a color television there are three electron guns. The fluorescent screen is coated with around a million tiny light-emitting dots arranged in triangles.

- In each triangle there is one dot that emits red light when hit by electrons, one which emits blue light and a third that emits green light.

- A metal shadow mask ensures that the electrons from one gun only hit red light emitting dots, electrons from another gun only hit blue dots, and electrons from the third gun only hit green dots.

- All colors are made by combining dots of these three colors in different intensities. For example, in a triangle of dots, if the electron beams to the red and green dots are intense while the electron beam to the blue dot is not then the dot will emit red and green lights strongly and appear yellow.

Television

1 Electron beam tracks screen

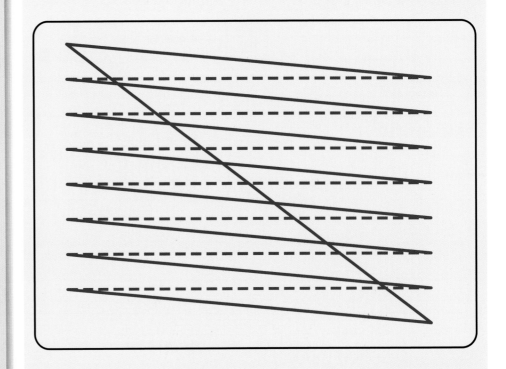

2 Color image formation

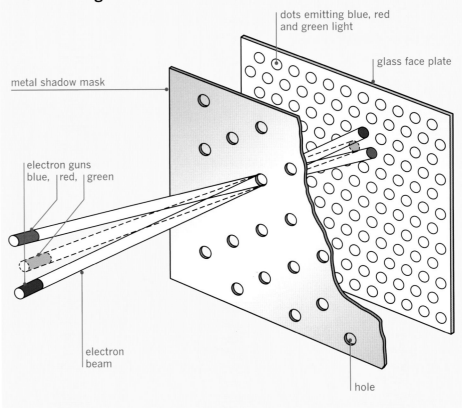

dots emitting blue, red and green light

glass face plate

metal shadow mask

electron guns
blue, red, green

electron beam

hole

AC theory 1

1 AC as sine wave

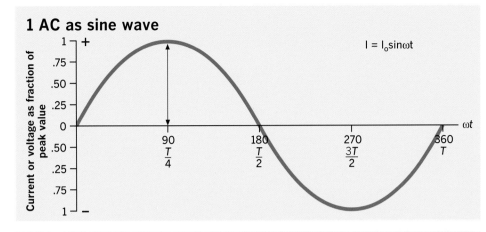

$I = I_0\sin\omega t$

2 Phase difference

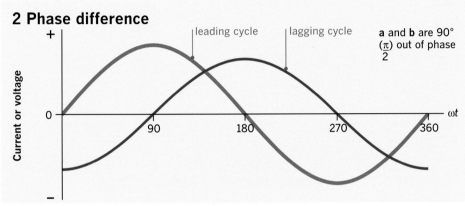

leading cycle　　lagging cycle

a and **b** are 90°
$\left(\dfrac{\pi}{2}\right)$ out of phase

3 Voltage across capacitor

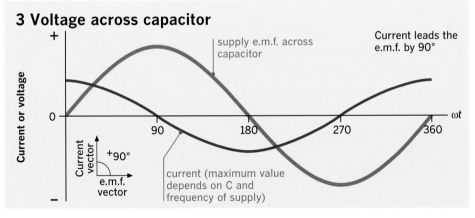

supply e.m.f. across capacitor

Current leads the e.m.f. by 90°

Current vector
+90°
e.m.f. vector

current (maximum value depends on C and frequency of supply)

4 AC in inductor

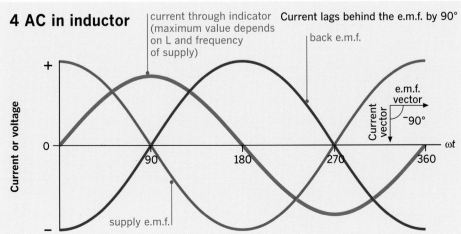

current through indicator (maximum value depends on L and frequency of supply)

Current lags behind the e.m.f. by 90°

back e.m.f.

e.m.f. vector
Current vector
−90°

supply e.m.f.

Key words

alternating current (AC)
amplitude
capacitance
capacitor

electromotive force (e.m.f.)
frequency
inductance
phase
sine wave

1 AC as sine wave

● An *alternating current* is conveniently represented as a *sine wave*.

2 Phase difference

● This shows two alternating currents which are out of phase, i.e. they do not reach maximum and minimum values at the same points.

3 Voltage across capacitor

● Alternating current flows around a circuit containing a *capacitor* because the capacitor plates are continually being charged and discharged and then charged the opposite way around by the alternating voltage.

● If the *amplitude* of the *current* is denoted by the amplitude of the voltage, V_m, and its *frequency* by f, instantaneous voltage, V, at time, t, is $V = V_m\sin\pi ft$.

● If C is the *capacitance* of a capacitor the charge on its plates is given by $Q = CV$ therefore $Q = CV_m\sin\pi ft$.

● The current flowing at any instant, I, equals the rate at which charge is accumulating on the capacitor plates.

$$I = \frac{dQ}{dt} = \frac{d(CV_m\sin\pi ft)}{dt} = 2\pi fCV_m\cos 2\pi ft$$

4 AC in inductor

● If the amplitude of the current is I_m, and frequency f, instantaneous current, i, at time, t, is:
$I = I_m\sin 2\pi ft$.
If L is the *inductance* of a coil the changing current sets up a back *electromotive force*, E, in the coil of magnitude

$$E = \frac{LdI}{dt} = \frac{Ld(I_m\sin 2\pi ft)}{dt} = 2\pi fLI_m\cos 2\pi ft$$

● To maintain the current the applied supply voltage must equal the back electromotive force.

Key words

capacitor
current
impedance
induction coil
phase

potential
difference
resistance
vector

1 Resistor and capacitor

- When an alternating *potential difference* (p.d.), V, is applied across a *resistance*, R, and a *capacitor*, C, connected in series the same *current*, I, flows through each component so the reference *vector* will be that representing the current. The p.d. across the resistor is in *phase* with the current while the that across the capacitor lags by 90°.
- The resultant voltage, $V = I\sqrt{(R_2 + X_c^2)}$ where X_c is the reactance of C.
- The impedance, Z, of the circuit is $\sqrt{(R_2 + X_c^2)}$. It is a measure of the opposition to the alternating current and is measured in ohms.
$$Z = \frac{V}{I} = \sqrt{(R_2 + X_c^2)}$$

2 Resistor and inductor

- Alternating p.d., V, is aplied across a resistance, R, and an *induction coil*, L, connected in series. The same current flows through each component so the reference vector will once again be that representing the current. The p.d. across the resistor is in phase with the current while the p.d. across the induction coil leads by 90°.
For this circuit the resultant voltage, $V = \sqrt{(R_2 + X_L^2)}$ where X_L is the reactance of L.
$$Z = \frac{V}{I} = \sqrt{(R_2 + X_L^2)}$$

3 Inductor, capacitor, resistor

- An LCR circuit contains an induction coil, a capacitor and a resistor in series. The p.d. across the induction coil leads the current (reference) vector by 90° while that across the capacitor lags by 90°.
$$V = I\sqrt{[R_2 + (X_L - X_C)^2]}$$
and the *impedance* is given by
$$Z = \frac{V}{I} = \sqrt{[R_2 + (X_L - X_C)^2]}$$

AC theory 2

1 Resistance and capacitor

Impedence diagram

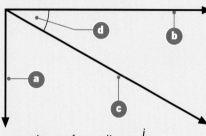

a reactance of capacitor $= \frac{j}{\omega C}$

b resistance $= R$

c impedence $= [R^2 + (\frac{1}{\omega^2 C^2})]^{\frac{1}{2}}$

d phase angle $= \tan^{-1}(\omega CR)$

2 Resistor and inductor

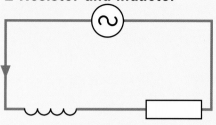

Impedence diagram

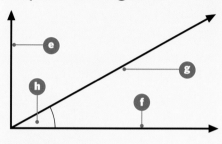

e reactance $= j\omega L$

f resistance $= R$

g impedence $= (R^2 + \omega^2 L^2)^{\frac{1}{2}}$

h phase angle $= \tan^{-1} \frac{\omega L}{R}$

3 Inductor, capacitor, resistor

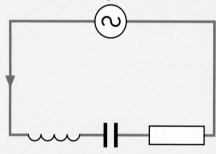

Impedence diagram

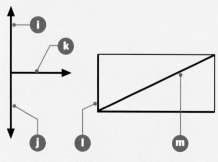

i reactance of $L = j\omega L$

j reactance of $C = \frac{j}{\omega L}$

k resistance $= R$

l total reactance $= j\omega L - \frac{j}{\omega C}$

m impedence $= [R^2 + (\omega L - \frac{1}{\omega C})^2]^{\frac{1}{2}}$

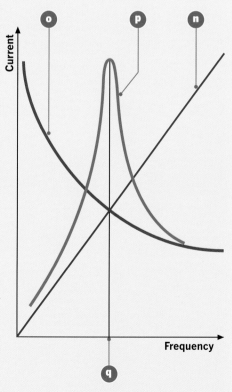

n capacitance on its own

o inductor on its own

p L and C in series (resistance in circuit comes from resistance of inductor)

q resonant frequency $= \frac{1}{2\pi} \sqrt{\frac{1}{LC}}$

R.C. network 1: AC response

Key words

frequency
high pass filter
short-circuit

1 Crossover circuit

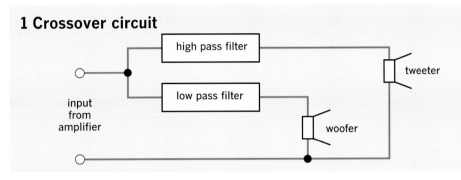

2 Low pass filter

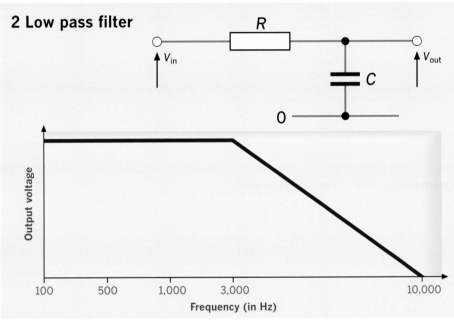

3 High pass filter

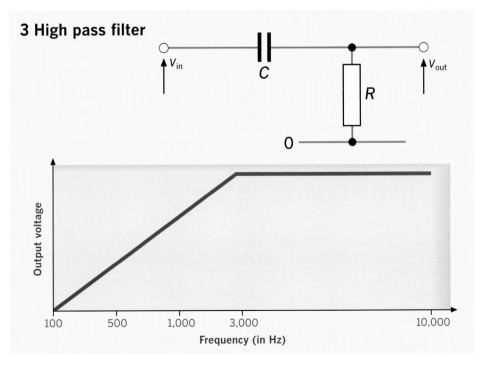

1 Crossover circuit

- More than one loudspeaker is needed to handle the full range of *frequencies*. In practice a large loudspeaker, called a woofer, deals with low frequencies while a smaller loudspeaker, called a tweeter, deals with high frequencies. Sometimes a third speaker may be present to deal with middle frequencies.
- The appropriate range of frequencies is directed to each speaker by a crossover circuit. The low pass filter passes low frequencies while blocking high frequencies. The high pass filter has the opposite effect.
- A common crossover frequency is 3 kHz. Frequencies above this go mostly to the tweeter while frequencies below this go mostly to the woofer.

2 Low pass filter

- In the low pass filter high frequencies in the input are *short-circuited* by the capacitor, **C**, and do not reach the output. **R** and **C** act as a potential divider across the input with **C** offering a much lower impedance to high frequencies than to low ones therefore there is very little high frequency voltage in the output.

3 High pass filter

- In the *high pass filter* **C** blocks out the low frequencies but allows high frequencies to pass to the output.

© Diagram Visual Information Ltd.

Key words

capacitor
frequency
resistance
square wave
waveform

R.C. network 2: AC response

1 Response of RC network to varying input frequency

- The time constant, **T**, for an R.C. network is equal to the product of the *capacitor* (expressed in farads) and *resistor* (expressed in ohms). When a *square wave* is input to an R.C. network the waveform of the output is dependent on the *frequency* of the *alternating current*.
- When the frequency is much less than **1/T** the capacitor has sufficient time to charge up and the output wave is very similar in shape to the input wave.
- When the frequency is much greater than **1/T** the capacitor has insufficient time to charge up and the output wave is triangular in form and greatly smoothed.
- When the frequency is equal to **1/T** the output *waveform* is triangular but not symmetrical.

2 Spike generator

- When the input is at +5V the capacitor becomes fully charged with positive charge to the left and negative charge to the right. When the input voltage drops to 0V, the capacitor discharges causing a negative spike as negative charge leaves it.
- When the input voltage jumps from 0V to 5V, negative charge is attracted to the left of the capacitor as it charges up and a positive spike occurs. As the capacitor becomes more charged the positive output falls.

1 Response of R.C. network to varying input frequency

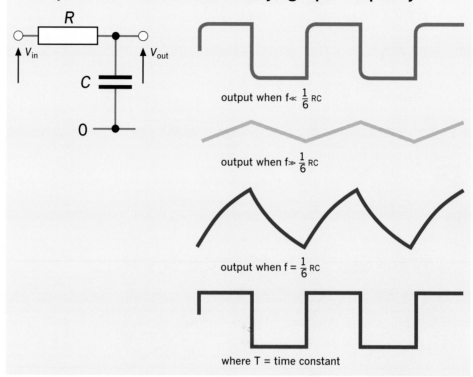

output when $f \ll \frac{1}{6}$ RC

output when $f \gg \frac{1}{6}$ RC

output when $f = \frac{1}{6}$ RC

where T = time constant

2 Spike generator

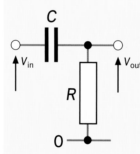

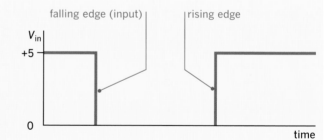

falling edge (input)   rising edge

V_{in}
+5

0   time

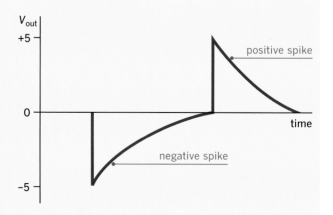

V_{out}
+5

positive spike

0   time

negative spike

−5

Electricity in the car

Key words

accumulator	potential
battery	difference
current	solenoid
earth	
electrical energy	

1 Wiring diagram for car

a storage battery
b current when dynamo is charging the battery
c alternator (dynamo)
d current from dynamo or battery
e ignition key switch
f fuses
g headlights and sidelights
h ignition coil
i windscreen wiper motor
j earth connection to chassis

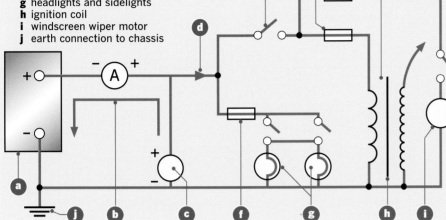

1 Wiring diagram for car

● A car is supplied with electricity from a storage *battery* or *accumulator*. The car chassis is connected to the negative terminal so circuits run from the positive terminal through the electrical device to *earth* on the chassis.
● *Electrical energy* is used for the ignition system and for a variety of accessories including lighting and windshield wipers. When the engine is running it drives an alternator which recharges the accumulator.

2 Starter motor circuit

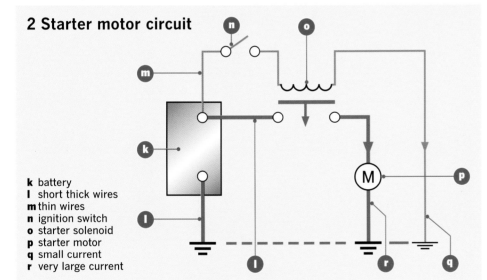

k battery
l short thick wires
m thin wires
n ignition switch
o starter solenoid
p starter motor
q small current
r very large current

2 Starter motor circuit

● A *current* of the order of 100 A is needed to drive the starter and thick wires are needed to carry such a current. To avoid having to run these wires to the ignition switch, the high current circuit is controlled by a low current circuit using a *solenoid*.
● When the low current circuit is completed by turning the ignition key, the solenoid throws a switch which completes the high current circuit causing the starter to turn over the engine until it starts running.
● Releasing the ignition key opens the low current circuit and reverses the action of the solenoid which, in turn, opens the high current circuit.

3 Ignition circuit

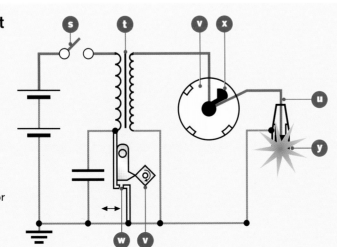

s ignition switch
t ignition coil
u spark plug
v parts of the distributor (cam and rotor)
w contacts
x rotor arm
y spark inside engine

3 Ignition circuit

● In a petrol engine, a mixture of petrol vapor and air is ignited inside a series of four (normally) cylinders using spark plugs.
● Current at a high *potential difference* is provided by an ignition coil. It passes through the spark plug causing a spark to jump across a gap at its base, igniting the gaseous mixture.
● The distributor and a series of high tension leads determine the sequence in which the spark plugs fire.

© Diagram Visual Information Ltd.

Circuit symbols 1

Components–symbols and function in circuits

● Electronic symbols are used in electric circuits in order to represent components. The use of these symbols is universal so a circuit can be read and understood by physicists who speak different languages.

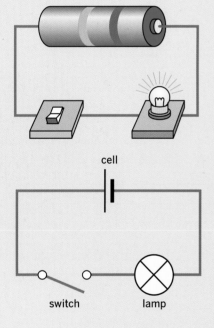

cell

switch   lamp

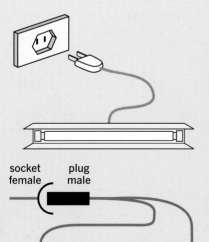

socket   plug
female   male

fluorescent
tube lamp

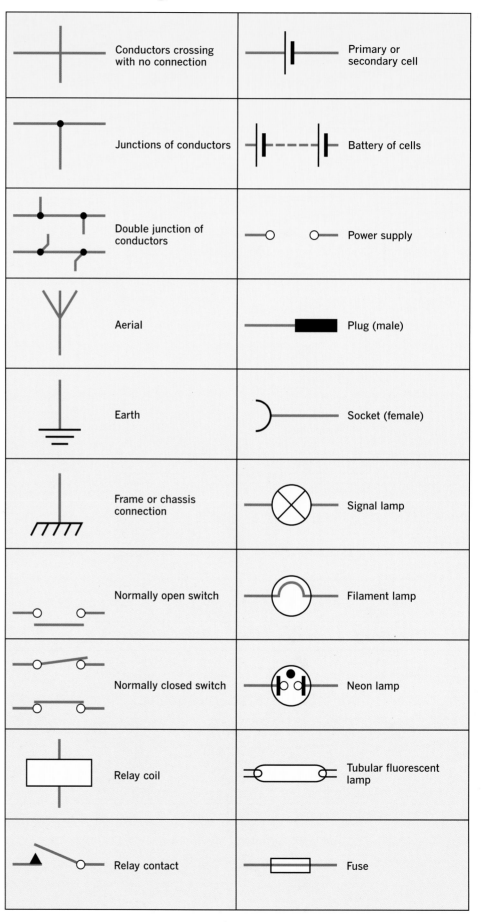

Symbol	Description	Symbol	Description
	Conductors crossing with no connection		Primary or secondary cell
	Junctions of conductors		Battery of cells
	Double junction of conductors		Power supply
	Aerial		Plug (male)
	Earth		Socket (female)
	Frame or chassis connection		Signal lamp
	Normally open switch		Filament lamp
	Normally closed switch		Neon lamp
	Relay coil		Tubular fluorescent lamp
	Relay contact		Fuse

Circuit symbols 2

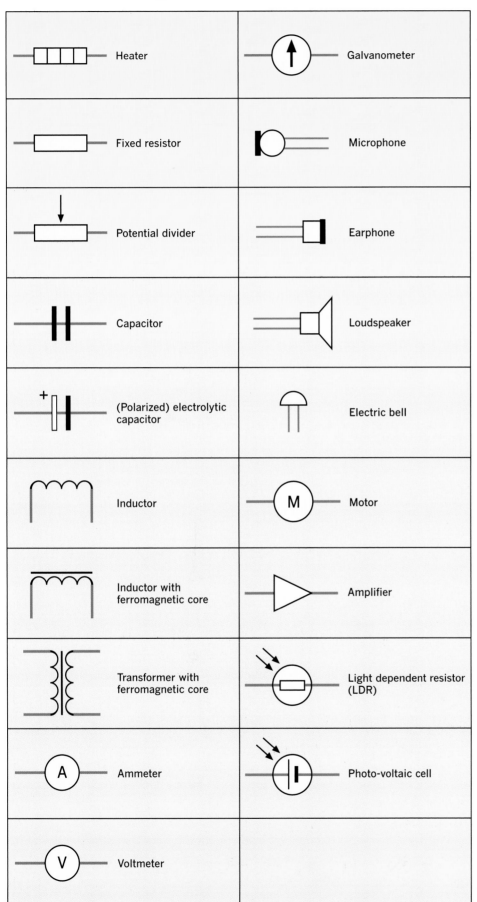

Heater	Galvanometer
Fixed resistor	Microphone
Potential divider	Earphone
Capacitor	Loudspeaker
(Polarized) electrolytic capacitor	Electric bell
Inductor	Motor
Inductor with ferromagnetic core	Amplifier
Transformer with ferromagnetic core	Light dependent resistor (LDR)
Ammeter	Photo-voltaic cell
Voltmeter	

Key words

amplifier	galvanometer
capacitor	light-dependent
cell	resistor (LDR)
electrolytic	
capacitor	

Components–symbols and function in circuits

● Electronic symbols are used in electric circuits in order to represent components. The use of these symbols is universal so a circuit can be read and understood by physicists who speak different languages.

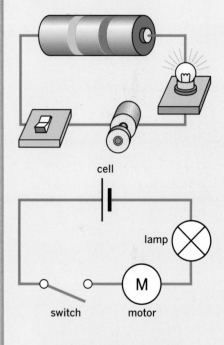

cell

lamp

switch   motor

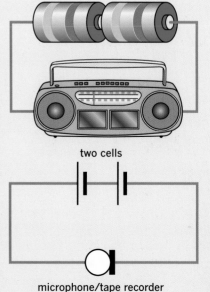

two cells

microphone/tape recorder

Key words

diode	*transistor*
light-emitting diode (LED)	*zener diode*
thermistor	
thyristor	

Semiconductor components

- Diodes and transistors are formed of semiconductor materials such as silicon and germanium crystals. The material is treated in one of two ways. Either an impurity such as arsenic is added, to give the material an excess of electrons, forming an n-type semiconductor, or an impurity such as boron is added to give the material fewer electrons (p-type semiconductor).
- A diode consists of an n-type layer fixed to a p-type layer.
- The connector from the p-type layer forms the anode and that from the n-type layer forms the cathode. When connected in a circuit in this way (forward bias), charge carriers in the diode move to the junction between the layers and current flows. If the diode is connected the opposite way, (reverse bias) either no current flows or, if a large voltage is applied, the diode breaks down.
- A bipolar transistor consists of three layers – either a layer of p-type material sandwiched between two n-type layers (n-p-n junction transistor) or a layer of n-type sandwiched between two p-type layers (p-n-p junction transistor). Each layer has a connector, they are called the base, the collector and the emitter.

Variability of components

- The function of many electronic circuits depends on small changes caused by sensors which operate within certain known ranges, such as thermistors, whose resistance falls with increased temperature. In order for circuits to function correctly in response to signals from sensors, some components, such as resistors can be adjusted to particular values.

Circuit symbols 3

Semiconductor components

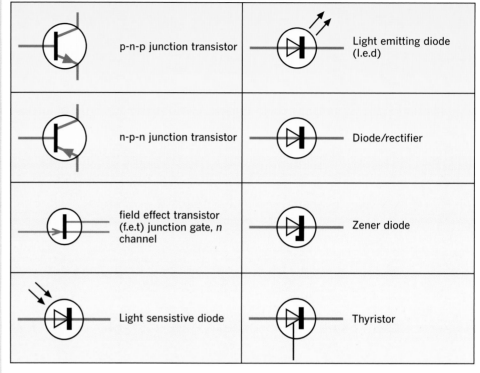

Symbol	Description
	p-n-p junction transistor
	Light emitting diode (l.e.d)
	n-p-n junction transistor
	Diode/rectifier
	field effect transistor (f.e.t) junction gate, *n* channel
	Zener diode
	Light sensitive diode
	Thyristor

Variability of components

The addition of variability to resistive, capacitative or inductive symbols is indicated as follows

Symbol	Description of symbol when placed across the component symbol
	indicates a variability of value which may, or may not, be continuous
	indicates that the component may be pre-set to a particular value
	indicates that it has an inherent non-linear variability

The following examples illustrate the use of these symbols

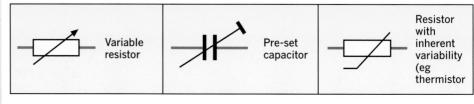

Variable resistor

Pre-set capacitor

Resistor with inherent variability (eg thermistor)

Semiconductor diodes

1 Diode

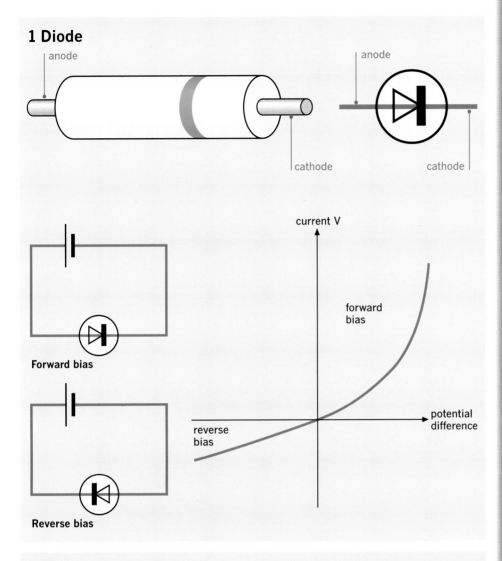

anode

cathode

anode

cathode

Forward bias

Reverse bias

current V

forward bias

reverse bias

potential difference

2 LED

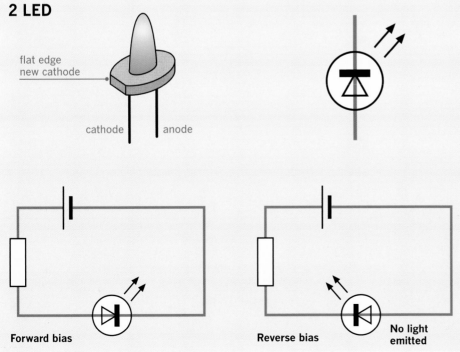

flat edge new cathode

cathode   anode

Forward bias

Reverse bias   **No light emitted**

Key words

anode
cathode
cell
current
diode

filament
light-emitting
   diode (LED)
resistance

1 Diode

- A *diode* allows *current* to pass in one direction only. The end marked with a band is the *cathode* which should be connected to the *cell's* negative terminal. The other end (*anode*) should be connected to the cell's positive terminal.
- When anode and cathode are connected to a cell's positive and negative terminals the diode is forward biased. Its *resistance* is very low and current flows through it. Conventional current travels in the direction of the arrow in the diode symbol.
- When the diode is connected in the opposite orientation it is said to be reverse biased. It has a very high resistance and does not conduct.
- When a diode is forward biased it does not begin to conduct until the turn-on voltage (about 0.6 V for silicon diodes and 0.1 V for germanium diodes) is reached. A small increase in voltage then causes a large increase in current.
- Every diode has a maximum forward current (forward current rating) which should not be exceeded or the diode overheats and may be destroyed.

2 LED

- A *light emitting diode* (*LED*) is made from gallium arsenide phosphide. LEDs look like tiny *filament* lamps and may emit red, yellow or green light when forward biased. They do not emit light when reverse biased.
- An LED should not be connected into a circuit without a series resistor to limit the current or it could be destroyed.
- LEDs are used as indicator or signal lamps in electronic equipment. They are smaller, more reliable, last longer, respond faster and need less current than filament lamps.

Key words

amplifier
battery
current
transistor

1 Bipolar transistor

- A bipolar *transistor* has three connections—the collector (C), the base (B) and the emitter (E).
- There are two main bipolar transistor types; the n-p-n and the p-n-p type.
- In the n-p-n type the base current enters by B and leaves by E. At the same time the collector current enters by C and leaves by E. The emitter current is a combination of the base and collector currents.
- When the switch is open the base *current* is zero. Neither lamp lights up indicating that the collector current is also zero although the *battery* is connected across the collector and emitter.
- When the switch is closed the base is connected to the positive terminal of the battery through the resistor. L_2 lights up but not L_1 showing that the collector current is much greater than the base current, which is too small to illuminate L_1.
- If the base current is considered as the transistor's input and the collector current its output, the transistor acts as an *amplifier* since the collector current is greater than the base current. The collector current tends to be 10 to 1000 times greater than the base current. The bipolar transistor is a current control device.

2 Field effect transistor

- A field effect transistor (FET) has three connections—the drain (D), the gate (G) and the source (S).
- In an FET the input voltage at the gate controls the output current at the drain. The input current is usually negligible due to the high input resistance of the FET compared to a bipolar transistor.

Transistors

1 Bipolar transistor

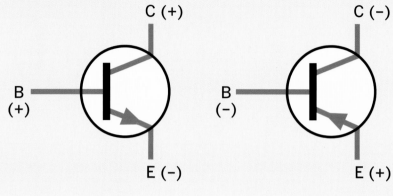

n-p-n type   p-n-p type

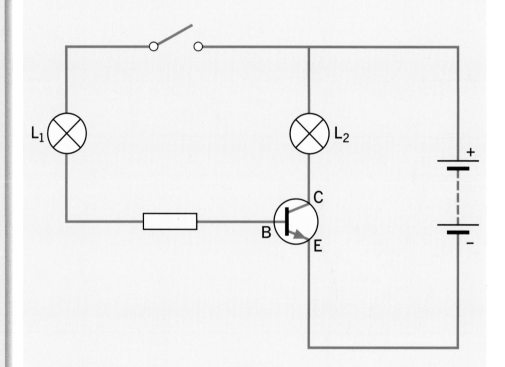

2 Field effect transistor

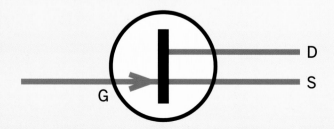

Integrated circuits

1 Integrated circuit

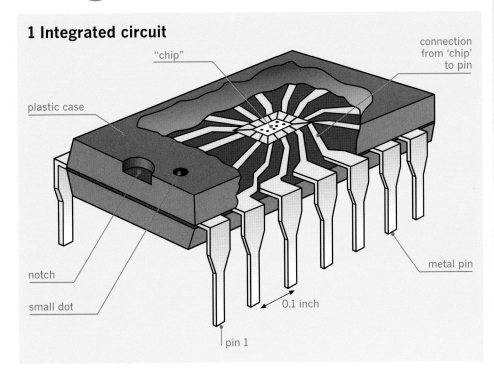

connection from 'chip' to pin

"chip"

plastic case

notch

small dot

metal pin

0.1 inch

pin 1

1 Integrated circuit

● An *integrated circuit* consists of integrated rather than discrete electronic components. A single integrated circuit may contain thousands of *diodes*, resistors, *transistors* and small *capacitors*, all etched onto a small chip of silicon.

2 Analog signal

● In linear and *analog* integrated circuits signals are often electrical representations of physical quantities, such as sound, which change continuously and smoothly over a range of values between some minimum and maximum points.

● This type of integrated circuit includes many kinds of amplifier circuit including the *operational amplifier* or op amp.

3 Digital

● *Digital* integrated circuits deal with signals which can have one of only two possible outputs; low (near 0 V) and high (near the supply voltage, typically 5 V).

● This type of integrated circuit includes *logic gates*, memories and *microprocessors*.

2 Analog signal

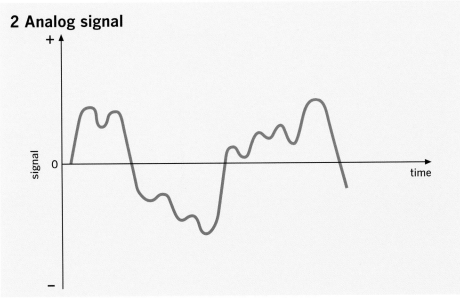

signal

0

time

3 Digital

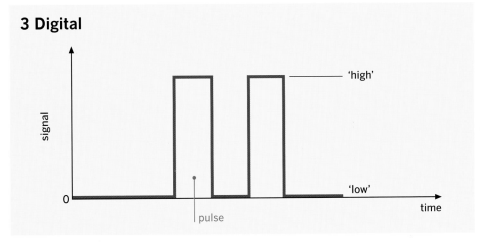

signal

'high'

'low'

0

pulse

time

Key words

logic gate
truth table

1 Logic gates

- The input to a *logic gate* can have only one of two values. It can be low e.g. near 0 V and indicated by "0," or it can be high e.g. close to the supply voltage of typically 5-6 V and indicated by "1."
- A *truth table* for a logic gate indicates the output for all possible inputs.
- Different logic gates are different shapes and the type is sometimes written on them in circuit diagrams.

2 Logic gates with truth tables

- AND gate—output is only high when both inputs are high, otherwise the output is low. A and B is written A.B.
- NAND (NOT AND) gate—logic output of any logic gate is reversed if the symbol is modified by adding a small circle to the base of the output. Output is low when both inputs are high. For all other combinations of input output is high.
- OR gate—logic output is high if either or both of the inputs are low. A or B is written A+B.
- NOR (NOT OR) gate—logic output is the reverse of an OR gate.
- EXOR (exclusive OR) gate—output is high when either input is high but not when both are high.
- NEXOR (NOT exclusive OR) gate—logic output is the reverse of an exclusive OR gate.
- NOT gate—sometimes called an inverter since output is always the logical opposite to the input. Output is high when inputs are low, and low when inputs are high.
- NOT gate from NAND gate—the inputs of a NAND gate can be linked to form a gate which has the same logic as a NOT gate.
- NOT gate from NOR gate—the inputs of a NOR gate can be linked to form a NOT gate.

Logic gates and their truth tables

1 AND

B	A	Output
0	0	0
0	1	0
1	0	0
1	1	1

2 NAND

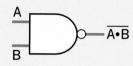

B	A	Output
0	0	1
0	1	1
1	0	1
1	1	0

3 OR

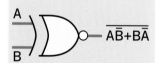

B	A	Output
0	0	0
0	1	1
1	0	1
1	1	1

4 NOR

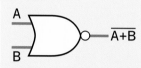

B	A	Output
0	0	1
0	1	0
1	0	0
1	1	0

5 EXOR

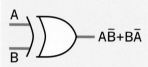

B	A	Output
0	0	0
0	1	1
1	0	1
1	1	0

6 NEXOR

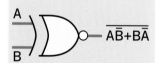

B	A	Output
0	0	1
0	1	0
1	0	0
1	1	1

7 NOT

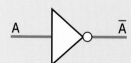

A	Output
0	1
1	0

8 NOT (from NAND)

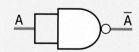

A	Output
0	1
1	0

9 NOT (from NOR)

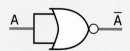

A	Output
0	1
1	0

NAND equivalents

Key words

logic gate

1 NOR gate

A	B	C	D	E	Q
0	0	1	1	0	1
0	1	1	0	1	0
1	0	0	1	1	0
1	1	0	0	1	0

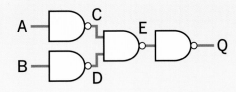

2 OR gate

A	B	C	D	Q
0	0	1	1	0
0	1	1	0	1
1	0	0	1	1
1	1	0	0	1

3 AND gate

A	B	C	Q
0	0	1	0
0	1	1	0
1	0	1	0
1	1	0	1

4 EXOR gate

A	B	C	D	E	F	Q
0	0	1	1	1	1	0
0	1	1	0	0	1	1
1	0	0	1	1	0	1
1	1	0	0	1	1	0

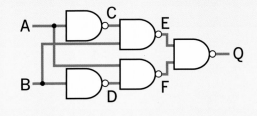

Combinations of NAND gates

- Combinations of NAND *logic gates* can have the same logic as a single logic gate.
- The logic of a combination of gates can be followed by considering the output of each gate.
- When both inputs to a logic gate are linked it is sometime shown only as one input.

1 NOR gate

- The logic of this combination of NAND gates is the same as a single NOR gate.

2 OR gate

- The logic of this combination of NAND gates is the same as a single OR gate.

3 AND gate

- The logic of this combination of NAND gates is the same as a single AND gate.

4 Exclusive OR (EXOR) gate

- The logic of this combination of NAND gates is the same as a single exclusive OR gate.

© Diagram Visual Information Ltd.

Combinations of NOR gates

- Combinations of NOR *logic gates* can have the same logic as a single logic gate.
- The logic of a combination of gates can be followed by considering the output of each gate.
- When both inputs to a logic gate are linked it is sometime shown only as one input.

1 NAND gate

- The logic of this combination of NOR gates is the same as a single NAND gate.

2 AND gate

- The logic of this combination of NOR gates is the same as a single AND gate.

3 OR gate

- The logic of this combination of NOR gates is the same as a single OR gate.

4 Exclusive OR (EXOR) gate

- The logic of this combination of NOR gates is the same as a single exclusive OR gate.

NOR equivalents

1 NAND gate

A	B	C	D	E	Q
0	0	1	1	0	1
0	1	1	0	0	1
1	0	0	1	0	1
1	1	0	0	1	0

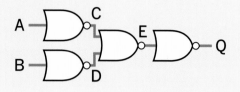

2 AND gate

A	B	C	D	Q
0	0	1	1	0
0	1	1	0	0
1	0	0	1	0
1	1	0	0	1

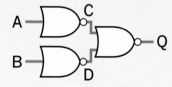

3 OR gate

A	B	C	Q
0	0	1	0
0	1	0	1
1	0	0	1
1	1	0	1

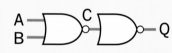

4 EXOR gate

A	B	C	D	E	F	Q
0	0	1	1	1	0	0
0	1	0	1	0	0	1
1	0	0	0	1	0	1
1	1	0	0	0	1	0

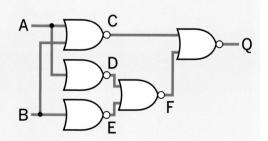

CMOS chips showing pin connections

Key words

bistable
Complementary
 Metal Oxide
 Semiconductor
 chip (CMOS)

logic gate

1 4001 quad 2-input NOR gate

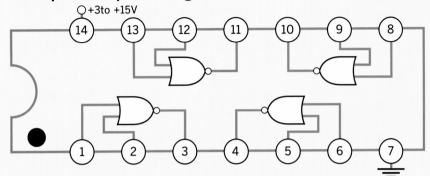

2 4002 dual 4-input NOR gate

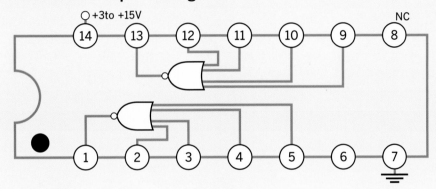

3 4010 hex non-inverting buffer

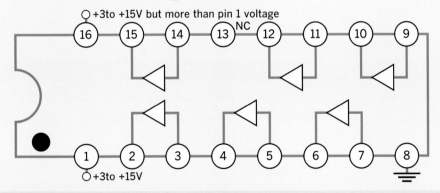

4 4044 quad R/S flip-flop (NAND logic)

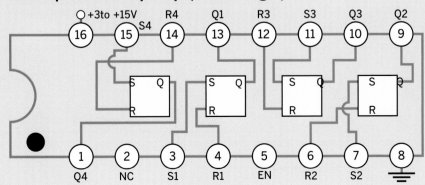

CMOS chips
- *CMOS chips* require supply voltage of 3–15 V and draw very low current but have a relatively slow switching speed.

1 4001 quad 2-input NOR gate
- Supply voltage is connected across pins 14 and 7 (pin 14 connected to positive terminal).
- The remaining pins are the inputs and outputs of four independent NOR gates. These could be connected to give the same logic as another single *logic gate*.

2 4002 dual 4-input NOR gate
- Supply voltage is connected across pins 14 and 7; pins 6 and 8 do not connect to any component of the integrated circuit.
- The remaining pins are the inputs and outputs of two 4-input NOR gates.

3 4010 hex non-inverting buffer
- Positive terminal of the supply voltage is connected to pins 16 and 1; pin 8 is connected to earth; pin 13 does not connect to any component of the integrated circuit.
- The remaining pins are the inputs and outputs of six non-inverting buffers.

4 4044 quad R/S flip-flop (NAND logic)
- An R/S *bistable* is a switching circuit with two outputs. One is high when the other is low. The outputs are complementary (changing low output to high changes high output to low).
- Each state is stable (bistable). A state is retained or stored until the bistable is triggered when one output flips from 0 to 1 and the other flops from 1 to 0 (alternative name—flip-flop).

© Diagram Visual Information Ltd.

Key words

Boolean algebra

Operators
- "+" denotes OR
- "•" denotes AND
- "‾" denotes NOT.

1 Basic functions
- OR function—when A is combined with 0 the output is always A no matter whether it is high or low. When A is combined with 1 the output is always 1. When A is combined with itself the output is always the value of A. When A is combined with not A the outcome is always 1.
- AND function—when A is combined with 0 the output is always 0 no matter whether it is high or low. When A is combined with 1 the output is always A. When A is combined with itself the output is always the value of A. When A is combined with not A the outcome is always 0.
- NOT function—NOT (NOT A) equals A.
- Commutation—functions using OR operators and AND operators can be performed in any order.

2 Association
- Brackets may be disregarded as operations may be performed in any order.

3 Distribution
- An operator is distributed over its terms (giving precedence to one operator over the other).

4 De Morgan's theorem
- Rule governing relations between pairs of logical operators when simplifying a long bar symbol.

Boolean algebra

1 Basic functions

$$0 + A = A$$
$$1 + A = 1$$
$$A + A = A$$
$$A + \overline{A} = 1$$

OR function

$$0 \cdot A = 0$$
$$1 \cdot A = A$$
$$A \cdot A + A$$
$$A \cdot \overline{A} = 0$$

AND function

$$\overline{\overline{A}} = A$$

NOT function

$$A + B = B + A$$
$$A \cdot B = B \cdot A$$

Commutation

2 Association

$$A + (B + C) = (A + B) + C$$
$$A \cdot (B \cdot C) = (A \cdot B) \cdot C$$

3 Distribution

$$A \cdot (A + B) = A \cdot B + A \cdot C$$
$$(A + B) \cdot (B + A) = A + B \cdot C$$

4 De Morgan's theorem

$$(\overline{A + B}) = \overline{A} \cdot \overline{B}$$
$$(\overline{A \cdot B}) = \overline{A} + \overline{B}$$

Combinational logic design 1

Key words

binary code   logic gate
light-dependent
  resistor (LDR)
light-emitting
  diode (LED)

1 Burglar alarm

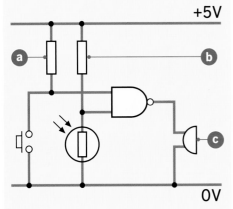

a,b pull-up resistor – to keep input high
when switch is open and no light is
shining on the LDR
Note: CMOS inputs must not float
c buzzer

2 Automatic night light

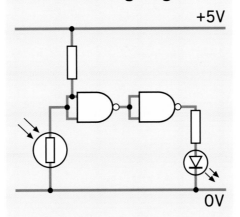

3 2-bit decoder

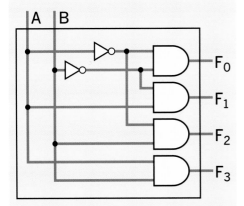

Truth table

B	A	F_0	F_1	F_2	F_3
0	0	1	0	0	0
0	1	0	1	0	0
1	0	0	0	1	0
1	1	0	0	0	1

4 2-bit encoder

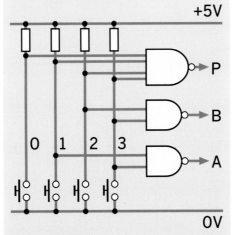

Truth table

0	1	2	3	B	A	P
0	1	1	1	0	0	1
1	0	1	1	0	1	1
1	1	0	1	1	0	1
1	1	1	0	1	1	1
1	1	1	1	X	X	0

1 Burglar alarm

- The *light-dependent resistor (LDR)*
  and the adjacent resistor act as a
  potential divider. In the dark the
  resistance of the LDR is high and both
  inputs to the NAND gate are high and
  the output is 0.
- When light shines on the LDR its
  resistance drops and that input to the
  NAND gate becomes low. The result is
  an output of 1 which causes the
  buzzer to sound.

2 Automatic night light

- During the day the LDR is illuminated
  and its resistance is low. The low input
  to the first NAND gate is inverted to
  give a high input to the second NAND
  gate. The high input to the second
  NAND gate is inverted to give a low
  output so the LED is not lit.
- As it goes dark the resistance of the
  LDR rises and gives a high input to the
  first NAND gate. This is inverted,
  giving a low input to the second
  inverting NAND gate. The resulting
  high output from the second NAND
  gate turns the *LED* on.

3 2-bit decoder and truth table

- A decoder converts a *binary* input
  into a form which can be displayed.
  The network of AND and NOT gates
  provide a different output for each
  different combination of inputs from A
  and B.

4 2-bit encoder and truth table

- An encoder converts an input into a
  binary output. Closing a switch causes
  the voltage across the wire to fall.
  Closing each different combination of
  the switches produces a unique output
  from A and B.

Combinational logic design 2

Key words

light-dependent
  resistor (LDR)
logic gate
resitance
thermistor

1 Switch for electric motor

- With the switch open, voltage across the NAND gate is high. This provides a low input to the NOT gate. The NOT gate provides a high output which activates the relay, completing the motor circuit.
- With the switch closed, voltage across the NAND gate is low. This provides a high input to the NOT gate. The NOT gate provides a low output which deactivates the relay, switching off the motor.

2 Fire alarm

- The resistance of a *thermistor* falls with increasing temperature.
- The resistor and thermistor act as potential dividers. At low temperatures the thermistor's *resistance* is high, thus the input to the NAND gate is high. The NAND gate acts as an inverter so its output is low.
- If there is a fire the thermistor's resistance falls. The input to the NAND gate becomes low, its output high and the buzzer is turned on.

3 Length detector

- The resistance of a light dependant resistor (*LDR*) falls with increasing brightness.
- When both LDRs are dark, voltage across them is high and inputs to the NAND gate are both high. This produces a high output at the second NAND gate, sounding the buzzer.
- If one LDR is moved towards a light its resistance falls, as does the voltage across it. When one input to the NAND gate is low its output is high; output of the second NAND gate will be low and the buzzer will not sound.

4 Non-sequential traffic lights

- The four possible inputs can be used to illuminate different combinations of lights.

1 Switch for electric motor

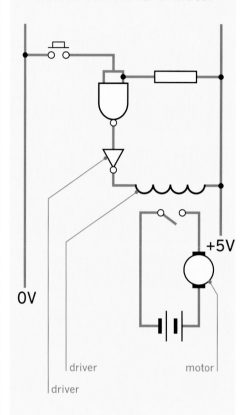

driver

driver

motor

0V

+5V

2 Fire alarm

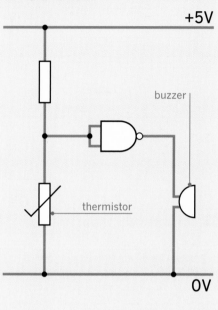

+5V

buzzer

thermistor

0V

3 Length detector

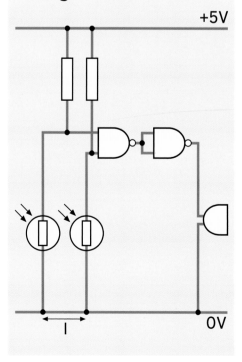

+5V

0V

I

4 Non-sequential traffic lights

A B

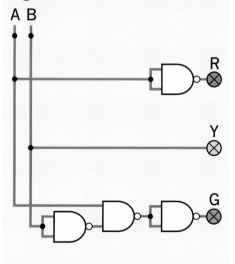

R

Y

G

A	B	R	Y	G
0	0	1	0	0
0	1	1	1	0
1	0	0	0	1
1	1	0	1	0

Sequential logic 1: the bistable

Key words

bistable
latch
logic gate
truth table

1 S̄-R̄ flip-flop

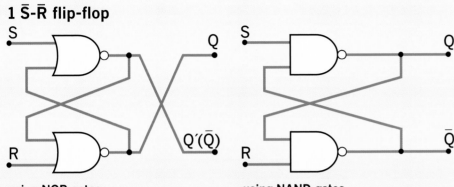

using **NOR** gates

using **NAND** gates

State	S	R	Q	Q̄
Set	1	0	1	0
	1	1	1	0
Reset	0	1	0	1
	1	1	0	1
Indeterminate	0	0	1	1
	1	1	?	?

truth table

2 R-S flip-flop

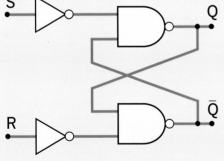

using **NAND** gates

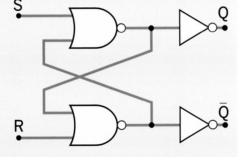

using **NOR** gates

State	S	R	Q	Q̄
Set	0	1	1	0
	0	0	1	0
Reset	1	0	0	1
	0	0	0	1
Indeterminate	1	1	1	1
	0	0	?	?

truth table

3 Circuit symbol

The bistable

- *Bistables* are used as *latches*, in counters, registers and memories.
- An R-S bistable has two inputs, R (for RESET), and S (for SET) and two outputs Q and Q̄.

1 S̄-R̄ flip-flop

- Using NOR gates—An R-S bistable can be made from two NOR gates connected so that the output from each gate is fed back as the input of the other.
- Using NAND gates—An R-S bistable can be made from two similarly connected NAND gates.
- *Truth table*—when S is at logic 1 and R is at logic 0 the bistable is in one stable state in which Q is at logic 1 and Q̄ is at logic 0. Even if R now becomes logic 1 the same state remains. When R is at logic 1 and S is at logic 0 the bistable flips into its second stable state in which Q is at logic 0 and Q̄ is at logic 1. Even if S now becomes logic 1 the same state remains. When S and R are both at logic 1, Q and Q̄ can be at either logic 1 or 0 depending on the state before this input condition existed. The previous output state is retained.

2 Reset-set (R-S) flip-flop

- The logic of the inputs can be reversed using inverters.

3 Circuit symbol

- The circuit symbol for a Reset-set (RS) flip-flop.

© Diagram Visual Information Ltd.

Key words

bistable
latch
logic gate

Sequential logic 2: examples using the bistable

1 The latched burglar alarm

- In many *latches* when the input goes low the output goes high. The output then stays high no matter what happens at the input i.e. it is latched to a high output. The output can only be reset to low by a reset switch.
- In this circuit the two NAND gates form an R-S *bistable*. Assuming that the inputs to the upper NAND gate are 1 and 1, the output will be 0 and the alarm does not sound.
- When the trip switch is closed the inputs to the upper NAND gate now become 0 and 1. The output is now 1 and the alarm rings.
- The inputs to the lower NAND gate become 1 and 1 giving an output of 0. This feeds back to the upper NAND gate so the inputs are 0 and 0 and the output remains 1.
- If the trip switch is immediately opened the inputs to the upper NAND gate are 1 and 0 so the output remains at 1 and the alarm continues to ring.
- The alarm can only be switched off by closing the reset switch. When this switch is closed the inputs to the lower NAND gate become 1 and 0 and the output becomes 1. This output feeds back to the upper NAND gate changing its inputs to 1 and 1. The output becomes 0 and the alarm ceases to sound.

2 Reversing an electric motor

- The two NAND gates form an R-S bistable. When the set switch is closed one of the relays is activated and the motor starts to rotate in one direction, continuing to do so even if the set switch is opened.
- When the reset switch is closed the first relay is deactivated and the second relay is activated, which reverses the direction of the motor's rotation.

1 The latched burglar alarm

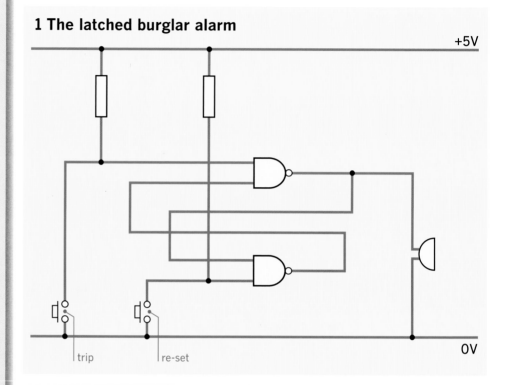

2 Reversing an electric motor

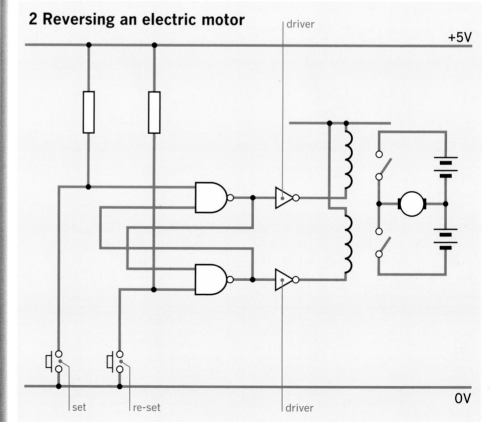

Clocked logic

Key words

bistable
clocked logic
square wave

1 The clocked bistable

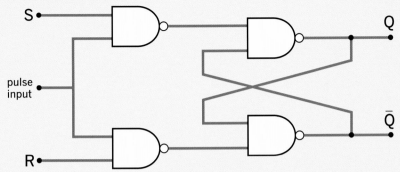

2 Timing diagram for clocked bistable

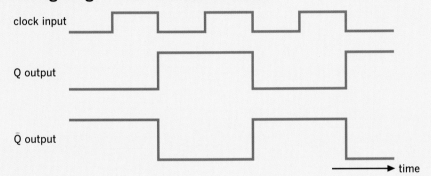

3 Debouncing using logic gates

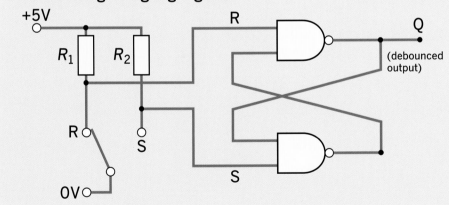

4 Circuit symbol for clocked flip-flop

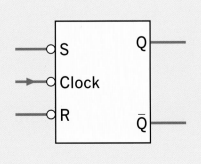

5 D-type flip-flop used as clocked bistable

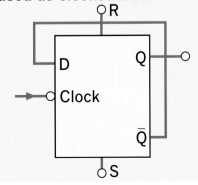

1 The clocked bistable

- Clock pulses are supplied by a pulse generator. This could be a mechanical switch turning a d.c. supply on and off or it could be a crystal-controlled oscillator which supplies a steady repetition frequency.
- Pulses should have a good *square wave* form i.e. they should have a fast rise and fall time. Any switches must be debounced.

2 Timing diagram for clocked bistable

- Each time the pulse falls it causes the *bistable* to toggle. The first pulse leaves $Q = 1$ and $\bar{Q} = 0$. During second clock pulse logic of outputs is reversed—$Q = 0$ and $\bar{Q} = 1$. Toggling continues with each pulse input.

3 De-bouncing using logic gates

- More than one pulse may result from using a mechanical to change the state of a bistable, due to the metal switch contacts not staying together at first but bouncing off each other.
- The effect of bounce contact is eliminated by using an R-S bistable in the debouncing circuit. When the switch is moved from R to S, the output Q remains at logic 0 even if bouncing occurs.

4 Circuit symbol for clocked flip-flop

- Circuit symbol for an R-S bistable is modified to show a clocked flip-flop.

5 D-type flip-flop used as clocked bistable

- In a D-type bistable one bit of data (0 or 1) is input at D for processing by the bistable. Pulses are applied to the clock input to control exactly when D input is processed. S is the set input allowing Q to be set to 1. R is the reset input allowing Q to be set to 0.

Key words

bistable
clocked logic
light-dependent
  resistor (LDR)
logic gate

1&2 Sequential traffic lights

- This type of *bistable* is rising-edge triggered. The change in voltage as the clock pulse rises from logic 0 to logic 1 changes the output logic.
- As clock voltage rises, output at Q is logic 1 and the red light shines. While clock is at logic 1 yellow light stays off (logic 1 is inverted to logic 0 by upper NOR gate). Inputs to lower NOR gate are 1 and 0, giving output 0 and green light stays off.
- As clock voltage falls to 0, output at Q remains 1, red light stays shining, but logic 0 is inverted to 1 by upper NOR gate and the yellow light comes on. Inputs to the lower NOR gate are now 1 and 1, giving output of 0 so green light stays off.
- When clock voltage rises to logic 1 again, output at Q becomes logic 0 and the red light goes off. The logic 1 is inverted to logic 0 by the upper NOR gate and the yellow light goes off. Inputs to lower NOR gate are now 0 and 0, giving output of 1, turning the green light on.

3 Dual system traffic lights

- Circuit containing several clocked bistables and NOR gates provides a dual system of traffic lights. Sequences are off-set—as one set of lights changes from red to green the other changes from green to red.

4 Interval timer

- When light shines on *LDR1* its resistance falls and input to upper NAND gate becomes logic 0. This is inverted to give output of logic 1 which sets the bistable. Output at Q is logic 1 and the counter starts.
- When the light moves from LDR1 to LDR2, resistance of the former rises while that of the latter falls, resetting the bistable, giving an output of logic 0 at Q which stops the counter.

Examples of clocked logic

1 Sequential traffic lights

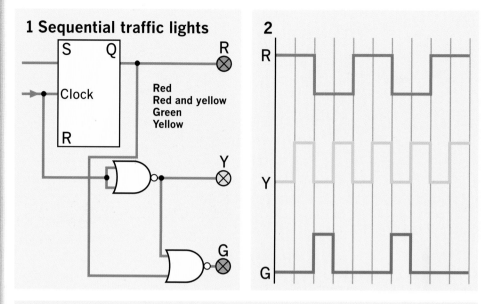

Red
Red and yellow
Green
Yellow

3 Dual system traffic lights

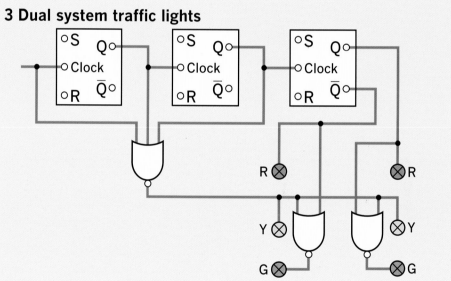

4 Interval timer

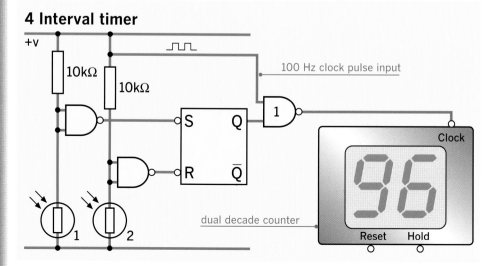

100 Hz clock pulse input

dual decade counter

Counting circuits 1

1 Binary up-counter

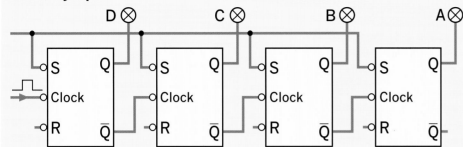

2 Counting table for binary-up counter

Pulse number	D	C	B	A
0	0	0	0	0
1	0	0	0	1
2	0	0	1	0
3	0	0	1	1
4	0	1	0	0
5	0	1	0	1
6	0	1	1	0
7	0	1	1	1

Pulse number	D	C	B	A
8	1	0	0	0
9	1	0	0	1
10	1	0	1	0
11	1	0	1	1
12	1	1	0	0
13	1	1	0	1
14	1	1	1	0
15	1	1	1	1

3 Binary-down counter

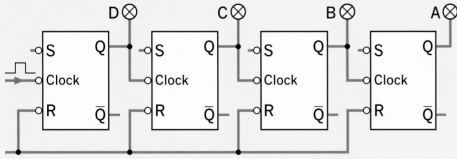

4 Dual decade counter

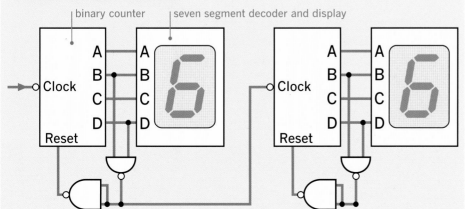

binary counter   seven segment decoder and display

Key words

binary code
bistable
clocked logic

Counting circuits

- Electronic counters consist of *bistables* connected so that they toggle when pulses to be counted are applied to their clock input.
- Counting is done in *binary code* using only 0 and 1. 0 and 1 correspond to the low and high states of binary output.

1 Binary up-counter

- In an up counter the count increases by one for each clock pulse.
- The Q output of each clocked bistable becomes the clock input of the next.

2 Counting table for binary-up counter

- The total count at any time is given by the states of:

D	C	B	A
2^3	2^2	2^1	2^0
8	4	2	1

A counter with four clocked bistables can count up to 1111 in binary (15 in base 10).

3 Binary-down counter

- In a down counter the count decreases by one for each clock pulse.

4 Dual decade counter

- The output of a binary counter is a sequence of 0s and 1s representing a number. This is decoded and different combinations of segments are turned on and off to represent each number.

Key words

battery	light-dependent
binary code	resistor (LDR)
bistable	
clocked logic	

1 Switching machine off for 5 s in every 20s

- The *binary* counter and timed *bistables* provide an output of 0 for 15 out of every 20 second period. This is inverted by the NOT gate which activates the relay, turning the motor on.
- For the remaining 5 seconds the output is 1. This is inverted by the NOT gate and thus deactivates the relay turning the motor off.

2 Reversing action of food mixer every 5 s

- This type of circuit is sometimes used in food mixers. Activating the relay does not turn the motor on or off, but reverses the direction of the current and thus the direction in which the motor rotates.

3 Flashing a lamp

- The output from a binary counter can be used to turn a lamp on and off a given number of times. When the switch is turned on in this circuit the lamp flashes 6 times.

4 Automatic light buoy

- Flashing lamps have many possible applications including providing warnings such as buoys which mark the position of an underwater hazard. The circuit can be modified using an *LDR* so that the light only flashes when it is dark which preserves the *battery*.

5 Batch counter

- Batches of articles can be counted either by depressing switches manually or having an arrangement in which a switch is triggered each time an article passes a sensor.

Counting circuits 2

1 Switching machine off for 5 s in every 20 s

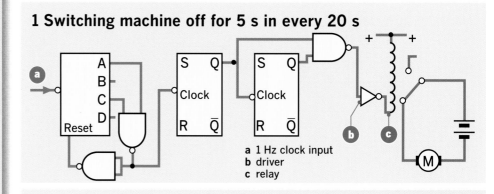

a 1 Hz clock input
b driver
c relay

2 Reversing action of food mixer every 5 s

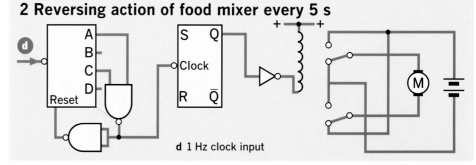

d 1 Hz clock input

3 Flashing a lamp

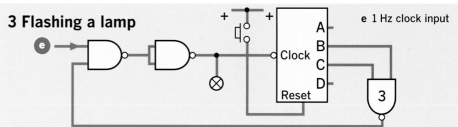

e 1 Hz clock input

4 Automatic light buoy

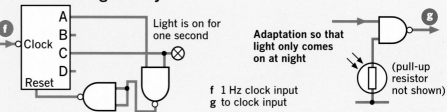

Light is on for one second

Adaptation so that light only comes on at night

(pull-up resistor not shown)

f 1 Hz clock input
g to clock input

5 Batch counter

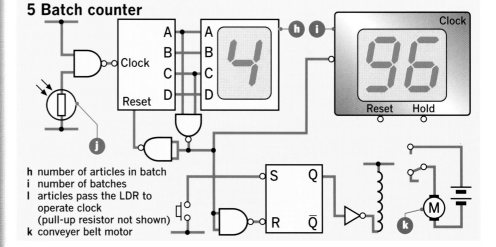

h number of articles in batch
i number of batches
l articles pass the LDR to operate clock (pull-up resistor not shown)
k conveyer belt motor

Operational amplifiers 1

1 Schematic circuit of the 741 op-amp chip

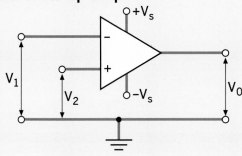

a non-inverting input
b inverting input
c output
d off-set null

2 Circuit symbol for op-amp

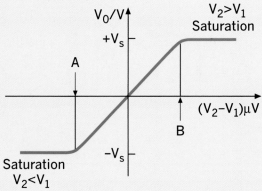

3 Transfer characteristic

Key words

capacitor
operational
  amplifier
transistor

1 Schematic circuit of the 741 op-amp chip

● *Operational amplifiers* or op-amps have many uses including as high gain voltage amplifiers of both a.c. and d.c. and as switches.

● The 741 op-amp chip contains around 20 *transistors* together with resistors and *capacitors* all etched onto a silicon chip. It requires a dual power supply which gives equal positive and negative voltages; $+V_S$, 0 and $-V_S$ where typically $+V_S$ = +15 V and $-V_S$ = -15 V. The centre point of the power supply, 0 V, is common to both the input and output circuits.

2 Circuit symbol for op-amp

● There is one output and two inputs; an inverting input (marked -) and a non-inverting input (marked +). The – and + input signs should not be confused with the polarity of the power supplies.

3 Transfer characteristic

● The polarity of a voltage applied at the inverting input is reversed at the output. A voltage applied at the non-inverting input gives an amplified voltage of the same polarity.

● If $V_2 > V_1$ i.e. the non-inverting input is greater than the inverting input then V_{out} is always positive.

● If $V_1 > V_2$ i.e. the inverting input is greater than the non-inverting input then Vout is always negative.

● If $V_1 = V_2$ then V_{out} = 0.

● An op-amp acts as a differential voltage amplifier. It amplifies the difference between V_1 and V_2.

● A and B show where saturation starts.

Operational amplifiers 2

Key words

amplifier
impedance
inverting
  amplifier
operational
  amplifier

1 Amplifier with negative feedback

- When an *op-amp* is used as an *amplifier* the output is fed back to the inverting input. The voltage at the output is of opposite polarity to the one from which the feedback was taken, thus the output and the gain of the amplifier is reduced i.e. the feedback is negative.
- Although negative feedback reduces the gain of the amplifier it results in a more stable amplifier whose gain can be accurately predicted. The amplifier has a better frequency response and output distortion is reduced.

2 Non-inverting amplifier

- In a non-inverting amplifier the input voltage is applied to the non-inverting input of the op-amp. The result is an output voltage of the same polarity as the input voltage.
- Negative feedback is obtained by feeding back to the inverting input a fraction of the output voltage developed across R_i in the potential divider formed by the resistors.

3 Voltage follower

- A voltage follower is a special case of the non-inverting amplifier in which all of the output is fed back tot he inverting input. The output voltage is equal to the input voltage but the circuit has an extremely high input impedance and low output impedance making it suitable as a buffer amplifier to match a high *impedance* source with a low impedance load.

4 Summing amplifier

- When an op-amp is connected as a multi-input amplifier it can be used to add a number of voltages, either d.c. or a.c. This type of circuit is used as a mixer in audio applications to combine the outputs of microphones, electrical instruments and special effects.

1 Amplifier with negative feedback

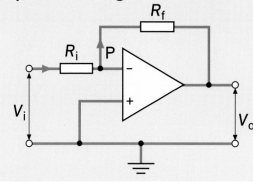

$$\frac{V_o}{V_i} = \frac{-R_f}{R_i}$$

2 Non-inverting amplifier

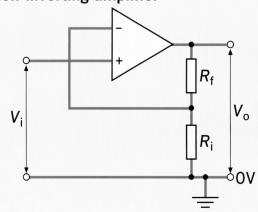

$$\frac{V_o}{V_i} = 1 + \frac{R_f}{R_i}$$

3 Voltage follower

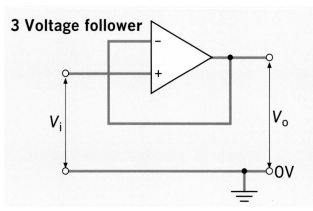

$$V_o = -V_i$$

4 Summing amplifier

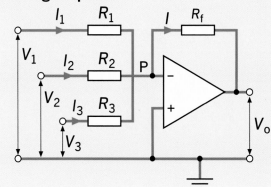

$$V_o = -\left(\frac{R_f}{R_1} V_1 + \frac{R_f}{R_2} V_2 + \frac{R_f}{R_3} V_3\right)$$

If $R_f = R_1 = R_2 = R_3$

Then $V_o = - (V_1 + V_2 + V_3)$

Operational amplifiers 3

Key words

capacitor	thermistor
light-emitting	transistor
diode (LED)	waveform
operational	
amplifier	

1 Simple integrating circuit

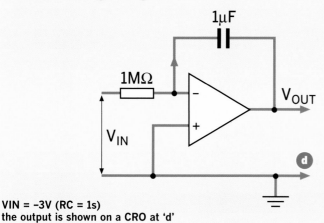

1μF

1MΩ

V_{IN}

V_{OUT}

d

VIN = –3V (RC = 1s)
the output is shown on a CRO at 'd'

2 Output of the integrator

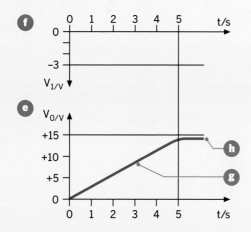

f

0 1 2 3 4 5   t/s

0

–3

$V_{1/V}$

e

$V_{0/V}$

+15

+10

+5

0

0 1 2 3 4 5   t/s

h

g

e input voltage   g saturation
f output voltage   h ramp voltage

3 Low temperature alarm

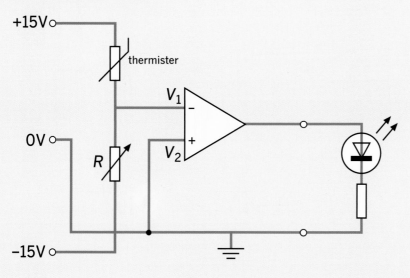

+15V

thermister

V_1

V_2

R

0V

–15V

1 Simple integrating circuit
- An *op-amp* is the basis of a ramp generator for producing a voltage with a sawtooth *waveform*.
- When steady input voltage V_{in} is applied through resistor **R**, after time t (s) the output voltage V_{out} is
  $V_{out} = -\ (1/CR) \int V_{in}\ dt$
  where **C** is in μF and **R** is in MΩ. Since the inverting input is used, negative sign indicates that output voltage is negative if input voltage is positive and vice versa.

2 Output of the integrator
- If input voltage of -3 V is applied, output voltage rises by +3 V per second. If a power supply of ±15 V is used the output voltage will be close to 15 V after 5 seconds when the op-amp becomes saturated. Input voltage is thus added up or integrated over time t to give a ramp voltage waveform whose slope is $-V_{in}$ when **CR=1s**.
- To reset output voltage to zero when it reaches its maximum value a *transistor* can be connected across the capacitor to short circuit the *capacitor* causing the output voltage to fall to 0 V when it receives a reset pulse.

3 Low temperature alarm
- An op-amp can act as a switch in a similar way to a transistor.
- The *thermistor* and the resistor **R** form a potential divider across the 15 V supply. The op-amp compares the voltage V_1 at the potential divider junction with V_2 which is 0 V.
- If the temperature falls below a certain value (determined by setting **R**) the thermistor's resistance becomes greater than that of **R**. There is a greater voltage drop across the thermistor than **R** thus V_1 becomes negative. $V_2 > V_1$ which switches V_{out} from around -15 V to + 15 V lighting the *LED*.

Key words

cathode ray
  oscilloscope
differential
  equation
feedback

operational
  amplifier

Differential equations

- The rate of change of a variable, y, with respect to time, t, is given by
$$\frac{dy}{dt}.$$
  Similarly, the rate of change of
$$\frac{dy}{dt}$$
  with respect to time is given by
$$\frac{d^2y}{dt^2}.$$

- Equations of the form
$$a\frac{d^2y}{dt^2} + b\frac{dy}{dt} = kx$$
  are described as *differential equations* and are solved by the process of integration.

- An *op-amp* is able to add up or integrate voltage over time and can therefore be used to solve differential equations.

1 Solving the differential equation

- The *feedback* to the first op-amp is to the inverting input thus a positive input provides an output which is negative.

- The feedback to the second op-amp is also to the inverting input thus the output is also inverted. Since the input is negative, the output is inverted and therefore is positive.

2 Producing oscillations

- Where the output from the second op-amp is negative, it is necessary to add a third op-amp which acts as an inverter to provide a positive output for display on a *cathode ray oscilloscope*.

Operational amplifiers 4

1 Solving the differential equation

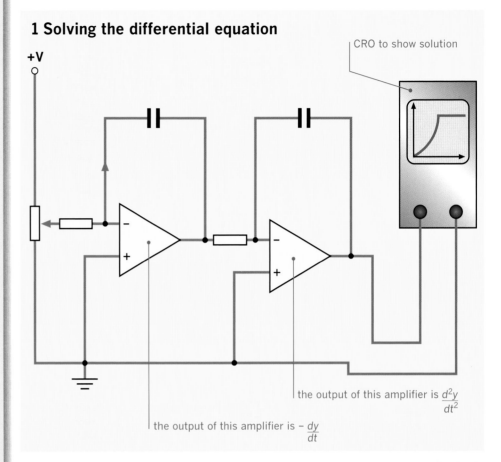

CRO to show solution

+V

the output of this amplifier is $\frac{d^2y}{dt^2}$

the output of this amplifier is $-\frac{dy}{dt}$

2 Producing oscillations

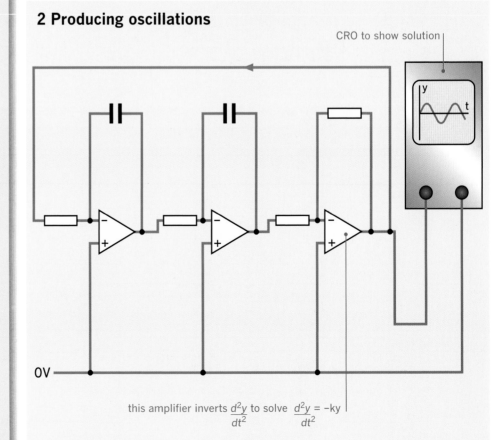

CRO to show solution

0V

this amplifier inverts $\frac{d^2y}{dt^2}$ to solve $\frac{d^2y}{dt^2} = -ky$

Operational amplifiers 5

Key words

capacitor	oscillator
feedback	waveform
frequency	
operational amplifier	

1 Wien network and oscillator

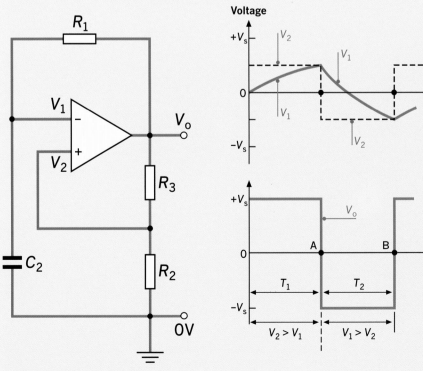

Wien network
Wien oscillator

Op amp oscillator circuit

2 Op-amp astable multivibrator

Op amp astable multivibrator

Op-amp as oscillator

- An *op-amp* can become an *oscillator* by feeding back the output to the input in such a way as to ensure that the *feedback* is in phase with the input i.e. positive, and that it is sufficient to make good energy losses in the circuit so the amplified output consists of undamped electrical oscillations.
- The action of the oscillator is to supply its own input and convert d.c. from the power supply to a.c. The resulting a.c. can have a variety of *waveforms* depending on the circuit.

1 Wien network and oscillator

- Sine waves in the audio *frequency* range (20–20,000 Hz) can be generated by an op-amp using a Wien network circuit.
- To obtain oscillations the network is used with the non-inverting input of the op-amp giving an output to the Wien network in phase with its input.

2 Op-amp astable multivibrator

- An op-amp voltage comparator in its saturated condition can work as an oscillator.
- Suppose output voltage V_0 is initially positive. A fraction of V_0, V_2, is fed back to the non-inverting input. V_0 is also fed back to the inverting input via resistor R_1, causing V_1 to rise as *capacitor* C_1 is charged.
- When V_1 becomes greater than V_2, the op-amp switches into negative saturation and V_0 is negative.
- Capacitor C_1 now starts charging in the opposite direction causing V_1 to fall rapidly until eventually becoming less than V_2. The op-amp then switches into positive saturation and V_0 is positive. This continues indefinitely at a frequency determined by the value of the capacitor.

Key words

alternating current (AC)	potential difference
current	rectifier
diode	transformer
electrolytic capacitor	

a.c. rectification

- A *diode* only allows *current* to flow in one direction, so diodes can *rectify*, or convert, *alternating* to direct current.

1 Half-wave rectification

- The negative half cycle of the a.c. is removed to give a varying d.c. Half-wave rectification is wasteful since half the electrical energy is lost as heat from the diode. Many loads require steadier d.c. than is produced by half-wave rectification.

2 Full-wave rectification

- In the center tap *transformer*, current passes through the upper diode on the first half of the cycle and through the lower diode on the second.
- The bridge rectifier is a bridge of four diodes. Current passes through opposite pairs of diodes during each alternating current half cycle.
- The negative half cycle of a.c. becomes positive, resulting in a varying d.c. in which none of the a.c. is lost.

3 Smoothing

- Variations in d.c. are smoothed by connecting a large *electrolytic capacitor* across the load. The capacitor charges as the current rises, and discharges as it falls. The capacitor smoothes the current by reducing the height of the current peaks while eliminating the points where current is zero.
- The amplitude of the ripple voltage is decreased if the value of the capacitor is increased A greater charge is held and the *potential difference* across the capacitor falls less when it supplies current. This amplitude also decreases when the output current drawn by the load decreases, because the potential difference across a capacitor is affected less the smaller the current drawn from it.

Rectifier circuits

1 Half-wave rectification

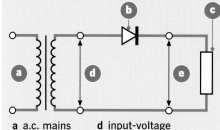

a a.c. mains
b diode
c load resistor
d input-voltage
e output-voltage

d input-voltage
e output-voltage

2 Full-wave rectification

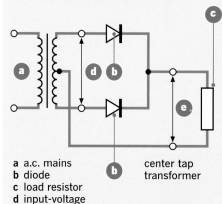

a a.c. mains
b diode
c load resistor
d input-voltage
e output-voltage

center tap transformer

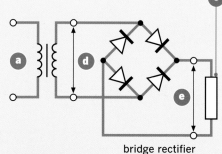

bridge rectifier

a a.c. mains
c load resistor
d input-voltage
e output-voltage

d input-voltage
e output-voltage

3 Smoothing

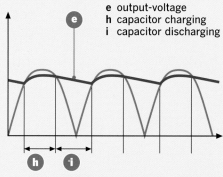

a a.c. mains
c load resistor
d input-voltage
e output-voltage
g smoothing capacitor

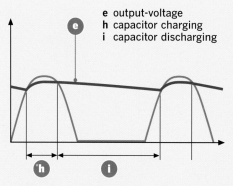

e output-voltage
h capacitor charging
i capacitor discharging

effect on smoothing on half-wave rectification

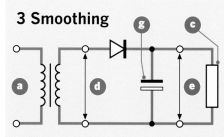

e output-voltage
h capacitor charging
i capacitor discharging

effect on smoothing on full-wave rectification

The microprocessor

1 Basic computer interconnections

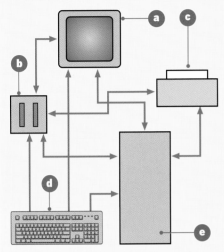

a VDU (Visual Display Unit)
b memory
c printer
d keyboard
e Central Processing Unit (CPU)

2 Interconnection via a bus

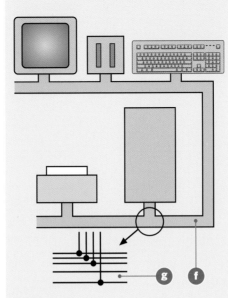

f the bus
g wires of the bus

3 Use of a tristate

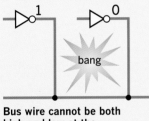

Bus wire cannot be both high and low at the same time

h input
i output
j normal inverter
k "enables" switch

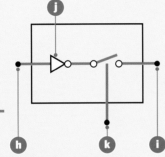

Basic layout of tri-state device

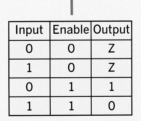

Input	Enable	Output
0	0	Z
1	0	Z
0	1	1
1	1	0

Circuit symbol of tri-state and truth table; Z means not connected

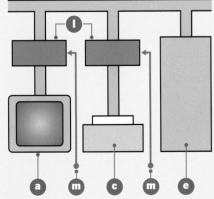

a VDU (Visual Display Unit)
c printer
e Central Processing Unit (CPU)
l tri-state
m enable control

Connection to the bus via tristate buffers

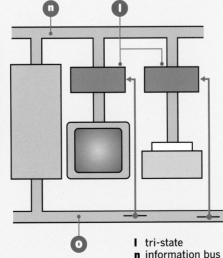

l tri-state
n information bus
o control bus

Addition of control bus to enable the buffers

Key words

bus
microprocessor

1 Basic computer interconnections

- A computer consists of input devices, such as a keyboard; output devices, such as a visual display unit (VDU) and a printer; a central processing unit (CPU) and memory. The CPU is connected to other parts of the system by three sets of wires called *buses* because they transport information.
- A clock generates timing pulses at frequencies of several megahertz which are used to synchronize the computer's operations so that they take place at the correct time and in the correct sequence.

2 Interconnection via a bus

- The one-way address bus carries signals from the CPU enabling it to access data in specific locations in the memory.
- The data bus allows two-way transfer of data between the CPU and other parts of the system.
- The control bus transmits timing and control signals to keep the different parts of the system working in step.

3 Use of a tristate

- To prevent interference between those parts of the system that are not sending signals to the bus and those that are, all parts have a tristate gate in their output. Each gate is enabled or disabled by a control unit.
- When the tristate gate is enabled, the output is low or high and signals can be sent to, or received from the bus.
- When the tristate gate is disabled, the output has such a high impedance that it is effectively disconnected from the bus and can neither receive or send signals. It thus does not upset signals already passing along the bus.
- Components are connected to the bus via tristate buffers.
- A control bus is used to enable the buffers.

Key words

amplitude
analog
digital
waveform

Information transmission

- Information can be represented and transmitted electrically either as an analog or as a digital signal.

1 Analog signal

- An *analog* signal represents a physical quantity which can vary continuously with time.
- The information carried by an analog signal is in the *amplitude* and *waveform* of the physical quantity.

2 Digital signal

- A *digital* signal consists of a sequence of binary code with 1 and 0 representing high and low voltages.
- Information in the signal is coded using the American Standard Code for Information Interchange (ASCII), a code consisting of 8 digits or bits.

3 Advantages of digital signal

- Signals weaken as they travel and require amplification. They also pick up stray voltages and currents which form noise, distorting the signal.
- Noise is amplified when analog signals are amplified.
- Digital signals can be regenerated as clean, noise free pulses.

4 Analog to digital conversion

- The analog voltage is divided into a number of levels. Measurements are taken regularly to find the level. Each level is represented by a binary code. A three-bit code can represent $2^3 = 8$ levels (0–7).
- The accuracy of the conversion increases with the number of voltage levels and the frequency of sampling.

Analog and digital signals

1 Analog signal

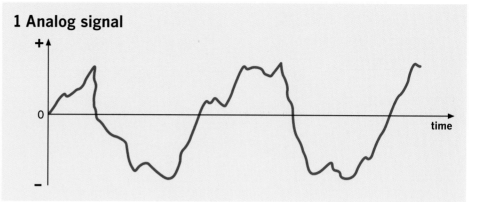

2 Digital signal

3 Advantages of digital signal

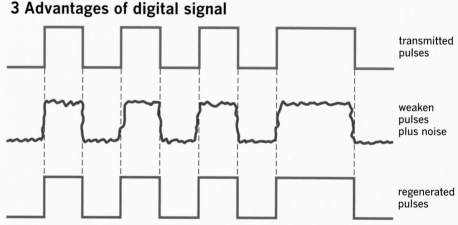

transmitted pulses

weaken pulses plus noise

regenerated pulses

4 Analog to digital conversion

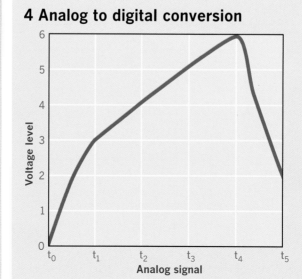

3-bit code	Voltage level
0 0 0	0
0 0 1	1
0 1 0	2
0 1 1	3
1 0 0	4
1 0 1	5
1 1 0	6
1 1 1	7

Sample time	Digital signal
t_0	0 0 0
t_1	0 1 1
t_2	1 0 0
t_3	1 0 1
t_4	1 1 0
t_5	0 1 0

ASCII code

© Diagram Visual Information Ltd.

Dec	Hex	ASCII	Dec	Hex	ASCII	Dec	Hex	ASCII
000	00	NUL	043	2B	+	086	65	V
001	01	SOH	044	2C	,	087	66	W
002	02	STX	045	2D	–	088	67	X
003	03	ETX	046	2E	.	089	68	Y
004	04	EOT	047	2F	/	090	69	Z
005	05	ENQ	048	30	0	091	6A	[
006	06	ACK	049	31	1	092	6B	\
007	07	BEL	050	32	2	093	6C	]
008	08	BS	051	33	3	094	6D	^
009	09	HT	052	34	4	095	6E	_
010	0A	LF	053	35	5	096	6F	'
011	0B	VT	054	36	6	097	70	a
012	0C	FF	055	37	7	098	71	b
013	0D	CR	056	38	8	099	72	c
014	0E	SO	057	39	9	100	73	d
015	0F	SI	058	3A	:	101	74	e
016	10	DLE	059	3B	;	102	75	f
017	11	DC1	060	3C	<	103	76	g
018	12	DC2	061	3D	=	104	77	h
019	13	DC3	062	3E	>	105	78	i
020	14	DC4	063	3F	?	106	79	j
021	15	NAK	064	40	@	107	7A	k
022	16	SYN	065	41	A	108	7B	l
023	17	ETB	066	42	B	109	7C	m
024	18	CAN	067	43	C	110	7D	n
025	19	EM	068	44	D	111	7E	o
026	1A	SUB	069	45	E	112	7F	p
027	1B	ESCAPE	070	46	F	113	56	q
028	1C	FS	071	47	G	114	57	r
029	1D	GS	072	48	H	115	58	s
030	1E	RS	073	49	I	116	59	t
031	1F	US	074	4A	J	117	5A	u
032	20	SPACE	075	4B	K	118	5B	v
033	21	!	076	4C	L	119	5C	w
034	22	"	077	4D	M	120	5D	x
035	23	#	078	4E	N	121	5E	y
036	24	$	079	4F	O	122	5F	z
037	25	%	080	50	P	123	60	{
038	26	&	081	51	Q	124	61		
039	27	'	082	52	R	125	62	}
040	28	(	083	53	S	126	63	~
041	29	)	084	54	T	127	64	DEL
042	2A	*	085	55	U			

Key words

binary code
bit

ASCII code

- An agreed code represents letters of the alphabet and other symbols.
- The American Standard Code for Information Interchange (ASCII) is a code consisting of 8 digits or *bits* giving an eight-bit code which allows a maximum of $2^8 = 256$ characters to be coded in binary. This provides sufficient different codes for all letters of the alphabet, both upper and lower case, numbers from 0 to 9 and a variety of punctuation marks and other symbols.

Key words

direct proportion
inverse-square
  law
radiation

1 Linear relationship

- A straight-line graph indicates that one variable is *directly proportional* to another. The mass of a piece of iron is directly proportional to its volume; doubling the volume doubles the mass.
- Since density = mass / volume, the gradient of the graph gives the density of iron; 31.6 / 4 = 7.9 kg m⁻³.

2 Square relationship

- The area of a square is equal to the product of its two sides (i.e., the area of a square is proportional to the square of its length).

3 Cubic relationship

- The volume of a cube is equal to the product of its three sides (i.e., the volume of a cube is proportional to the cube of its length).

4 Similar figures

- If the linear dimensions of similar objects are in the ratio of **1:x** then the ratio of their areas will be **1:x²**. If the length of the larger figure is twice that of the smaller figure its area will be four times greater than the smaller figure.
- For similar 3-dimensional objects if the linear dimensions are in the ratio **1:x** then the ratio of their volumes will be **1:x³**.

5 Inverse-square relationship

- According to the *inverse-square law*, the intensity of an effect is reduced in inverse proportion to the square of the distance from the source. This law is true for most types of *radiations*, including light, and fields.
- From the graph, it can be seen that light intensity 10 m from the light source is four times greater than the intensity at 20 m.

Function and scaling

1 Linear relationship

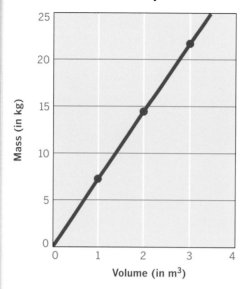

2 Square relationship

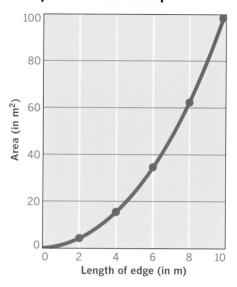

3 Cubic relationship

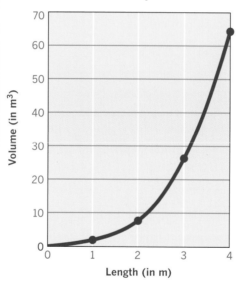

4 Similar figures

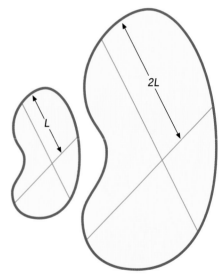

5 Inverse-square relationship

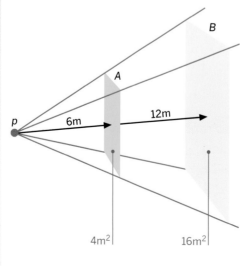

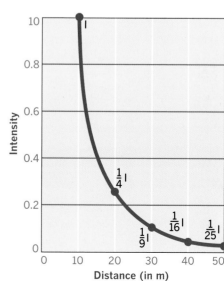

Motion in a straight line

1 Uniform and non-uniform motion

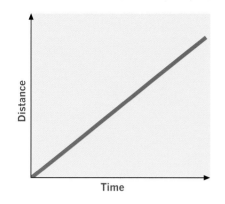

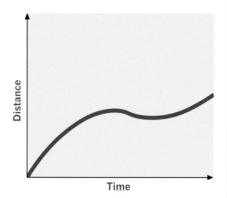

2 Constant speed

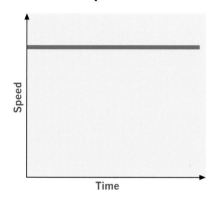

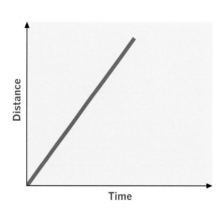

3 Constant acceleration

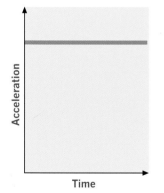

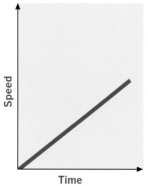

4 Falling object

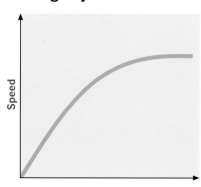

5 Bouncing ball

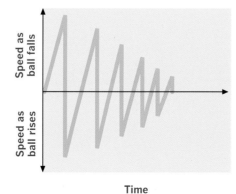

Key words

acceleration
direct proportion
gravity
terminal velocity

1 Uniform and non-uniform motion

- Distance traveled by a body in uniform motion is *directly proportional* to time.
- Distance traveled per unit time by a body in non-uniform motion may continually increase or decrease.

2 Constant speed

- Speed is the ratio distance:time. A body in uniform motion moves at a constant speed.

3 Constant acceleration

- The speed of a body moving with constant acceleration increases at a uniform rate. Acceleration is the ratio speed:time. The graph of speed against time is a straight line (speed is directly proportional to time).

4 Falling object

- A falling object is acted on by *gravity* pulling it downwards, and by air friction, opposing its movement.
- Gravity is initially dominant and the object's speed increases. Air friction increases as the object moves faster, until it equals the force of gravity. There is no net acceleration and the object continues falling at a constant speed—its *terminal velocity*.

5 Bouncing ball

- The ball *accelerates* as it is pulled towards the ground by gravity; its speed rapidly falls to zero when it hits the ground. It leaves the ground moving at maximum speed in the opposite direction then slows as it reaches maximum height where it momentarily stops.
- Some energy is lost as heat to the ground each time this is repeated so the ball eventually stops bouncing.

Key words

velocity

1 Position–time graph for particle with continuously changing velocity

- Determination of the particle's *velocity* at point **d**.
- Velocity is the ratio of displacement (change of position) to time; velocity in meters per second (ms⁻¹) = displacement in meters (m) / time in seconds (s)
- If a particle's velocity is calculated using the distance traveled over a period of time, the resulting figure is actually the average velocity over that time period. It may be that the body never actually travels at this velocity during the particular time period.

2 Considering the particle's instantaneous velocity

- The particle's actual velocity at a particular point in time is called its instantaneous velocity. This can only be found by considering a very small change in displacement over a very short time period.

Instantaneous velocity 1

1 Position-time graph for a particle with a continuously changing velocity

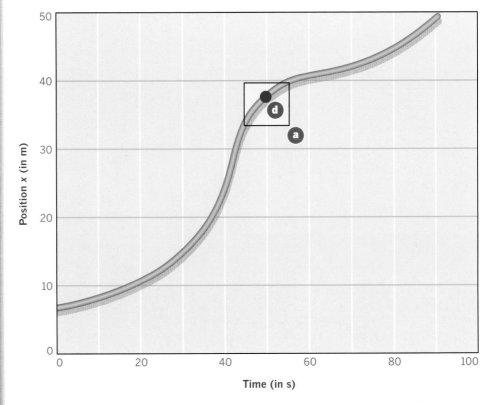

2 Considering the particle's instantaneous velocity

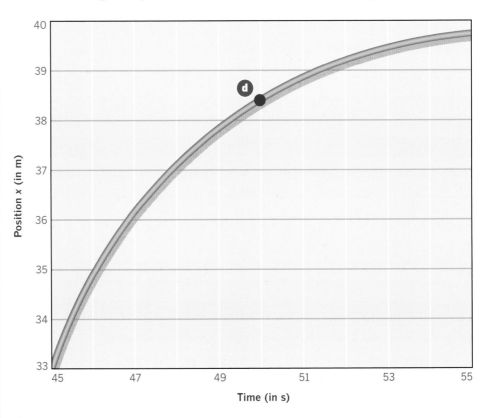

The marked area (**a** in the top diagram) is enlarged 10 times.

Instantaneous velocity 2

Key words

gradient
tangent
velocity

1 Gradient of position–time graph

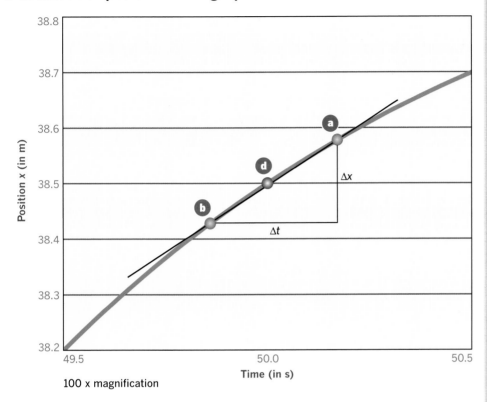

100 x magnification

2 Tangent to position–time graph

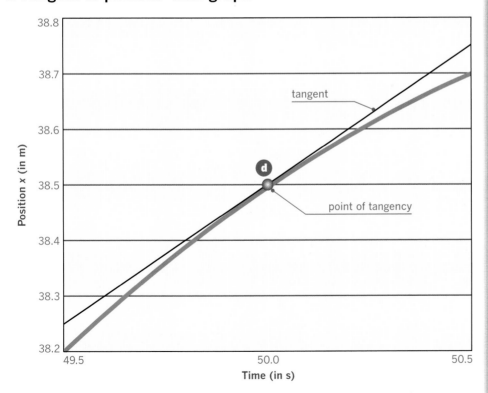

With 100 x magnification, the curve and its tangent are indistinguishable near the point of tangency **d**.

1 Gradient of position–time graph

- *Velocity* is given by the *gradient* of a position–time graph.
- The Greek prefix delta, Δx, its lower case alternative δ, or the letters D or d are used to denote a small change in a variable.
- Δx is thus a small change in displacement during Δt, a small change in time.
- Instantaneous velocity at a point in time can be obtained by finding the gradient of the curve at that point in time.
- If the scale of the graph is magnified, it can be seen that its gradient at point d is approximately equal to $\Delta x/\Delta t$ where Δx is the distance between points **a** and **b**, and Δt is the time interval between these points.

2 Tangent to position–time graph

- Provided Δx and Δt are small enough, the section of the curve approximates to a straight line and thus the gradient at **d** equals the *tangent* drawn at that point.

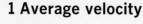

Key words

acceleration
gradient
tangent
velocity

Instantaneous velocity and acceleration

1 Average velocity

- Average *velocity* between points **a** and **b** = Δx / Δt

2 Instantaneous velocity

- Instantaneous velocity at point **e** is found by drawing the *tangent* to **e**, **ced**.
- Velocity is the gradient of this line (32m / 60 s = 0.53 ms⁻¹)

3 Instantaneous positive acceleration

- *Acceleration* is the ratio of velocity to time. Acceleration in meters per second² (ms²) = velocity in meters (ms⁻¹) / time in seconds (s)
- The acceleration of a body calculated from its change in velocity over a period of time gives the body's average acceleration over that time period. It may be that the body never actually accelerates at this rate at any time during the time period.
- The actual acceleration at a particular point in time is called the instantaneous acceleration. It is found by considering a very small change in velocity over a very small period of time.
- Acceleration is given by the slope of a velocity–time graph. Instantaneous acceleration at a point in time is obtained by finding the gradient of the curve at a point in time.
  Tangent of **f** gives slope h/i
  Thus **acceleration = 30 ms⁻¹ / 2 s = 1.5 ms⁻²**

1 Average velocity

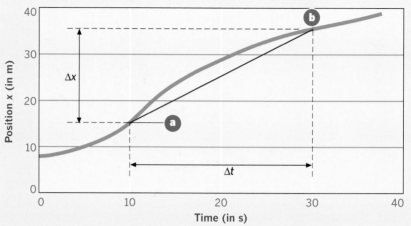

2 Instantaneous velocity

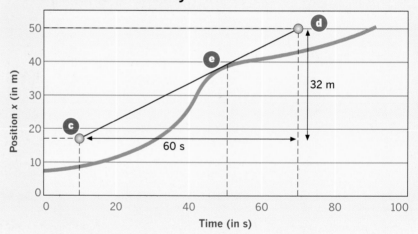

3 Instantaneous positive acceleration

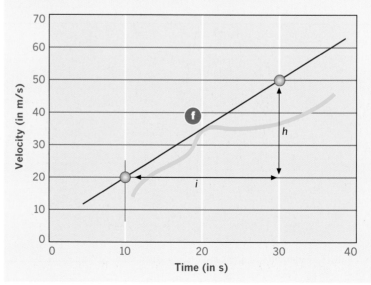

Addition and subtraction of vectors 1

1 Position specified by two coordinate numbers

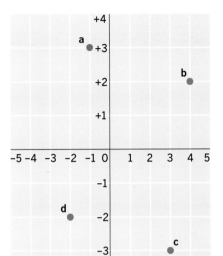

2 Position specified by directed line segment or position vector

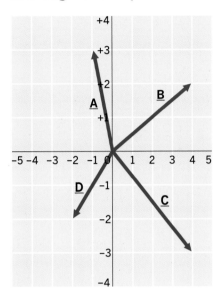

3 Displacement vector and resultant

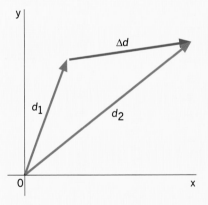

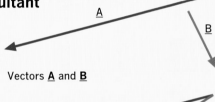

Vectors **A** and **B**

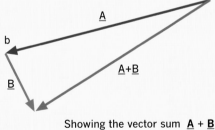

Showing the vector sum **A** + **B**

4 Subtraction of two vectors in a plane

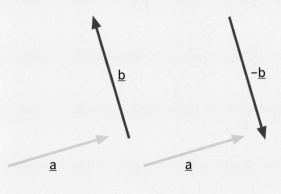

Vectors **a** and **b**

Drawn as vectors **a** and **−b**

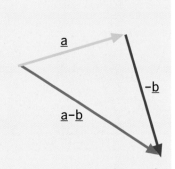

Showing the sum **a** + (**−b**) = **a** − **b**

1 Position specified by two coordinate numbers

- On a *Cartesian* axis the position of a point is given by two coordinate numbers or coordinates; one along the horizontal (often designated **x**) axis and one along the vertical (often designated **y**) axis. The **x** coordinate is always given first.
- The point where the axes intersect is called the origin. The x coordinate is positive to the right of the origin and negative to the left of the origin. The y coordinate is positive above the origin and negative below the origin.

2 Position specified by directed line segment or position vector

- A point can also be defined by a *position vector*. This is a straight line from the origin to the point.

3 Displacement vector and resultant

- A *displacement vector* has both magnitude (length) and direction. It can be represented by an arrow. The sum, or *resultant*, or two vectors is found by drawing the vectors as two sides of a triangle. The resultant is obtained by drawing in the third side.

4 Subtraction of two vectors in a plane

- Reversing the arrow representing a vector reverses the direction of the vector but does not alter its magnitude. If the vector b is represented by an arrow pointing in one direction, the vector -b is represented by an arrow of equal length pointing in the opposite direction.

Key words

vector

1 Vector addition

- If a swimmer attempts to cross a river both the force created by the swimming stroke and the flow of the water act on him. Each force can be represented by an arrow on a *vector* diagram.

- If the swimmer sets off perpendicular to the flow of the river he will arrive at a point on the opposite bank downstream from where he started. In order to arrive at a point on the opposite bank directly opposite where he started, he needs to swim at a suitable angle upstream.

2 Components and vectors

- Any vector can be resolved into a pair of perpendicular vectors or component vectors. If the vector, A, makes an angle q with the horizontal then the component vectors are Acosq in the direction parallel to the horizontal and Asinq in the direction perpendicular to the horizontal.

3 Vectors in three dimensions

- Motion in 3-dimensions can be expressed as a combination of three vectors in directions perpendicular to each other.

4 Further illustrations of components

- When a vector moves parallel to or perpendicular to a line one or other of the component vectors is equal to zero since the angle is 0° in which case sin 0° = 0, or 90° in which case cos 0° = 0.

Addition and subtraction of vectors 2

1 Vector addition

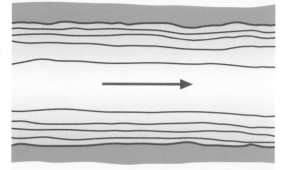

Swimming across a river with a current of ½ mi/h (V_c)

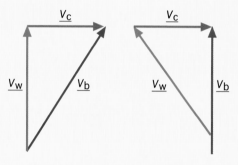

If you swim with a velocity of 1 mi/h (V_w), your velocity will be V_b relative to the bank

If you now swim upstream at the angle shown, your velocity will be 0.86 mi/h at right angles to the bank

3 Vectors in three dimensions

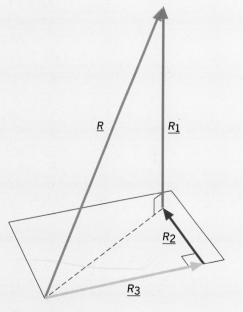

The vector $\underline{R}$ has the three components $\underline{R_1}$, $\underline{R_2}$ and $\underline{R_3}$

2 Components and vectors

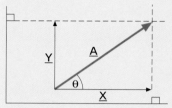

Components of a vector:
$\underline{X}$ is the component of $\underline{A}$ in x direction $\underline{Y}$ is the component of $\underline{A}$ in y direction
Magnitude of $\underline{X}$ = A cos θ
Magnitude of $\underline{Y}$ = A sin θ

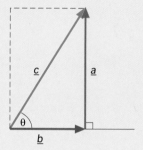

Finding a vector if components are known:
$\underline{a}$ = 20 ms⁻¹ in north direction
$\underline{b}$ = 10 ms⁻¹ in east direction
Resultant $\underline{c}$ = 22 ms⁻¹ with θ = 64°

4 Further illustrations of components

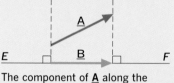

The component of $\underline{A}$ along the line EF is $\underline{B}$

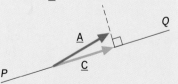

The component of $\underline{A}$ along the line PQ is $\underline{C}$

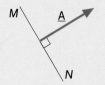

The component of $\underline{A}$ along the line MN is zero

The international system of units: base units

Key words

SI

Name of base SI unit	Definition
meter	The length equal to 1,650,763.73 wavelengths in vacuum corresponding to the transition between the levels $2p_{10}$ and $5d_5$ of the krypton-86 atom.
kilogram	The unit of mass; it is equal to the mass of the international prototype of the kilogram. (This prototype is in the custody of the Bureau International des Poids et Mesures at Sèvres, France.)
second	The duration of 9,192,631,770 periods of radiation corresponding to the transition between the two hyperfine levels of the ground state of the cesium-133 atom.
ampere	That constant current which, if maintained in two straight parallel conductors of infinite length, of negligible circular cross-section, and placed 1 meter apart in vacuum, would produce between these conductors a force equal to 2×10^{-7} newton per meter of length.
kelvin	The unit of thermodynamic temperature is the fraction $\frac{1}{273.16}$ of the thermodynamic temperature of the triple point of water.
candela	The luminous intensity, in a given direction, of a source that emits monochromatic radiation of frequency 540×10^{12} hertz that has a radiant intensity in that direction of 1/683 watt per steradian.
mole	The amount of substance of a system which contains as many elementary entities as there are atoms in 0.012 kilogram of carbon-12.

Note: When the mole is used, the elementary entities must be specified and may be atoms, molecules, ions, electrons, other particles, or specified groups of such particles.

Physical quantity	Name of base SI unit	Symbol for unit
length	meter	m
mass	kilogram	kg
time	second	s
electric current	ampere	A
thermodynamic temperature	kelvin	K
luminous intensity	candela	cd
amount of substance	mole	mol

Physical quantity	Name of supplementary SI unit	Symbol for unit
plane angle	radian	rad
solid angle	steradian	sr

1 International System of Units: base units

- Scientific quantities are measured using the *SI* system (Système International d'Unités). There are seven base units—the meter, kilogram, second, ampere, Kelvin, candela and mole. All other SI units are derived from these.
- The name of each unit is represented by a symbol. Some units are named after famous scientists. In this case the name of the unit is written in lower case while the symbol for the unit is written as an upper case letter
- For example, thermodynamic temperature is measured in kelvins but the symbol for this unit is K; electrical current is measured in amperes but the symbol is A.
- The radian and the steradian are supplementary SI units used in angular measurement.

Key words

SI

1 International System of Units: derived units

- Most units are derived from two or more of the seven base units.
- Some derived units are always expressed in terms of base units. For example: **speed = distance expressed in meters divided by time expressed in seconds**. The unit of speed is therefore the meter per second or ms^{-1}.
- Other derived units are named. For example: **pressure = force expressed in newtons divided by area expressed in square meters**. The unit of area is therefore the newton per square meter or Nm^{-2} (although this is same as the pascal or Pa).
- The same series of prefixes can be added to any unit to change its value by multiples of 10. For example, the prefix kilo indicates a factor of 10^3 or 1,000, therefore **1 kilometer = 1,000 meters**. Similarly, the prefix micro indicates a factor of 10^{-6} therefore **1 microgram = 0.000 001 gram**.
- In order to avoid confusion, the correct use of upper case and lower case for prefix symbols is important. For example, m (milli) is the symbol representing 10^{-3} while M (mega) represents 10^6.

The international system of units: derived units

Physical quantity	Derived SI unit	Symbol for unit	Unit expressed in termsof base
frequency	hertz	Hz	$1Hz = 1s^{-1}$
force	newton	N	$1N = 1Kgms^{-2}$
pressure and stress	pascal	Pa	$1Pa = 1Nm^{-2}$
work, energy, heat	joule	J	$1J = 1Nm$
power	watt	W	$1W = 1JS^{-1}$
electric charge	coulomb	C	$1C = 1As$
electrical potential difference, electromotive force	volt	V	$1V = 1JC^{-1} = 1WA^{-1}$
electric resistance	ohm	Ω	$1\Omega = VA^{-1}$
electric conductance	siemens	S	$1S = 1\Omega^{-1}$
electric capacitance	farad	F	$1F = CV^{-1}$
magnetic flux	weber	Wb	$1Wb = 1Vs$
magnetic flux density (magnetic induction)	tesla	T	$1T = Wbm^{-2}$
inductance	henry	H	$1H = WbA^{-1}$
luminous flux	lumen	lm	$1lm = 1cdsr$
illuminance	lux	lx	$1lx = 1lm\ mm^{-2}$
activity (of a radioactive source)	becquerel	Bq	$1Bq = 1s^{-1}$
absorbed dose (of ionizing radiation)	gray	Gy	$1Gy = 1Jkg^{-1}$
dose equivalent (of ionizing radiation)	sievert	Sv	$1Sv = 1Jkg^{-1}$

Factor by which the unit is Multiplied	Prefix	Symbol	Factor by which the unit is Multiplied	Prefix	Symbol
10^{-1}	deci	d	10^1	deca	da
10^{-2}	centi	c	10^2	hecto	h
10^{-3}	milli	m	10^3	kilo	k
10^{-6}	micro	μ	10^6	mega	M
10^{-9}	nano	n	10^9	giga	G
10^{-12}	pico	p	10^{12}	tera	T
10^{-15}	femto	f	10^{15}	peta	P
10^{-18}	atto	a	10^{18}	exa	E

The international system of units: symbols and conventions

Key words

SI

Quantity	Symbol	Name of unit	Symbol
length	l		
breadth	b		
height	h		
thickness	d		
radius	r		
diameter	d		
distance along path	s, L	meter	m
wavelength	e		
mean free path	l, e		
radius of gyration	k		
focal length	f		
object distance	u		
image distance	v		
mass	m	kilogram	kg
mass of molecule	m	tonne	t
electron mass	m_e		
proton mass	m_p	atomic mass unit	u
neutron mass	m_n		
atomic mass	m_a		
relative atomic mass	A_r		–
relative molecular mass	M_r	(no unit, purely numerical)	
amount of substance	n	mole	mol
molar mass	M	kilogram per mole	kg mole^{-1}
concentration of solute B	C_B	mole per meter cubed	mol m^{-3}
		mole per decimeter cubed	mol dm^{-3}
Time	t	second	s
period	T	minute	min
radioactive	$T^{1/2}, t^{1/2}$	hour	h
time constant	τ		

International System of Units: some symbols and conventions

- The scientific community generally refers to certain quantities using specific symbols such as l for length, r for radius, f for focal length. Such lengths use the SI unit of measurement, the meter.
- Some quantities use non-SI units but are recognized for general use. For example, the atomic mass unit is 1/12 the mass of one atom of carbon-12 (approximately 1.66×10^{-27} kg, equivalent to the mass of a proton).
- The mole is defined as the amount of a substance which contains the same number of entities (for example atoms or molecules) as there are atoms in 0.012 kg of carbon-12. This number (6.023×10^{23}) is also known as Avogadro's number. A mole of a substance therefore is the amount of the substance which contains 6.023×10^{23} particles of that substance.
- The half-life of a radioactive substance ($T^{1/2}$) is the time taken for one half of the original quantity to decay. Half lives vary from fractions of seconds to millions of years.

Key words

absolute zero The lowest possible temperature.

absorption The assimilation of radiation into a body with its partial or complete conversion into another form of energy.

acceleration A measure of how a body's velocity changes with time.

accommodation The adjustment of the focus of the eye to form a sharp image on the retina.

accumulator An electric battery that stores energy when an electric current from an external source causes a reversible chemical change.

action at a distance Forces such as gravity and magnetism that can affect objects with which they are not in direct contact. The space through which the forces operate is called a field.

adiabatic change A change that occurs without thermal transfer to a system.

alpha particle A particle released during radioactive decay.

alternating current (AC) A continuous electric current that varies in strength, regularly reversing its direction.

amplifier An electronic device for increasing the strength of a varying electrical signal.

amplitude The size of the maximum displacement from the equilibrium position of an oscillation or wave.

amplitude modulation Used in radio transmissions: a wave motion that varies the amplitude of the carrier wave is added to carry the signal to a receiver.

analog A continuous representation, of any kind, of a varying quantity.

angle of incidence The angle between an incident ray striking a reflecting or a refracting surface and the normal at the point of incidence.

anion An ion that has a negative charge.

anode The positive electrode toward which negative particles, such as electrons or negative ions, are attracted. It is the electrode carrying the positive charge in a solution undergoing electrolysis.

aperture The useful or effective diameter of a lens or curved mirror.

aquifer Water-bearing rock.

area A measure of the extent of a surface.

asymptote A curve becoming a straight line at infinity.

atom The smallest particle of an element that can exhibit that element's properties. An atom has a small massive nucleus of protons and neutrons surrounded by a cloud of electrons.

auditory nerve A nerve that conveys sound impulses to the brain.

basal metabolic rate The minimum energy required to maintain life.

battery Two or more electrical cells connected in series or parallel.

beat The interference effect between two waves of almost, but not quite, identical frequency.

binary code The representation of numbers in a positional system using the integers 0 and 1.

biogas Combustible gas formed by decomposition of organic matter.

bistable An electronic circuit that can have one of two stable states. Bistables are often called flip-flops or latch circuits.

bit Each digit of a number (0 or 1) in binary code is called a bit (from *binary digit*).

black body A theoretical body that absorbs all the radiation, of whatever kind, that falls on it. It is also a perfect emitter of radiation.

boiling point The temperature at which a liquid changes to the gas state. It depends on atmospheric pressure.

bolometer An electrical instrument used in the measurement of heat radiation. It utilizes platinum's characteristic change in resistance with temperature.

Boolean algebra A way of organizing logical operations (AND, OR, NOT) into a system of symbolic logic. It is the basis of the electronic logic gates used in digital computers.

bus A system of electrical connections or wires that carry related data or instructions between the various parts of a computer. Also known as a highway.

capacitance A measure of the ability of an object to store electrical charge as its potential rises.

capacitor A device, consisting of a pair of metal plates separated by an insulator (dielectric), that can store an electric charge.

carrier wave The electromagnetic wave of regular frequency, emitted from a transmitter, on which a second wave is superimposed by altering either its magnitude (amplitude) or the number of its cycles per second (its frequency). This superimposition on the plain wave is called modulation.

Cartesian coordinates Any system of locating a point on a plane by specifying the distance along two axes (usually a horizontal X axis and a vertical Y axis), or a point in space by specifying the distance along three axes (X, Y, and Z). The axes intersect at the origin.

cathode The negative electrode from which negative particles, such as electrons or negative ions, emerge. It is the electrode carrying the negative charge in a solution undergoing electrolysis.

cathode ray oscilloscope An instrument used to display electrical signals on a phosphorescent screen.

cation An ion having a positive charge, which is attracted by the negatively charged electrode, the cathode, during electrolysis.

caustic curve A curve or surface caused when parallel light rays strike a concave mirror. The rays are reflected in such a way that they intersect to form a curve.

cell A vessel, used either to produce electricity or to perform electrolysis, containing two electrodes surrounded by an electrolyte.

Celsius A scale of temperature that has 100 divisions between the lower fixed point (the melting point of pure ice) and the upper fixed point (the boiling point of pure water).

center of curvature Center of the sphere of which a mirror or lens forms a part.

center of mass The point at which the whole of the mass of a body can be considered to be concentrated and to act for gravitational or other purposes. The center of mass is the same as the center of gravity.

chain reaction A reaction in which one event leads to a second, and so on, often used to describe a nuclear reaction.

charge (electric charge) The property of certain atomic and subatomic particles that causes forces of attraction and repulsion between them. The electron has the smallest unit of negative charge, the proton an equal amount of positive charge.

chemical energy The energy stored in the bonds between atoms and molecules that is released during a chemical reaction.

chirp A signal or pulse of radiation whose frequency changes with time.

clocked logic Logic gates used in a circuit that generate pulses at precisely controlled intervals.

cochlea Part of the inner ear.

combustion The chemical term for burning, usually in oxygen.

commutator A device used both to change the direction of current flowing in the armature coil of a DC motor and in a generator to convert AC/DC.

Complementary Metal Oxide Semiconductor chip (CMOS) An electronic chip with very low power consumption that can operate on low-supply voltages.

compression The result of applying force or pressure to a body so that it becomes smaller or shorter.

concave Curving inward, like the interior of a sphere. A concave lens is thinner at its center than at its periphery and causes incoming light rays to diverge. A concave mirror is a converging mirror.

condense The process by which a vapor becomes a liquid.

condenser An apparatus in which a vapor is converted to a liquid.

conduction (1) (electrical) The movement of free electrons from atom to atom in a metallic conductor that transfers electrical energy. (2) (thermal) The transfer of heat energy through a substance from a region of high temperature to low. Energy is transferred by the vibrations of adjacent molecules.

conductor A material that is able to conduct heat and electricity.

conservation of energy, law of In a closed system, energy remains constant. Energy can be neither created nor destroyed.

control rod A rod which absorbs neutrons, used in a nuclear reactor to maintain the reaction at the correct level.

convection The transfer of heat energy in fluids by motion of the fluid.

convex Curving outward, like the outside of a sphere. A convex lens is thicker at its center than at its periphery. It causes rays to converge. A convex mirror causes rays to diverge, magnifying the image.

cornea The transparent convex membrane covering the front of the eye.

corona A luminous electrical discharge seen around the surface of a charged conductor which causes ionization of the surrounding air.

corrosometer An application of the Wheatstone bridge, used to measure a material's susceptibility to corrosion.

couple Two equal and parallel forces that act together in opposite directions, tending to turn an object.

critical angle The smallest angle of incidence of a light ray passing from a dense to a less dense material, at which light only just reappears.

current A flow of electric charges through a conductor.

damping The reduction in amplitude of any oscillating or vibrating system as a result of energy dissipating through friction or in any other way.

decibel (dB) A unit of comparison between an arbitrary standard power level and any other level. In sound levels, one decibel is about the smallest difference perceptible.

demodulation The retrieval of the information content of a modulated carrier wave. Demodulation occurs in every radio receiver.

density Mass per unit volume of a substance. In SI units, kg/m^3. Nearly all materials change volume with changes in temperature, so density is a function of temperature. In the case of gases, it is also a function of pressure.

Dewar flask A flask designed to prevent its contents losing or gaining heat by conduction (the walls of the flask contain a vacuum), radiation (the walls are silvered), or convection (the contents are isolated so there can be no convection currents).

diatonic scale A series of eight musical sounds or notes (doh ray me fah soh lah te doh') where the frequency of doh' is twice that of doh.

dielectric A substance having very low electrical conductivity, used as an insulator. In a capacitor, the air or insulating material between plates is the dielectric.

differential equation An equation which contains derivatives of a function.

diffraction Spreading or bending of waves that pass the edge of an obstacle or pass through a small opening. Light diffracted by a narrow slit produces a set of interference fringes.

diffraction grating A piece of transparent film or glass printed or engraved with many thousands of closely spaced opaque parallel lines.

digital The method of representing information as a sequence of discrete numbers.

diode A component of an electrical circuit that allows current to pass in only one direction.

diopter A measure of lens power.

dipole (1) Two point charges, equal in magnitude but opposite in sign, separated by a small distance. (2) A molecule in which electrons in the bonds move toward the more electronegative atom.

direct proportion The relationship between two variables which are a constant multiple of each other.

dispersion The separation of a beam of mixed frequencies. Shorter wavelengths are bent most.

displacement vector The vector describing an object's change of position.

diverging lens Alternative name for concave lens.

dynamo A machine that converts mechanical energy to electrical energy.

earth (electrical) The electrical connection by a conductor between an electrical appliance and Earth.

eddy current The electric current induced in a conductor cut by a changing magnetic field.

efficiency The ratio of the energy output of a machine to the energy input. Thermal efficiency is the ratio of the work done to the heat supplied by the fuel.

electrical energy The energy acquired from moving electric charges.

electric field (1) An area in which forces are exerted on electric charges. (2) (strength or intensity) A field produced around a charged object. Electric fields can be described as having lines of electric force or field lines.

electricity The term used to describe the effects of electric charges. Moving charges cause electric current, stationary charges cause static electricity.

electrode A conductor that allows current to flow through an electrolyte, gas, vacuum, dielectric, or semiconductor.

electrolysis The process by which an electrolyte is decomposed when a direct current is passed through it between electrodes.

electrolyte A substance that forms ions when molten or dissolved in a solvent and that carries an electric current during electrolysis.

electrolytic capacitor Small capacitor with large capacitance values. Electrolytic capacitors must be connected correctly with respect to electrical polarity.

electromagnet A magnet produced by the effect of a current flowing in a coil surrounding a soft-iron core.

electromagnetic induction The production across a conductor, moving relative to a magnetic field, of an induced e.m.f.

electromagnetic radiation Energy radiated through space in the form of oscillating electric and magnetic fields at right angles to each other and to the direction of propagation, at a speed of 3.00×10^8 m/s–1.

electromagnetic spectrum The range of frequencies of electromagnetic radiation—gamma radiation, X-rays, ultraviolet, visible light, infrared, microwaves, and radio waves.

electromagnetism The magnetic force produced by electricity, and the electric effects produced by magnetic fields.

electromotive force (e.m.f.) The power of an electric cell to push electrons around a circuit.

electron A basic subatomic particle. It is very light, has a negative charge, and orbits around the nucleus of an atom.

electroscope A device used to detect if an object is charged and, if so, whether the charge is positive or negative.

electrostatic precipitator Used to clean gas emissions of suspended solid particles.

electrostatics The study of the effects of stationary electric charges.

endoscope A medical instrument used to make internal examinations of the body without surgical intervention.

energy The ability of a system to do work. There are two fundamental forms of energy: potential (due to position) and kinetic (due to motion). Other forms of energy—chemical, electrical, heat, light, mechanical, nuclear, sound—can be described in terms of the fundamental forms and are largely interchangeable.

energy levels Bands of allowed energies, each representing many quantum states, that electrons can occupy in an atom.

epicenter The point on Earth's surface immediately above the focus of the seismic waves associated with an earthquake.

equilibrium A state of stability where forces acting on a body cancel each other out.

Eustachian tube Tube connecting the middle ear with the pharynx.

evaporation The process in which a liquid changes state to a vapor.

exothermic An exothermic reaction is a chemical reaction that releases heat to the surroundings.

expansion A physical process in which there is an increase of an object's length, area, or volume.

explosimeter An application of Wheatstone bridge used to measure the strength of an explosion.

exponential A function that varies with the power of another quantity.

exponential decay A property decaying by the same ratio in equal time intervals is said to undergo exponential decay.

Fahrenheit scale A temperature scale where the melting point of ice is 32° and the boiling point of water is 212°.

feedback The return to an amplifier as an input of a signal obtained from the output of the amplifier.

fermentation Anaerobic respiration of organic substances.

ferromagnetic A material, such as iron, steel, nickel, or cobalt, that can be made into a strong magnet.

fiber optics A branch of optics concerned with the transmission of light along optical fibers.

filament A thin high-resistance wire through which an electric current passes; in an electric light bulb the filament becomes white hot.

fission A process during which a heavy atomic nucleus disintegrates into two lighter atoms that together have less mass than the total initial material. The mass lost is liberated as energy ($E = mc^2$).

fluorescence The emission of radiation from certain substances that have been irradiated by light or other radiations.

flux The strength of a field (magnetic or electrical) in a given area. It is the product of the area and the part of the field strength that is at right angles to the area.

focal length The distance from the center of a lens to its focal point.

focus (principal focus or focal point) The point on the principal axis through which rays of light parallel to the principal axis are refracted.

force Any influence that causes a resting body to move or that changes the momentum of a moving body.

fossil fuel A fuel such as coal, petroleum, or natural gas formed by the decomposition of living organisms in prehistoric times.

frequency The number of complete cycles of a periodic motion passing a point in a given time.

frequency modulation A system of modulating a carrier wave used for transmissions in the very high frequency (VHF) and microwave bands.

friction The force that tends to oppose motion between surfaces in contact.

fundamental (harmonics) The component having the lowest frequency in a complex vibration (fundamental frequency or first harmonic).

fuse An electrical safety device. It is a short length of low melting point wire, which breaks if excessive current flows in a circuit.

fusion (nuclear) The process by which two or more light atomic nuclei join, forming a single heavier nucleus that is lighter than the components. The mass lost is liberated as energy ($E = mc^2$)

galvanometer A sensitive instrument for measuring small electric currents.

gamma radiation Very shortwave electromagnetic radiation emitted as a result of radioactive decay.

gas law The equation $PV = nRT$, where P is the pressure, V is the volume, n is the number of moles of gas present, T is the temperature measured in kelvin, and R is the universal gas constant.

Gauss's law When a closed surface is in an electric field, the total electric flux at right angles to that surface is proportional to the sum of the electric charges within the surface.

gear wheel A toothed wheel that transfers turning motion (torque) from one shaft to another.

generator A machine that converts mechanical energy to electrical energy.

geothermal energy Power generated making use of the heat energy in rocks within Earth's crust.

global warming Certain gases (known as greenhouse gases), such as CO_2 form a layer in Earth's atmosphere. Shortwave infrared rays from the Sun pass through this layer heating Earth, which radiates longer-wave infrared radiation. This is trapped in Earth's atmosphere, causing increased temperatures.

gradient The slope of a tangent to a curve at a given point.

gravitational field The area of space around a body in which its mass attracts another body.

gravitational potential The change in potential energy for a unit mass that moves into an object's gravitational field.

gravity The effect of gravitational attraction between Earth (or other heavenly body) and a body in its gravitational field.

half-life A substance that decays exponentially by the same ratio in equal intervals of time. The constant ratio is the half-life.

Hall effect The production of a transverse voltage difference in a conductor, caused by the disturbance of the lines of electrical current flow, which occurs on the application of a magnetic field perpendicular to the direction of current flow.

harmonic (overtone) The part of a complex vibration that is a simple multiple of the fundamental.

heat pump A closed system containing a working fluid that transfers heat from an external source.

helical motion Moving in a spiral.

high pass filter An electronic device that allows frequencies above a certain level to pass with little hindrance.

hydraulic jack A machine that uses a piston in a fluid filled cylinder to raise heavy weights over short distances.

hydraulics The science that relates to the flow of fluids.

hydroelectric plant A power station where the kinetic energy of falling water is converted to electrical energy.

ignite To heat a mixture of gases to the temperature at which combustion occurs.

impedance The total resistance to alternating current flow in a circuit.

inductance The extent to which an element of a circuit forms a magnetic field when carrying an electric current.

induction The change in a body's electric or magnetic state caused by its nearness to a field.

induction coil A form of electrical transformer used to produce a high-voltage, low-current alternating current from a low-voltage source of direct current.

inertia The tendency of a body to oppose a change in its motion.

infinity A point that is so far away from an optical system that the light emitted by it falls in parallel rays.

infrared Electromagnetic radiation with a greater wavelength than the red end of the visible spectrum.

infrasound Very low frequency sound.

insulation The process of inhibiting the flow of energy by placing nonconductors or insulators in its path.

insulator A component that impedes the flow of energy.

integrated circuit A complete electronic circuit on a silicon or other chip.

interference The interaction between waves of the same frequency emitted from different sources.

interference fringes The variation in disturbances produced by waves of the same frequency from different sources; they appear as alternate light and dark bands.

internal combustion engine An engine in which energy is produced by the combustion of a gas-and-air mixture.

internal energy A body's total energy resulting from the relative motions and kinetic and potential energies of all its component particles.

inverse-square law The intensity of radiation decreases with the square of the distance from its source.

inverting amplifier An amplifier whose output is the inverse of its input.

ion An electrically charged atom or group of atoms.

ionizing radiation Any electromagnetic or particle radiation that causes ionization in a medium when passing through it.

isotope Atoms of the same element having the same atomic number but containing different numbers of neutrons, giving different mass numbers.

Kelvin scale A temperature scale that has no negative values. Its lower fixed point is absolute zero.

Kepler's laws (of planetary motion) (1) Each planetary orbit is an ellipse with the Sun at one focus. (2) A line from the Sun to the planet covers equal areas in equal times. (3) The square of a planet's orbital period is proportional to the cube of its mean distance from the Sun.

laser A device that produces a narrow high energy beam of intense monochromatic light.

latch An electronic circuit that can store a single binary digit (bit) until the next clock pulse arrives.

laws of reflection When an incident light ray is reflected at a surface it is reflected in the same plane as the incident ray and the normal. The angle of reflection equals the angle of incidence.

lens A shaped piece of transparent material that bends light by refraction.

lever A simple machine consisting of a rigid beam turning about a pivot. A force applied to the beam moves a load at another point on the beam.

light-dependent resistor (LDR) An electronic device the resistance of which decreases when light falls on it.

light-emitting diode (LED) A semiconductor junction that produces a cold light when a small electric current passes through it.

KEY WORDS

Lissajous figures Patterns formed on an oscilloscope screen when the electron beam is moved simultaneously by the electric fields of two sinusoidal voltages at right angles to each other.

logic gate An electronic circuit that processes information coded in terms of voltage levels, usually representing "1" or "0," or "True" or "False."

longitudinal wave A wave motion the displacement of which is in the direction of its propagation.

Magnadur A material made from ferromagnetic compounds, used to make permanent magnets.

magnet An iron-containing body with domains sufficiently well aligned to produce an external magnetic field and to experience a turning force (torque) when placed in another magnetic field.

magnetic field A space in which a magnetic force can be detected by its effect on iron-containing bodies or on charged particles.

magnetism The field of force caused by (1) the alignment of the magnetic moments of atoms in the same direction (ferromagnetism); or (2) the movement of an electric charge (electromagnetism).

magnification The comparison of the size of an object to the size of the image produced by an optical system.

mass The measure of a body's resistance to acceleration. Mass, unlike weight, does not change when it is subjected to different gravitational forces.

mechanical advantage A measure of the effectiveness of simple machines, such as the lever.

melting point The temperature at which a pure solid changes state from solid to liquid at a certain pressure.

microprocessor A computer's central processor unit in a single integrated circuit chip.

microwaves Electromagnetic radiation lying in the spectrum between radio waves and the infrared.

moderator A material used in a nuclear reactor to slow fast neutrons so that they will undergo fission reactions. Graphite and heavy water are used as moderators.

modulation The process of superimposing a signal carrying information onto a carrier wave in radio transmissions.

molecule The smallest part of an element or chemical compound that can exist independently with all the properties of the element or compound.

moment The turning effect of a force around a point.

momentum A body's momentum is the product of its mass and velocity.

monochromatic light Electromagnetic radiation having only one wavelength and hence one color.

mutual inductance The generation of an e.m.f. in one system of conductors as a result of changing magnetic flux in an adjacent system of conductors.

neutral A conductor having neither negative nor positive electric charge.

neutron One of the two major components of the atomic nucleus. The neutron has a mass very close to that of the proton but has no electric charge.

Newton's laws of motion (1) A body will continue at rest or in a state of constant velocity unless acted on by an external force. (2) The rate of change of a body's momentum is proportional to the force applied and is in the direction of the force. (3) Action and reaction are equal and opposite.

Nicol prism Used to obtain plane-polarized light. It consists of two crystals of calcite cemented together with Canada balsam.

node A point on a standing wave where there is zero displacement.

nonmetal An element that is not a metal. Non-metals readily form negative ions and are poor conductors of heat and electricity.

normal A term meaning perpendicular to, or perpendicular to the tangent of a curve at a particular point.

n-type Semiconductor material treated to contain an excess of negative charge carriers (electrons).

nuclear energy (atomic energy) Energy released as a result of changes in the nuclei of atoms. Mass lost in these changes is converted to energy.

nucleus The small (about 10^{-14} m diameter) core of an atom.

nuclide A particular isotope of an element, identified by the number of protons and neutrons in the nucleus.

objective lens The lens nearest to the object in an optical instrument.

octave Interval between two frequencies which have the frequency ratio 2:1.

Ohm's law The ratio of the current (I) in a metallic conductor at constant temperature to the potential difference (V) between its ends is constant—the resistance (R) of the conductor.

operational amplifier (op-amp) General-purpose voltage amplifiers.

orbit The path of a heavenly body (or artificial satellite) circling another as a result of the attraction of gravity.

oscillation A rapid backward-and-forward repetitive motion in a fluid or solid that behaves elastically.

oscillator An electronic circuit that converts direct current electricity into an alternating current.

ossicles Small bones in the middle ear.

parabolic reflector A concave reflector, a section across which is a parabola.

parallel Two or more electrical components connected between the same points in a circuit are said to be connected in parallel.

pendulum An elongated body free to swing on a pivot, under the influence of gravity, about a horizontal axis.

permittivity The electric flux density produced in a material that is excited by a source of e.m.f.

pharynx A muscular tube which is part of the alimentary canal between the mouth and the gullet.

phase The point in a cycle of any periodic function or periodic quantity reached at a specific time.

photoconductive cell A passive semiconductor device the electrical resistance of which changes in proportion to the intensity of light falling on it.

photon A packet of electromagnetic radiation that can be considered as either a particle or a wave.

photovoltaic cell Photovoltaic cells, commonly known as solar cells, convert light energy to electrical energy. They consist of layers of p- and n-type silicon crystal. When light strikes the junction between the layers, electrons flow through the structure creating a potential difference.

piston A round plate, attached to a rod, that moves within a cylinder in a pump or engine.

pivot (or fulcrum) The point of support about which a lever turns.

plane A flat surface.

polarization Of a radiated wave, being oriented in a predictable direction perpendicular to the direction of propagation.

Polaroid Trade name for a transparent plastic sheet containing many minute double-refracting crystals with parallel axes, which produces plane-polarized light when ordinary light falls on it.

position vector (directed line segment) It represents the displacement of a point from a reference point.

potential difference The difference in electrical potential between two points on a circuit or in an electric field.

potentiometer An instrument used to give an accurate measurement of e.m.f. or potential difference.

power The rate of doing work or the rate at which energy is transferred.

pressure The force acting per unit area. In a liquid at rest, pressure increases with depth and acts equally in all directions.

primary colors Red, green, and bluish-violet. When light of these three colors is mixed, white light is formed.

principal axis The line that passes through the central point of the lens.

principle of superposition When a wave at its point of maximum positive amplitude meets another of equal amplitude at its point of minimum amplitude, the result is zero. If the maxima of two waves meet, the resulting wave is the sum of both waves.

prism A block of transparent material with a triangular cross section.

proton One of the basic particles of the atom, found in the nucleus with the neutron. It has a positive charge and is similar in mass to the neutron.

p-type Semiconductor material treated to contain an excess of positive charge carriers (sometimes referred to as "holes").

pulley A simple machine for raising loads, consisting of a grooved wheel over which a rope or chain passes.

pyrometer An instrument for measuring high temperatures.

radiation The transmission of energy by the movement of waves and particles in all directions. It does not require a medium in which to travel.

radioactivity The spontaneous disintegration of certain isotopes, accompanied by the emission of radiation.

radio waves A form of electromagnetic radiation.

radius A straight line joining the center of a circle to a point on its circumference.

rarefaction The opposite of compression for longitudinal waves.

Rayleigh criterion The criterion for the resolution of interference fringes, spectral lines, and images.

Rayleigh's scattering law When electromagnetic radiation is reflected off atoms there is a change in phase but not frequency.

rectifier A device allowing electric current to flow freely in one direction only.

reflecting telescope A telescope that brings light rays to a focus using a mirror.

reflection The process by which radiation incident on a surface does not penetrate the surface but bounces back.

refracting telescope A telescope that brings light to a focus using lenses.

refraction The change of direction of electromagnetic radiation, such as light, on passing from one medium to another.

refractive index The constant representing the amount of refraction occurring when electromagnetic radiation passes from one medium to another.

relay (electrical) An electromechanical switch.

resistance A measure of the extent to which a material can oppose the passage of an electric current.

resolving power The potential an optical instrument has for producing distinguishable images.

resonance The state of a body subjected to a periodic disturbance at a frequency close to or equal to the frequency at which it naturally vibrates or oscillates.

respiration The process in living organisms by which chemical energy in food is liberated.

resultant The single vector representing the sum of a set of vectors.

retina The light-sensitive area of the eye consisting of rod and cone cells.

Richter scale A logarithmic scale used to indicate the magnitude of earthquakes.

satellite A small body orbiting a larger one under the influence of gravity.

scalar A quantity that has magnitude but not direction.

secondary colors Magenta, cyan, and yellow. Each is formed from two different primary colors.

seismic wave A shock wave produced by an earthquake or explosion.

self inductance If the current in a circuit changes, the magnetic flux linked to the circuit changes and induces an e.m.f. the direction of which opposes the change causing it.

semiconductor Covalent crystals the resistance of which is between that of insulators and conductors. Current is carried by free electrons, leaving positively charged holes behind.

short-circuit An electrical connection of negligible resistance that bypasses a part of an electrical circuit.

SI *Système International* (d'Unités): a system of coherent metric units used in science.

simple harmonic motion Vibrational motion, in which acceleration toward a point is proportional to the distance from it.

sine wave The projection on a plane surface of the graph of a point moving around a circle at uniform speed, and the graph of the function $y = \sin x$ or $y = \cos x$.

solar panel A grouping of solar cells used to collect energy from sunlight using the photovoltaic effect to create electricity by absorbing the Sun's energy.

solenoid A coil of insulated wire, cylindrical in shape, with its length longer than its diameter.

sonar A system used to detect and locate objects using reflected sound waves.

sonometer An apparatus that is used to study the vibrations of a wire or string.

sound waves A series of alternate compressions and rarefactions (longitudinal waves) of a medium through which energy is transmitted.

spectrograph An instrument that makes a photographic record, a spectrogram, of a spectrum used in analysis.

spectrum The arrangement of electromagnetic radiation into its constituent wavelengths.

speed of electromagnetic waves All electromagnetic waves travel at a speed of 3×10^8 meters per second in a vacuum.

spherical aberration The distorted image formed by a lens or mirror when rays striking a lens or a mirror at different distances from the center do not come to a focus at the same point.

square wave An electrical waveform that alternates between a high and a low voltage, changing very suddenly from one to the other.

stationary wave (or **standing wave**) The interference pattern formed by two waves of the same type that have the same frequency and amplitude and are traveling at the same time in opposite directions.

strain A body's temporary or permanent distortion when a stress is applied to it.

stroboscope An instrument used to study vibrating or rotating objects.

tangent A line or plane that touches a curve or surface.

temperature A measure of the degree of heat of a system on a particular scale.

tension A body in equilibrium is under tension if a force is tending to stretch it.

terminal velocity The constant velocity acquired by a body falling freely through a fluid when acted on by a constant force or forces.

thermal conductivity A measure of the ease with which a material conducts heat energy.

thermal equilibrium The state of a body where no net heat flow occurs between it and its surroundings.

thermal radiation The emission of infrared radiation.

thermionic valve A glass or metal tube containing gas (or a vacuum) and two or more electrodes. The cathode is heated.

thermistor (or **thermal resistor**) A semiconductor the resistance of which is very sensitive to temperature.

thermocouple An instrument used for measuring temperature consisting of a pair of wires or semiconductors joined at each end.

thermopile (or **pile**) An instrument consisting of a number of thermocouples connected in series.

thyristor A semiconductor power switch.

tidal energy Energy represented by the water moving under the influence of gravity, following the pull of the Sun and Moon and forming tides.

torque The turning moment exerted by a force acting on an object at a distance from the axis of rotation and at a tangent to it.

transformer A device that changes an alternating current of one voltage to an alternating current of another voltage by electromagnetic induction (mutual induction).

transistor A semiconductor device that amplifies electric currents flowing through it. They usually consist of three layers of n-type and p-type semiconductors.

transverse wave Wave motions where the vibration or displacement is perpendicular to the direction of propagation.

triple point The conditions of temperature and pressure at which the three phases of a substance—solid, liquid, and gas—are in equilibrium.

truth table A table that shows all the possible inputs and outputs for a digital circuit in which logical operations take place.

turbine A machine that extracts energy from a moving fluid. The rotation of the turbine shaft can be used to generate electricity.

ultrasound Sound waves with a higher frequency than that detectable by the human ear (above 20 kHz).

ultraviolet light Electromagnetic radiation of shorter wavelengths than visible light, but of longer wavelength than X-rays.

vacuum A region devoid of matter—in practice it is considered to be a region of very low pressure.

valve A device controlling the passage of fluid in a pipe in one direction.

van de Graaff A machine using electrostatics to produce a very high voltage.

vapor Gas that is below the temperature at which it can be liquefied by pressure.

vaporization The process of change of state of a solid or liquid to a vapor.

vector A quantity that has both size and direction.

velocity Speed in a specified direction, a vector quantity.

virtual image An image produced by diverging rays that appears to be in a particular place but cannot be produced on a screen.

virtual ray A ray that appears to come from a virtual image but does not actually exist.

viscosity A measure of a fluid's inability to flow. The more viscous a fluid, the less easily it flows.

voltameter An electrolytic cell used to measure electric current.

wave A way in which energy is transferred through a medium as a series of periodic oscillations.

waveform The shape of a wave.

wavelength The distance between two corresponding points on a wave.

weight The force exerted on a body by Earth's gravitational pull.

Wheatstone bridge An apparatus for measuring electrical resistances.

work The transfer of energy occurring when a force is applied to a body to cause it to move.

X-rays Electromagnetic radiation of a frequency between that of ultraviolet light and that of gamma rays.

Young's double slit experiment Demonstrates light and dark patterns (Young's fringes) caused by interference between two light sources.

zener diode A simple semiconductor device used in voltage regulation.

Internet resources

There is a lot of useful information on the internet. Information on a particular topic may be available through a search engine such as Google (http://www.google.com). Some of the Web sites that are found in this way may be very useful, others not. Below is a selection of Web sites related to the material covered by this book.

The publisher takes no responsibility for the information contained within these Web sites. All the sites were accessible in March 2006.

The ABCs of Nuclear Science
A brief introduction to nuclear science with experiments and a glossary from the Nuclear Science Division, Lawrence Berkeley National Laboratory.
   http://www.lbl.gov/abc/

About Physics
Includes links to a glossary, encyclopedia, experiments, periodic table, chemical structure archive, chemistry problems, and articles.
   http://physics.about.com

Antimatter: Mirror of the Universe
A Web site that explains what antimatter is and where it is made. Produced by CERN.
   http://livefromcern.web.cern.ch/livefromcern/antimatter

Atomicarchive.com
Explores the history of nuclear weapons and the science behind them.
   http://www.atomicarchive.com

The Atoms Family
Teaches the different forms of energy using the spooky Addams Family theme.
   http://www.miamisci.org/af/sln

A Walk Through Time
A history of time measurement from prehistoric days to the present from the National Institute of Standards and Technology.
   http://physics.nist.gov/GenInt/Time

Beginner's Guide to Aerodynamics
An explanation of aerodynamics for beginners through interactive animations, equations, and text. Produced by NASA's Glenn Research Center.
   http://www.grc.nasa.gov/WWW/K-12/airplane/
   bga.html

Constants and Equations Pages
A collection of constants and equations, including the periodic table, unit conversions, SI units, and mathematical symbols.
   http://www.tcaep.co.uk

Cosmic Evolution from Big Bang to Humankind
A Web site that traces the cosmic origin and evolution of matter and energy from the Big Bang to the present.
   http://www.tufts.edu/as/wright_center/
   cosmic_evolution

Eric Weisstein's World of Physics
An online encyclopedia with excellent graphics; a good source for equations.
   http://scienceworld.wolfram.com/physics

Exploring the Nature of Matter
A comprehensive Web site sponsored by the Thomas Jefferson National Accelerator Facility. Contains information on current research as well as teacher and student resources, including a table of elements, glossary, hands-on-activities, and games and puzzles.
   http://www.jlab.org

Fear of Physics
A friendly, non-technical Web site for students, which includes a physics dictionary and covers 200 homework and exam questions.
   http://www.fearofphysics.com

Inquiring Minds
Exploring particle physics and the physics of the universe with the Fermi National Accelerator Laboratory.
   http://www.fnal.gov/pub/inquiring

INTERNET RESOURCES

Introduction to Particle Physics
Information on accelerators, detectors, antimatter, the Big Bang, dark matter, and the top quark from the Rutherford Appleton Laboratory
http://hepwww.rl.ac.uk/Pub/Phil/contents.html

NIST Reference on Constants, Units, and Uncertainty
The National Institute of Standards and Technology's guide to fundamental physical constants, SI units, and uncertainty-of-measurement results.
http://physics.nist.gov/cuu/Constants

The Official String Theory Web Site
Patricia Schwarz explains theoretical particle physics in lay terms.
http://www.superstringtheory.com

Open Directory Project: Physics
A comprehensive listing of internet resources in the field of physics.
http://dmoz.org/science/physics

Physics Central
Links to information on experiments, physics in daily life, biography, history, and reference resources from the American Physical Society.
http://www.physicscentral.org

Physics Classroom
Online Tutorials for high-school students on a variety of basic physics concepts, including Newton's laws; work, energy, and power; momentum and its conservation; and waves.
http://www.physicsclassroom.com

Physics.org
Links to information on experiments, physics in daily life, biography, history, and reference resources.
http://www.physics.org

Physics Timeline
A comprehensive list of "firsts" and discoveries in Physics from the sixth century BCE to today.
http://www.weburbia.com/pg/historia.htm

Physics Web
A Web site aimed primarily at the professional physicist but including many current stories about the state of physics research as well as links to teaching and learning resources.
http://physicsweb.org

Physics Zone
A resource for learning introductory level algebra-based physics.
http://www.sciencejoywagon.com/physicszone

Physlink.com: Physics and Astronomy Online
Comprehensive physics and astronomy online education, research, and reference Web site; includes an "Ask the Expert" resource.
http://www.physlink.com

ScienceMaster
News, information, links, columns, and homework help in all major areas of science.
http://www.sciencemaster.com

Science News for Kids
Science Service Suggestions for hands-on activities, books, articles, Web resources, and other useful materials for students ages 9–13.
http://www.sciencenewsforkids.org

Scientific American
The latest news in science.
http://www.sciam.com

The Soundry
Information on the perception, physics, and applications of sound, with a timeline of audio engineering.
http://library.thinkquest.org/19537

Stephen Hawking's Universe
Information on the history of the universe and unanswered questions in cosmology.
http://www.pbs.org/wnet/hawking

Index

Index of subject headings.